Russell Banks

Twayne's United States Authors Series

Frank Day, Editor
Clemson University

TUSAS 680

RUSSELL BANKS
Nathan Farb

Russell Banks

Robert Niemi

Saint Michael's College

Twayne Publishers
An Imprint of Simon & Schuster Macmillan
New York

Prentice Hall International
London • Mexico City • New Delhi • Singapore • Sydney • Toronto

Twayne's United States Authors Series No. 680

Russell Banks
Robert Niemi

Twayne Publishers
An Imprint of Simon & Schuster Macmillan
1633 Broadway
New York, NY 10019

Library of Congress Cataloging-in-Publication Data

Niemi, Robert.
    Russell Banks / Robert Niemi.
        p.   cm. — (Twayne's United States authors series ; TUSAS 680)
    Includes bibliographical references and index.
    ISBN 0-8057-4018-X (alk. paper)
    1. Banks, Russell, 1940–   —Criticism and interpretation.
    I. Title.   II. Series.
    PS3552.A49Z783   1997
    813′.54—dc21   96-50231
                                                                                 CIP

10 9 8 7 6 5 4 3 2 1

Printed in the United States of America

For Elena and Gretchen

Contents

Preface

In broad historical terms, twentieth-century American fiction tends to divide into two main traditions that have periodically traded dominance on the cultural scene. For want of more precise terminology, one tradition might be referred to as *socially conscious fiction* (e.g., realism, naturalism, the proletarian novel, the so-called nonfiction novel, grit lit, etc.). The other tradition might be termed *avant-garde fiction* (e.g., modernist and postmodernist narratives, metafiction, etc).

Neither type of writing exists in pure form, of course. The most inner-directed and aesthetically self-conscious narratives can scarce avoid reflecting larger social concerns (albeit often obliquely). Nor is realism in its various guises exempt from the requisites of artistic coherence and psychological credibility. Yet there *are* real differences between these two modes, differences that are *ideological* at base because they bespeak opposing views as to the primacy of the autonomous individual—in fiction narratives, in society, in life itself.

In politically conservative periods, when market values hold even greater than usual sway (the twenties and eighties come to mind), American fiction has tended to reflect and reinforce the zeitgeist of the era by displaying formalist, aestheticist, and individualist propensities. In more turbulent times, when status-quo values and institutions are undergoing a series of jolting legitimation crises (the thirties and sixties, for example), socially engaged writing quite understandably gains ascendency.

What does not usually change, though, is an individual writer's allegiance to one general mode or the other. For example, it is highly unlikely that an avant-garde fantasist, fabulist, romancer, or experimentalist will become a hard core realist, or vice versa. Though he or she may range far afield in terms of style, setting, and subject matter, the writer writes from within the peculiar and enduring mentality of his or her social class origins, even if those origins have been consciously transcended or, more likely, unconsciously repressed. In short, there is no danger that Dorothy Allison will metamorphose into Ann Beattie, or that John Irving will evolve into Denis Johnson.

My point is that the American social system of de facto class (and race) apartheid tends to produce myopically class-specific fiction. Reading any one of a hundred "serious" contemporary novelists, one can learn a great deal about the manners and mores of a particular social class. What is unusual, though, is to find a writer who is willing and able to write *across* class boundaries, one who knows how to dolly back for a revealing long shot of the American class structure in its looming totality. Russell Banks is such a writer.

By virtue of an extraordinarily salutary interplay between historical timing, social background, and personal temperament, Banks has proven almost singularly equipped to probe the normally taboo realities of social class in contemporary American society. Hailing from the New England white working class, Banks is intimately familiar with his perennial subject: the structure and psychology of proletarian life, especially its tendency to both absorb and generate toxic levels of verbal, emotional, and physical violence.

Born in 1940, Banks came of age in the late fifties, when American culture, historically authoritarian and puritanical, was being thawed by the warm currents of a countercultural revolution instigated by the emergence of the Beats, youth culture, and the white adoption of black musical forms. Attending a southern university at the height of the Civil Rights movement in the mid sixties, Banks was soon schooled in the liberationist politics of that era. A few years later as an apprentice writer, Banks mastered the metaphysical and linguistic subtleties of seventies metafiction. All of these timely influences, combined with Banks's considerable intellectual gifts, have produced a writer with an unusually high degree of political and aesthetic sophistication. Such savvy has enabled Banks to balance his narratives between chronicle and social critique. By often writing in a dual voice—a voice that moves both *inside* and *outside* blue-collar experience—Banks has proven adept at conveying the buried realities of life at the margins while also managing to foreground social class as a vital factor in the shaping of individual consciousness and fate.

Both messages need all the cultural air play they can get; they have not yet received their fair due. Despite a prolific and increasingly successful literary career that has produced a dozen books and numerous awards (including a Pulitzer Prize nomination), Russell Banks has never been the object of a book-length study—until now. Accordingly, this book is fairly comprehensive in scope. Following a detailed overview of Banks's life and literary career, I have explicated and evaluated all of Banks's poetry, collected short fiction, and novels in an effort to systematically examine his complex evolution, from counterculture aesthete to committed social critic. Above all, I have tried to show that Russell Banks is a *political* writer through and through, a writer devoted to telling the often horrifying truth about life in the modern world—not in an effort to titilate or shock or indulge in fashionable despair, but in hopes of illuminating a dark time for better times to come.

Acknowledgments

Quotations from *15 Poems, Waiting to Freeze: Poems, 30/6, Snow: Meditations of a Cautious Man in Winter, Searching for Survivors, Hamilton Stark, The Book of Jamaica,* and *Trailerpark* reprinted by permission of Russell Banks. Copyright © 1978 by Russell Banks.

Grateful acknowledgment is also due to the following for permission to quote material that appears in this book: HarperCollins, for quotations from *Continental Drift,* copyright © 1985, *Success Stories,* copyright © 1986, *Affliction,* copyright © 1989, *The Sweet Hereafter,* copyright © 1991, and *Rule of the Bone,* copyright © 1995; Sun & Moon Press, for quotations from *The Relation of My Imprisonment,* copyright © 1983, and *Family Life,* copyright 1988; University of Illinois Press, for quotations from *The New World: Tales,* copyright © 1978.

The author gratefully acknowledges the cheerful and generous cooperation of Russell Banks. Without such cooperation, this study would have been drastically diminished. Sincere thanks to Professor Frank Day of Clemson University for his excellent editorial work on the manuscript. Thanks also to Annie Dawid (Evergreen College, Oregon) and Donovan McDonough (Saint Michael's College), who also read the manuscript in progress and provided many useful suggestions. Thanks to Stewart Arnold and Dr. Joseph Ferdinand (Saint Michael's College) for providing background information on Haitian voodoo iconography. Finally, thanks to Saint Michael's College for providing me with research funds and the Inter-library Loan Department at Durick Library for obtaining hard-to-find materials.

Chronology

1940   March 28: Russell Earl Banks is born in Newton, Massachusetts, first of four children to Earl and Florence (Taylor) Banks.

1952   Earl Banks abandons his family; Florence Banks moves, with her children, to Barnstead, New Hampshire, and takes a job as a bookkeeper; subsequently sues Earl Banks for divorce.

1956   April: Banks and a friend named Dario Morelli steal Morelli's father's car and drive cross-country; they return home six weeks later.

1958   September: begins freshman year at Colgate University (Hamilton, New York) but drops out after nine weeks.

1959   January: hitchhikes to Florida to join Fidel Castro's revolution against Cuban dictator, Fulgencio Batista, but settles in central Florida instead; August: Banks marries Darlene Bennett, the daughter of a carpet installer.

1960   May 13: first daughter, Leona "Lea" (Stamm), born; Banks and Bennett move to Boston.

1961   Banks and Bennett separate; Banks returns to Florida and lives at Islamorada Key; moves to Key West near the end of the year; meets an ex-convict and an AWOL sailor in Key West and teams up with them to drive a travel-bureau car across the southern United States and into Mexico; eventually delivers the car in Los Angeles; visits mother in California then hitchhikes back to New Hampshire.

1962   February: Banks and Bennett divorce; Banks living in Keene, New Hampshire, working as a plumber and writing in his spare time; October 29: marries Mary Gunst.

1963   Attends Breadloaf Writers' Conference in Bennington, Vermont; works on his writing with Nelson Algren.

1964   July 7: second daughter, Caerthan, born; September: Banks enrolls at the University of North Carolina (Chapel Hill).

1966   Cofounds (with William Matthews) Lillabulero Press, Inc., and becomes editor and publisher of *Lillabulero*, "a periodical of Literature and the Arts."

1967   Graduates Phi Beta Kappa from University of North Carolina with an A.B. in English; publishes a chapbook entitled *15 Poems* with William Matthews and Newton Smith (Lillabulero Press).

1968   Awarded Woodrow Wilson Fellowship; returns to New Hampshire; begins teaching at Emerson College (Boston) and at the University of New Hampshire (Durham); May 17: third daughter, Maia, born; Banks's brother, Christopher, is killed in a train wreck near Santa Barbara, California.

1969   Publishes second chapbook, *Waiting to Freeze* (Lillabulero Press).

1970   January 13: fourth daughter, Danis, born.

1974   Publishes third chapbook, *Snow: Meditations of a Cautious Man in Winter* (Granite Press).

1975   Visiting Professor at New England College (Henniker, New Hampshire); publishes first and second books, *Searching for Survivors* (Fiction Collection), a collection of short stories, and *Family Life* (Avon), a novel; *Lillabulero* ceases publication after nine years.

1976   Writer in residence at Princeton University and Sarah Lawrence University; awarded Guggenheim Fellowship and Sarah Lawrence Award for Fiction (from Sarah Lawrence University and Fiction International).

1976–1977   Spends 18 months, with family, in Jamaica (on Guggenheim); subsequently divorced Mary Gunst.

1978   Publishes third and fourth books: *The New World* (University of Illinois Press), a second collection of short stories; *Hamilton Stark* (Houghton Mifflin), his second novel.

1979   Banks's father, Earl, dies of "massive alcoholic trauma to the liver" at the age of 63.

1980   Publishes fifth book: *The Book of Jamaica* (Houghton Mifflin), his third novel.

1981   Publishes sixth book: *Trailerpark* (Houghton Mifflin), his third collection of short stories.

1982   Marries Kathy Walton, an editor at Harper & Row; Banks and Walton move to Brooklyn, New York.

1983   Publishes seventh book: *The Relation of My Imprisonment* (Sun & Moon Press), his fourth novel.

1985   Publishes eighth book: *Continental Drift* (Harper & Row), his fifth novel; book wins John Dos Passos Award for Fiction; voted one of "the best books of 1985" by *Library Journal;* is also nominated for a Pulitzer Prize.

1986   Publishes ninth book: *Success Stories* (Harper & Row), his fourth collection of short stories.

1988   Divorced from Kathy Walton; marries Chase Twitchell, a poet; publishes a revised edition of *Family Life* (Sun & Moon Press).

1989   Publishes tenth book: *Affliction* (Harper & Row), his sixth novel.

1991   Publishes eleventh book: *The Sweet Hereafter* (Harper & Row), his seventh novel.

1995   Publishes twelfth book: *Rule of the Bone* (Harper-Collins), his eighth novel.

Chapter One

Success Story: The Life and Career of Russell Banks

There's no success like failure. And failure's no success at all.

Bob Dylan

A Zigzag Pattern

Russell Earl Banks was born on 28 March 1940 in Newton, Massachusetts, the first of four children to Florence (Taylor) Banks, a homemaker, and Earl Banks, a plumber (as was Banks's grandfather). By his own admission, Russell Banks "was not an attractive baby, unusually long and skinny, big-headed and bald" until he was 18 months old.[1] Banks also had crossed eyes, brought on, according to his mother, by whooping cough that refused to abate: " 'You wouldn't stop coughing, you couldn't, and your eyes got crossed then,' she reports" (Banks, 34).

The dubious notion that pertussis crossed her son's eyes Banks sees as typical of his mother, whom he has described, rather bluntly, as a woman "who projects her needs and desires onto the world and reports back, more or less accurately, what she sees there" and as "a truthful but somewhat deluded and self-absorbed person, some would say a narcissistic person, and for that reason [she] has always been a lonely, unreliable witness" (Banks, 34).

If Florence Banks has had a tendency to distort reality to suit her fancies, the late Earl Banks was, according to his son, an out-and-out liar, who "lied consciously, almost perversely, like a bored nihilist, but he rarely drew me in and thus was not so dangerous to me" (Banks, 34). Banks's father was also an alcoholic and a philanderer, and he and his wife subjected themselves and their children to a home life of unremitting turmoil. Recently Banks recalled that his "parents fought constantly; they drank too much; they were violent, especially my father . . . They were like hysterical children, stuck in a permanent tantrum. Everyone cried and shouted a lot. There was never enough money, and they were always packing up and moving out of an old place, where

1

things had gone wrong, into a new [place], where everything 'would improve' " (Banks, 37).

But things didn't improve. When Banks was 12 years old, his father went off to live with a girlfriend, abandoning the family forever. Florence Banks sued for divorce and took custody of the four children. Forced back into the workplace, she took a job as a bookkeeper: poorly paid drudgery that made life a constant, desperate struggle for survival. Always short of rent money, Florence and her young brood moved from house to house, apartment to apartment, in and around Wakefield, Massachusetts. Looking back on that period, Banks notes that "although the physical violence and the drunkenness ended [with the divorce], the financial insecurity was worse" (Banks, 37).

Charged by his departing father with the obligation to be "the man of the house," young Russell tried his best to live up to duties that should never be thrust on a child, especially by the man who shirked them. Banks's sister, Linda Weir, recalls her oldest brother as having been extremely protective toward his siblings: "He was always the responsible one. He was like a father, and he took that responsibility very seriously."[2] Banks himself suggests that his willingness to take charge, to assume a manly role while still just a boy, was probably forged out of the vicissitudes of his earliest years: "There was a high level of chaos in the family. I remember feeling the need to protect myself from these chaotic adults and tried to organize my life as much as possible. I was also cross-eyed and self-conscious as hell about that. All this may have forced the appearance of maturity on me" (Brown, 54).

Though morally and intellectually precocious, young Banks exhibited an opposing trait: a tendency to run away. Even as a toddler, Banks was given to wandering away from home. At the age of 5 or 6 his "favorite book was Toby Tyler, the story of a boy who ran off and joined the circus" (Banks, 37). When he was 9 Banks was picked up by police at the Concord, New Hampshire, airport; he had bicycled there with a knapsack on his back, intent on stowing away on an airplane, destination left to chance. At 16 Banks made a more serious and paradoxical attempt to escape from home. A self-described whiz kid at Wakefield High School, Banks applied, in January of 1956, to transfer to a first-class prep school: Phillips Andover Academy. Shortly thereafter, though, he and a friend named Dario Morelli stole Morelli's father's car and headed west on Route 66. They eventually worked their way across the country to Pasadena, California. There, Morelli, a Catholic, confessed the adventure to a priest, who turned the two boys in to their parents.

However, the damage had been done. Banks's disappearance from home for nearly two months had been a terrible emotional ordeal for his family. And perhaps Banks had also managed to hobble his own future, or at least sidetrack it, by missing out on a full scholarship to Andover, proffered and then withdrawn, during his absence (Banks, 37).

Looking back on the incident as an adult, Banks has come to two conclusions. He believes that, in abandoning his beleaguered family, he was unconsciously imitating his father's flight four years before. Banks also sees the running away as directly related to the application to prep school. In his own words, the application was a "concerted attempt" to lift himself "up by his own bootstraps." Cross-country flight was its negation. The two actions formed "a zigzag pattern . . . a life of advance-and-retreat, of achievement and self-sabotage, of commitment and betrayal," a pattern yet to come to full crisis (Banks, 43).

That happened two years later, in 1958, when Banks won a full academic scholarship to Colgate University, a prestigious (and, at that time, all-white and all-male) college in Hamilton, New York. This was the proverbial opportunity of a lifetime for a hardscrabble kid—possible entry into the middle class or beyond—but Banks soon found himself overwhelmed and desperate. Almost 30 years later he described the experience in a quasi-autobiographical narrative sardonically entitled "Success Story": "In this Ivy League school . . . among the elegant, brutal sons of the captains of industry, I was only that year's token poor kid, imported from a small . . . mill town like an exotic herb, a dash of mace for the vichyssoise. It was a status that perplexed and intimidated and finally defeated me, so that after nine weeks of it, I fled in the night."[3]

Banks returned to Massachusetts, to face the shock and deep disappointment of his family, friends, and high school teachers. He later recalled that his distraught mother "seemed always to be red-eyed from weeping" (*SS*, 53). The "zigzag pattern" had returned with a vengeance. Inevitably, perhaps, because Colgate presented the same, unbearable moral dilemma he had faced with the prep school application. On the one hand, it was natural for a gifted teenager to want out of an impoverished, demoralized home life. On the other hand, going off to college amounted to a massive betrayal of home and heritage, but not because he was leaving his struggling family to their own devices (he had their blessings, after all); it was their vicarious hope in his success that was betrayed. In addition, the issue was more subtle than that. Going to college meant embracing a creed utterly alien to the die-hard, working-class ethos of the Bankses. As Banks told an interviewer, "I come from a people who viewed success as a criticism of their life . . . if you're moving up, there's a kind of betrayal of the family. My father made a mockery of anybody who aspired to move up, unless you moved up as a wheeler dealer. That was a little different. If you could finagle a piece of real estate or a used car lot into something more lucrative, that would be all right. But to move up in the sense of moving into the world of ideas and trying to live your life through language—that was a betrayal" (Brown, 64). Leaving home was one thing. But leaving home *and* crossing the great divide of social class was the ultimate, terrifying apostasy. Better just to leave home, an act well within the family tradition.

One winter morning just after the 1958 Christmas holidays, Banks slung a duffel bag over his shoulder and left his mother's home in Wakefield to begin hitchhiking his way south. He had only a few dollars in his pocket but was inspired by Jack Kerouac's *On the Road,* which justified the trip on "religious, metaphysical, social, and political terms."[4] In "Success Story," Banks describes *this* leavetaking as "an exquisite pleasure, like falling into bed and deep sleep after having been pushed beyond exhaustion. Now, I thought the morning I left . . . *now* I can start to dream my own dreams, not everyone else's" (*SS,* 54).

Just 18, Banks dreamt a strange, exotic dream: to join Fidel Castro's guerrilla war against Cuban dictator Fulgencio Batista. Wesley Brown, an interviewer of Banks, is surely right in pointing out that this adventure "was not [based on] an ideological decision; for Banks, Castro was a romantic figure who represented a rejection of both an upwardly mobile middle-class existence and the grinding poverty of working-class life" (Brown, 66). Banks was nothing like a Marxist revolutionary; he was just a lost teenager in search of a role model to help him "locate his identity," as Wesley Brown aptly puts it.

Banks only got as far as Miami. Then, he confesses, he "got scared": "I realized I didn't know anything. I didn't know Spanish. I didn't know how to get across to Cuba [or] what I would do if I did. I didn't have the foggiest idea where things were leading. And I didn't trust chaos enough, or happenstance enough to keep going."[5] At a loss as to what to do with himself, Banks hitchhiked up to Saint Petersburg. There he found work as a furniture mover at a downtown hotel, the only healthy young man among a crew of "seven or eight men . . . over forty, terminally alcoholic, physically fragile and itinerant" (*SS,* 57). After a few weeks, Banks quit the hotel. His next job was as an "assistant window trimmer," dressing mannequins and constructing facades for the display department at Maas Brothers, a chic, downtown department store.

Also working at Maas was a pretty, 17-year-old salesgirl and bathing suit model by the name of Darlene Bennett, the daughter of a local carpet installer. The two began to date and quickly fell in love. Many years later, Banks explained that his attraction to Bennett was almost reflexive: "She was a sweet girl who loved me. At a time when I felt, in all other respects, [like] a worm ... a man without character, without ability, without promise, without anything going for him, there was this very pretty young woman who thought I was just terrific" (19 May 1993). In the late summer of 1959, only a few months after they met, Banks and Bennett married.

The young couple moved into an apartment in Lakeland. Banks, still only 19, had high hopes that his marriage would "be a Fresh Start," a "new life [that] would cancel the old life and create a new me" (*SS*, 88). Within a matter of weeks Bennett became pregnant. With the benefit of hindsight, Banks now understands all the haste as an unconscious compulsion: "Like a lot of kids from a broken family I was trying to repair that break by creating my own family, prematurely. I was out there getting married and [my wife] pregnant as fast as I could, to make the family that I had lost. Without any awareness of this at the time" (19 May 1993).

Banks's job at Maas had ended about the same time he got married, in an excruciatingly embarrassing but funny incident recounted in "Success Story" (*SS*, 52–76). After constructing a heavy four-by-eight-foot wooden panel for a bathing suit display, Banks attempted to transport it to an upper floor. Sad to say, the object proved too tall to clear the ceiling of the mezzanine at the top end of the store's escalator. In a horrendously loud, shattering impact, both ceiling and escalator were mangled. Fired on the spot, Banks next found work as a display artist at Webb's City, a sprawling discount department store that he has recently described as "a sort of precursor to Kmart" (19 May 1993). Later, Banks worked on displays at a Montgomery Ward's in Lakeland and as a shoe salesman at a suburban shopping mall.

As the year waned and his young wife grew more obviously pregnant, Banks's own anxieties reached unbearable levels. As he tells it, "[By the end of 1959] I really wanted to get the hell out of Florida and out of this trap that I could see myself settling into. The trap had several boxes in it. I was in the marriage box, soon to be a family box. I was in an educational and cultural box, trapped in a small town in central Florida, putting clothes on mannequins. I was going crazy with boredom and frustration and loneliness" (19 May 1993). Finally, in February of 1960, Banks packed his very pregnant bride and their few belongings into his old Packard and headed north to Boston.

After settling into a small basement flat on Queensborough Street in Boston's Back Bay, Banks found work in a bookstore and, as he later put it, "sort of eased into a community of young artists, painters, musicians, writers and hangers-on—most of them wannabes—between the ages of twenty and thirty. A lot of them had been or were going to the New England Conservatory [of Music] or Boston Museum of Fine Arts or Boston University theater schools" (19 May 1993). Coming out of the cultural wasteland of suburban Florida, Banks found Boston "a very exciting place to be": "That's when I really began to take myself seriously for the first time as an artist and I first began to write, seriously, at that point" (19 May 1993).

An important influence was Leo Giroux Jr., an unpublished writer several years Banks's senior.[6] Later characterized by Banks as "loud, garrulous, and insecure," Giroux was a troubled man, perhaps manic-depressive, but apparently well read and always eager to converse about literature. Giroux gladly assumed the role of Banks's mentor, advising his charge that, in order to be a serious writer, one first had to read his way through a wide swath of classic writers. He even supplied a reading list, which included the likes of Céline, Isak Dinesen, and Stephen Crane, writers Banks hadn't even heard of at that time. Looking back on those days, Banks sees his friendship with Giroux as an important but short-lived moment in his development as a writer: "Our lives touched, when I was twenty and he was twenty-seven or so, and there was a wonderful spark that jumped from his life to mine. And then there was too great a gap between us for that spark to cross, either way, again" (19 May 1993).

Meanwhile, Banks's marriage was, in his own words, "under enormous stress." At the stage when sexual infatuation needs to be replaced by deeper bonds, both he and Darlene were discovering that they had next to nothing in common beyond extreme youth and naïveté. The birth of a daughter, Leona (nicknamed Lea), on 13 May 1960 only added to the pressures. Six months later Banks initiated the inevitable break, very much against his wife's wishes. Heartbroken, panicked, and full of resentment, Bennett had no choice but to return to Florida with the baby and live with her parents. Shortly thereafter, Bennett remarried and put up a wall of silence that Banks made no effort to penetrate; there was no contact between either party for many years. It was as if Banks had never been married or fathered a child, an act of desertion not unlike his father's, as he later admitted to Wesley Brown: "I essentially replicated my father's behavior toward me and my siblings, in that I abandoned [Lea] for no clear reasons. I was able to explain my behavior in various ways, as I'm sure my father rationalized his behavior" (Brown, 68).

Six months later Banks met, through mutual friends, a lively, attractive but volatile Emerson College theater major named Mary Gunst. Banks had just turned 21 when the two entered into a stormy romance that he was not well equipped to handle. In the throes of what he has come to feel was a delayed reaction to the physical and emotional battering he had suffered in his upbringing, and full of guilt over the breakup of his marriage, Banks soon found himself on the verge of collapse: "I was coming undone ... my emotional equilibrium was achieved and maintained with great difficulty. I had, that summer, what today we'd probably call a nervous breakdown" (19 May 1993).

Depressed to the point of paralysis, Banks did what he had done so many times before to save himself. He put some belongings into his duffel and lit out—for Florida once again, as if drawn instinctually to warmer climes. But beyond escape there was also a positive motivation. He later told an interviewer that he "had to pull away from that Boston crowd. I was getting much more serious as a writer, and I couldn't do that staying up until 4, smoking dope, drinking wine, and snapping fingers to the cadence of 'Howl.' "[7] Intent on solitude in order to write and to get his life back together, Banks ended up at Islamorada Key, 50 miles north of Key West. There he spent the latter half of 1961 living in a trailer, writing during the day, and pumping gas at night at a filling station next to the trailer park. Still in possession of Leo Giroux's reading list, Banks continued his self-education, loading up on works by Melville, Hawthorne, Henry James, and other American classics when the bookmobile from Miami made its weekly stop.

Restless again near the end of the year, Banks hitchhiked down to Key West, which he remembers, with great fondness, as "a Caribbean kind of town, really quite wonderful ... The town itself had not turned into the tourist trap that it has become. It was a navy base, a sailor town—bars and whorehouses. All kinds of flotsam and jetsam, ne'er-do-wells and drop-outs from the continent ended up there. It was sort of a last jumping off place before you got into the Caribbean" (19 May 1993). Low on money, Banks stayed in a dollar-a-night rooming house (actually a whorehouse) and began to look for work. Unable to find any, he was about to move on when he met up with two other men living in the same building: a young sailor from Oklahoma, AWOL from the base, and a slightly older man, a barker at strip shows in Atlantic City, fresh from a jail term in New Jersey. Card sharps with lots of money, both men wanted out of Key West, but neither could obtain a legal driver's license, which Banks had. So, for mutually expedient reasons, the three teamed up to drive "an old German Opal" from Miami across country for delivery to its owner in Los Angeles. What followed was a much wilder version of Banks's cross-country junket with Dario Morelli five and a half years earlier.

The trip, which should have taken only about a week, took three months. The three lingered in New Orleans for six weeks, staying at a motel populated by strippers the barker knew, then proceeded across Texas and into Oklahoma, to drop off the sailor at his parents' home. Banks and the convict then headed into northern Mexico, "stopping at these little towns, sitting around getting drunk, acting like fools and wastrels," as Banks remembers it (19 May 1993). Long after it was probably reported stolen, the car finally made its appearance in Los Angeles in the spring of 1962. Banks phoned the owner to notify him of its whereabouts in a store parking lot, with the keys tucked into the sun visor.

Banks then proceeded down to San Diego to visit his mother, who had relocated there, two years before, to take a job as a bookkeeper at Raytheon Corporation. Though he was glad to see his sister, Linda, and his brother, Chris, relations with his mother were strained, and he didn't much like southern California. After a few months, Banks called his father, who was then living in Concord, New Hampshire. His father advised him to come back East and "learn a useful trade, stop all this goofing around, and settle down and become a useful citizen," which Banks recalls as seeming "like a very good idea at that point" (19 May 1993).

After a series of hitchhiking adventures of the sort "made into a cliché by Kerouac," Banks arrived in New Hampshire, whereupon his father got him into the union as a plumber's apprentice (19 May 1993). Banks settled into a small apartment above the Apple Tree Bookstore on Warren Street in Concord—his "bachelor digs"—and bought a 1932 black Ford pickup truck. A pipe fitter by day, Banks was a fledgling writer, working on a novel, in his off-hours, which also included frequent forays into Boston to see his bohemian friends in the Back Bay and enjoy the city's bookstores, arts, and nightlife. It was a starkly bifurcated life but manageable all the same.

Less manageable was Banks's relationship with Mary Gunst, with whom he had been in touch ever since he had fled Boston the previous summer, even though both had come to the understanding that their troubled romance was, in Banks's words, "a broken one." By the time Banks returned to New England, Gunst was no longer living in Boston; she had transferred to Virginia Commonwealth University in Richmond for her senior year. That October, Banks phoned her to break off the relationship once and for all. The next night he found Mary Gunst at his doorstep; at a moment's notice she had dropped out of school to be with him. Shortly thereafter, on 29 October 1962, Banks and Gunst were married. They lived in Concord for the next year.

During that period Banks finished his first attempt at a novel, which he has since described as "quite simply awful, despite a few striking paragraphs here and there."[8] He took a week off from work in late August 1963 to attend the Breadloaf Writers' Conference near Middlebury, Vermont, then under the direction of poet John Ciardi. On the staff at Breadloaf was Nelson Algren, winner of the first National Book Award in 1949 for *Man with the Golden Arm,* and, at age 54, the unofficial dean of American proletarian fiction. As he was paid to do, Algren read Banks's manuscript and, as Banks recalls, "quickly located those few striking paragraphs and pointed them out to me and made it clear that I was supposed to do the rest myself (and what more can an apprentice writer ask of a master anyhow?)" (Banks, 1990, 34). After that, Algren, who didn't drive, suggested that the two of them escape the stuffy atmosphere of the colony, where writers drank sherry "with their little fingers in the air" (Banks, 1990, 34). The pair convened to a bar in Middlebury and cemented their friendship over beers. Banks, who recalls Algren as "large-hearted, funny, angry, lonely," entered into a mentor-acolyte relationship with him even more important than the one he had had with Leo Giroux (Banks, 1990, 34). Banks now credits Algren (who died in 1981) as having "validated me as a writer. [He] said this is real writing, you're a real writer. He said it in public, he declared it to me privately. And he allowed me to have access to him personally in a way which let me learn how to behave in the world as an adult writer" (19 May 1993).

Chapel Hill

Mary Gunst's well-to-do parents had not exactly taken to Banks with open arms. But after the marriage, the Gunsts came to reconcile themselves to their somewhat scruffy son-in-law. Before the birth of Caerthan in July of 1964—the first of three daughters Gunst and Banks would

have together—Banks's mother-in-law offered to pay his way through
college, an offer that Banks has since pronounced "one of the purely
generous acts I've encountered in my life" (Wilkie, 27). There was only
one stipulation: that Banks attend a college in the South so that Mary
could be near her family. Banks gladly accepted the offer and considered
Duke and the University of Virginia but finally chose the University of
North Carolina at Chapel Hill because it was coed, less formal, and
more cosmopolitan than the other schools. He enrolled there in September 1964, "the year," as Banks puts it, "that Chapel Hill kind of became
the Berkeley of the South. I walked in there expecting to go to a sleepy
but interesting southern town and a large but nonetheless fairly elite
state university. Instead I walked into a hotbed of radicalism. The Civil
Rights movement was everywhere and the anti-war movement was just
starting" (19 May 1993).

Banks recalls "two significant events" happening to him within a
week of his arrival, incidents that signaled the true beginning of "the
Sixties" for him personally. At a small gathering on campus, another
student, just back from Morocco, produced an attaché case entirely
filled with hashish. Later that week, Banks attended a racially integrated party in a house out in the country, an affair that was soon broken up by Ku Klux Klan gunfire. Coming from New Hampshire, where
there were relatively few blacks, Banks was shocked by the intense
racism that still permeated Chapel Hill, supposedly "the most liberal
city in the upper South" (Wilkie, 27). The experience radically altered
his views on race. As he told an interviewer, "until then, black people
had been exotic, mysterious, to me. They were more emblematic, symbolic to me than real. It wasn't really until Chapel Hill that I managed
to understand black Americans as human beings, and with that came an
understanding of the political reality of their lives" (Wilkie, 27).

Six years after the Colgate fiasco, Banks made the most of his second
chance at college. Majoring in English, he handled his course work with
great energy and skill, graduating Phi Beta Kappa in 1967 (in less than
three years). The same kind of striving marked Banks's literary interests
outside the classroom. In 1966 he and a close friend, poet William
Matthews, cofounded Lillabulero Press, to publish poetry chapbooks
and a little magazine, also entitled *Lillabulero,* "a Periodical of Literature
and the Arts" (along with poetry and fiction, the first four numbers also
featured loose-leaf portfolios of artwork). With Banks, Matthews, and
occasionally Newton Smith as editors, *Lillabulero* published a mix of
established and younger writers, all of whom were politically and aes-

thetically antiestablishment to varying degrees. Contributors included Gary Snyder, Robert Creeley, Nelson Algren, Malcolm Cowley, Diane Wakoski, Greg Kuzma, Margaret Randall, and Andre Codrescu.

Banks remembers the magazine as "a great focus for our chaotic energies and ambitions. We thought of ourselves as young Turks. Before long the magazine turned out, to our surprise, to have a following that wasn't just Chapel Hill."[9] Banks understates the case; quickly earning a national reputation for excellence, *Lillabulero* achieved and steadily maintained a circulation of about 1,000 copies throughout its eight-year life span.[10]

Banks also got himself published. In 1967 he and his coeditors, William Matthews and Newton Smith, each contributed five poems to *15 Poems,* a Lillabulero Press chapbook.[11] Banks's poems are artless in the extreme, plainspoken prose verse on the most prosaic subjects: the view from his bed, a maudlin drunk singing in a bar, a girl failing to catch a frisbee, a disappointing beach trip, and eight mournful haiku on a favorite Banks topic—the rigors of New England in winter. Mostly bad poetry, of which little can be said except that it is earnest and heart-felt.

More interesting is a short story that Banks published in the July 1967 issue of *Lillabulero,* entitled "The Adjutant Bird" (after a Kipling tale). Therein Banks recounts the true story of Yankee sea captain Frederick Tudor, who pioneered the shipping of ice from New England to the American South, the West Indies, and even India in the early 1800s. Banks's fascination with Tudor is telling in several ways. One attraction, no doubt, was the sheer oddity of Tudor's story. Marketing ice in the tropics before modern refrigeration was, to say the least, a strange, quixotic venture. Then there was the heroic element. Tudor eventually succeeded, through sheer will, courage, perseverance, and ingenuity, traits that Banks could well appreciate. On a deeper level, Tudor's story centers on a theme that had already marked Banks's life and would occupy an increasingly important place in his subsequent work: the intersection of alien worlds, especially the northern and southern hemispheres. Finally, there's the rich metaphor of the ice itself: a substance as fragile and elusive as truth, only precious where it is most evanescent.

Returning to the Wound

Though Banks and Mary Gunst were quite happy living in Chapel Hill, neither of them wanted to join the ranks "of that population that, after graduation, hangs around" town.[12] So in the summer of 1968, shortly after the birth of their second daughter, Maia, they left North Carolina for Northwood Narrows, New Hampshire. A small town in the southeastern corner of the state, Northwood was about a half an hour's drive west of Durham and not far from Barnstead, where Banks grew up. The choice was not accidental, of course. Though he now sees the move as hardly "a single-minded, obsessive return," Banks clearly had deep emotional ties to the area (12 August 1993). Furthermore, New England real estate was then extraordinarily cheap. A large house could be had for as little as $25,000, which is exactly what Banks and Gunst paid for "a pretentious Victorian farm house" that Banks despised but his wife loved (12 August 1993). Without much difficulty, Banks secured jobs teaching writing at Emerson College, Boston, and at the University of New Hampshire in Durham.

Joining Banks and his family in the move to Northwood were Doug Collins and his wife. Collins was a Lillabulero Press cohort and close friend with whom, Banks recalls, he "was able to share ideas and gained ideas from" (12 August 1993). Shortly thereafter, Banks and Collins were joined by the poet Charles Simic, who came to teach at the University of New Hampshire and whom Banks describes as his "fellow reader." In an intensive, self-imposed discipline much like graduate study, both would read the same books—detective fiction for awhile, then, perhaps, pre-Socratic philosophy or theoretical physics—and discuss ideas and responses.

The return to New Hampshire was soon manifest in Banks's writing. In 1969 Banks published his first poetry chapbook, *Waiting to Freeze,* through his own press, Lillabulero.[13] As the title suggests, the 10 poems contained therein are steeped in the bleak atmospherics of New England in winter, a real landscape but also the psychic terrain of Banks's troubled youth. In a poem entitled "Purchase," Banks speaks directly to his need to keep on returning to New England

> [f]or chances
> To bicker with memories,
> To re-enter the lists
> Armed with the cool gigantic force
> Of dead anger,
> Making messes of the past,

> Remaking everything
> In my own images.

As Banks later told Wesley Brown, "I can see my life as a kind of obsessive return to the 'wound' ... Going back again and again trying to get
it right, trying to figure out how it happened and who is to blame and
who is to forgive" (Brown, 68).

Returning to the "wound" seems to have had salutary effects. Banks's
family was filled out with the birth of a fourth daughter, Danis, in January of 1970. And his literary endeavors proceeded apace. That same
year, one of Banks's stories was chosen for inclusion in *Best American
Short Stories*. Three years later he won the Fels Award for fiction. Shortly
thereafter, while serving as visiting professor at New England College in
Henniker, New Hampshire, Banks published a longer poem entitled
Snow: Meditations of a Cautious Man in Winter, a comic novella, *Family
Life,* and his short story collection *Searching for Survivors*.[14]

Snow picks up where *Waiting to Freeze* leaves off. Written in short,
spare lines, the poem begins as a meditation on the hardness of New
England winters. But, halfway through, memory takes over and the
cold, snowy landscape once again becomes the primal scene of the poet's
traumatic childhood: "*Hands!* I'd looked for / *hands!* Fisted, / like knot-
ted wet rope. / Hands pounding down on me, the / face fading above."
Suddenly reliving the horror of his past, the speaker—clearly Banks—
engages in guilty self-interrogation:

Are you, have you ever been, a *violent* man?

> Yes. Of course. My father
> beat me. He was a champion youth.
> A brawler in the ring, as they tell it now,
> But a precise boxer in the streets.
> I was neither,
> I fear.
> But I would have settled for either. Listen can't we talk
> about something else for a change? Yes,
> I was, have been, am still,
> a violent man. But I've only beaten

> women and men.
> I've never been anything
> but kind to children

Here the poem's real subject emerges: how Banks's father's beatings instilled violence in him, which he, in turn, inflicted upon others. Banks admitted as much to Wesley Brown: "When I was much younger, I was a violent man ... I was violent against the people I loved. But I was never violent against my children. That's as specific as I can be" (Brown, 70).

The sombre and deeply personal tone of *Snow* finds marked contrast in *Family Life*, an absurdist fable set in contemporary North America but featuring fairy tale characters: King Egress the Hearty (sometimes "The Bluff"), his wife, Naomi Ruth, their three sons, Princes Egress, Dread, and Orgone, and various other zanies. Highly episodic and virtually plotless, *Family Life* superimposes the hip psychobabble of seventies pop culture unto the medieval folktale genre for comic effect. Yet Banks's underlying intention is serious: to satirize the inane self-importance of the domestic melodrama, a narrative impulse that has come to dominate contemporary American culture across all its media. The critics were mystified and not at all amused; they savaged the book, finding it "impenetrable," "heavy-handed and pretentious," "appallingly clumsy."[15] If *Snow* was too private and esoteric to add to Banks's fledgling literary reputation, *Family Life* actually damaged it.

Banks was, however, on firmer ground with *Searching for Survivors*, a collection of 14 stories dedicated to the memory of his younger brother, Christopher, who was killed at the age of 17 in 1968, when the freight train he was riding in was destroyed in a mud-slide outside of Santa Barbara, California, a tragedy movingly recounted in the collection's closing story, "Searching for Survivors (II)." Also of note are three stories that feature, in varying degrees of irony, one of the heroes of Banks's adolescence, the late Che Guevara (to whom Banks had already paid homage in a 1969 poem).[16]

The collection, which won the St. Lawrence Award for short fiction, was generally well received by critics. *Publishers Weekly* cited Banks's talent for the "evocation of place, his feel for the Yankee sensibility and New England landscape."[17] Thomas LeClair, writing in the *New York Times Book Review*, was equally generous in his assessment: "Some of the stories are journeyman stuff and several are Barthelmean oddments, but the best are as deceptive as wisdom. In them invention seems off-hand and natural, artifice and circumstance one. Without being small, Banks's stories have an assurance few younger—or established—writers can match."[18]

Bipolarity

After the publication of *Searching for Survivors* Banks's career noticeably gathered momentum. In 1976 he applied for and won a coveted Guggenheim Fellowship. A few years earlier Banks had had the opportunity to rent a vacation house in Jamaica, where he became "deeply attracted to the culture, the people, and fell in love with the place" (Thiébaux, 121). He used the $25,000 Guggenheim grant to install himself and his family in an estate on Jamaica rented out by whites who had fled Michael Manley's new regime for Canada. The Bankses stayed on the island for more than a year, from May 1976 to September 1977.

In the course of his stay, Banks finished two book-length manuscripts and several short stories. When he wasn't writing, Banks took pains to adapt to the island and its culture. As he told Wesley Brown, "I used to hang out with a bunch of guys in Jamaica who played dominoes. I made a point of getting good at it. It was a way of learning patois, and people forgot I was an American and started dealing with me as if I were just another guy playing dominoes. At some point, I realized that these men—carpenters, stone masons, upholsterers and cab drivers—did the same things as the men I knew growing up" (Brown, 68).

Banks also ventured into the back country, where he made friends among the Maroons, a religious sect descended from Ashanti slaves who had successfully rebelled against the British in the late eighteenth century. At the same time, Banks supplemented his travels with extensive reading on the history of Jamaica and Caribbean life in general. As he told an interviewer, "Like most fiction writers, I'm really a library rat, and look for excuses to research something" (Thiébaux, 121).

Banks's wife and children returned to Northwood in June of 1977. Banks stayed on in Jamaica until September. He would later recall that by the time he returned home, the marriage, "which had been coming undone for some years ... was pretty much kaput" (12 August 1993). Despite deep bonds of affection, there were fundamental differences in temperament that made a parting of the ways inevitable. Jamaica had catalyzed the break: "we really kind of went our separate ways down there. I had my interests and my life and the children were the main thing that kept us together" (12 August 1993). Barely a month after returning home, Banks moved out of the house. He bought a small farmhouse just down the road, to remain close to the children, who now ranged in age from 7 to 13.

Out of a marriage, Banks also found himself out of work. During his absence, Banks's teaching job at the University of New Hampshire was discontinued. Luckily, Banks was able to secure a tenure-track position at New England College in Henniker, where he had been visiting professor three years earlier. And his literary career continued to flourish with the publication, in 1978, of two books he had worked on in the Caribbean: *Hamilton Stark*, his second novel, and *The New World: Tales*, his second collection of short fiction.[19]

Hamilton Stark is set in New Hampshire, though much of it was written in Jamaica. Indeed, *Hamilton Stark* shows every evidence of being another attempt by Banks to understand himself by reimagining his New England past: a daunting, perhaps impossible project, given the enormous complexity of any individual's identity. Banks acknowledges as much by beginning with a quote from Kierkegaard: "The individual has a host of shadows, all of which resemble him and for the moment have an equal claim to authenticity."

Banks's title character, Hamilton Stark, is his case in point. A five-times married misanthropic Yankee who is fond of dumping his garbage on his property and then shooting at it with a high-powered rifle, Stark is a veritable mass of contradictions: "self-centered, immature, violent, cruel, eccentric, and possibly insane," but also meticulously well groomed, funny, handsome, ferociously quick witted, relentlessly honest, and a great dancer to boot. Husky, turbulent Stark is partly self-caricature but mostly a kind of mythic portrait of Banks's father, Earl.

Banks's unnamed narrator (another version of the author) is in love with Stark's daughter, Rochelle. Obsessed with "Ham" in all his abominable glory, both are writing, or attempting to write, books about the man. In the end, though, the subject proves too elusive for satisfactory closure. Tracking Stark on his weekly trek to the summit of Blue Job Mountain, the narrator loses him altogether and is left, in the largest sense, with "Nothing. *Unimaginable nothing.*"

In the final analysis, *Hamilton Stark* is an epistemological thriller, a self-deconstructing detective novel/(auto)biography that embraces indeterminacy without lapsing into solipsism or despair. Banks's methods reinforce his message. Though there is nothing extraordinary about his prose, which might be described as a kind of witty naturalism, with lots of sly authorial asides, the overall structure of the novel is self-consciously postmodern. As critic Ann Birstein has pointed out, the book resembles a kaleidoscope of constantly shifting patterns, with Banks "using every literary device at hand, including a formal introduction to the novel, an elaborate study of the geography and history of the region, Hamilton's reminiscences, tape recordings by his [ex-]wives, various addenda, philosophical digressions, footnotes," and the like.[20] Though some critics found so many obvious displays of artifice cloying, most reviewers felt that Banks had managed to apply sophisticated metafictional techniques wisely and well.

As for *The New World*, Banks divides the book into two parts, each containing five stories. The first section, headed "Renunciation," features realistic tales of contemporary American life. Focusing especially on the vagaries of sexual relationships, Banks offers no easy moral judgments, only the studied irony so evident in *Hamilton Stark*. The second half of the collection, "Transformation," is decidedly more experimental in style and subject matter, a neat bifurcation reflecting Banks's as yet unresolved ambivalence regarding the uses of realism versus metafiction. In four of these five stories, Banks employs a narrative technique perfected by E. L. Doctorow, which involves casting historical figures in imaginary situations.[21] Simon Bolívar, Jane Hogarth (wife of William Hogarth, the painter), Edgar Allan Poe, and Jamaicans Bernardo de Balbuena (seventeenth-century Spanish prelate and poet) and Mosseh Alvares (a Sephardic goldsmith)—all are taken out of the abstract, distant past and depicted in intensely intimate, living terms. In effect, history shades into fiction and fiction melds into history. Banks's central theme, though, is the enduring human need to reinvent the self in order to escape or transcend the constrictions of one's actual circumstances. This means creating a "new world" out of the imagination, just as the "discovery" of the Americas opened up vast horizons for a culturally exhausted Old World Europe.

Stylistically sophisticated and conceptually daring, *The New World* was deemed "pretentious" in some quarters, a charge critics often leveled at Banks's earlier work, probably because of its cerebral, ratiocinative properties.[22] Other reviewers were able to see beyond Banks's fondness for complex contrivance. Finding the collection's "strongest and most common trait ... a wonderful exercise of the imagination," Robert Kiely pronounced Banks a writer who "deserves watching."[23] *Publishers Weekly* was even more enthusiastic: " 'The New World' is ... the kind of unequivocally brilliant performance that one can't ever be sure of seeing twice in any writer's career."[24]

With *Hamilton Stark* Banks had examined, from almost every conceivable point of view, the myriad and contradictory facets of an individual personality. In his next novel, *The Book of Jamaica* (1980), Banks applied the same sort of perceptual intensity to the entire culture of Jamaica, his setting and subject.[25] This time, however, formal pyrotechnics were eschewed in favor of a relatively straightforward narrative style and structure. The only significant innovation Banks allowed himself was a declension of his unnamed narrator's voice, which begins in the first person, eventually shifts to the second, and ends in the third, as the narrator is inexorably drawn out of himself and into the life of the island. Not surprisingly, that narrator is loosely based on Banks himself: a 36-year-old New Hampshire college professor and novelist on a grant to study the Maroons. Aptly described by critic Darryl Pinckney as "extravagantly sincere, alert to cultural differences, and filled with racial guilt," Banks's narrator is the archetypal liberal academic, well meaning but rather smug in his relentless "grasping after certainty."[26]

The island, however, is a "text" not easily read by an outsider. Indeed, mysteries abound, not least of which is a decades-old murder that might have involved Jamaica's most famous white resident, the notoriously roguish actor, Errol Flynn. For the narrator (and for Banks), Flynn is a powerfully evocative symbol of all that is wrong with the affluent West: its casual brutality, its decadence, its flagrant disrespect for other cultures. Yet Banks refuses to settle for easy moral dichotomies. His narrator's growing identification with the miserably exploited Maroons culminates in an ill-advised attempt to mediate a treaty dispute, an act of friendly meddling that only results in violence and terror. The man the natives come to call "Johnny" (the Jamaican name for a trusted foreigner) leaves the island less certain than ever as to what he had experienced.

Most critics were deeply impressed by *The Book of Jamaica*. Jerome Klinkowitz called it a "truly excellent novel" and "the breakthrough novel for commercially innovative fiction in America."[27] The reviewer for *Booklist* applied Banks's own description of the Jamaican taste in music to the novel as a whole: "impeccable and serious, knowledgeable and refined."[28]

With his next book, *Trailerpark* (1981), Banks once again trained his sights on New England working-class life.[29] A collection of 13 interrelated stories, *Trailerpark* is strongly reminiscent of Sherwood Anderson's *Winesburg, Ohio* in form, content, and overall mood. Each of the stories deals with one of the dozen or so denizens of Granite State Trailerpark (in central New Hampshire), all of whom are "generally alone in the world." There are "widows and widowers, divorcees and bachelors and retired Army officers, a black man in a white society, a black woman there, too, a drug dealer, a solitary child of a broken home, a drunk, a homosexual in a heterosexual society—all of them, man and woman, adult and child, basically alone in the world." Indeed, Banks's main theme is the terrible isolation of the poor, a condition that breeds anomie, derangement, and various forms of suicidal behavior. But, as critic Jonathan Yardley has pointed out, "the natural human instinct is to seek community," an instinct that finds "these utterly unconnected people ... drawn together by the accident of living in the same place; the trailer park, grim and dreary as it may be, is a neighborhood. And into it Banks has crowded a small but vibrant cast of characters, a human comedy in microcosm."[30]

One commentator rightly noted that *Trailerpark* "was a more thorough-going exploration of literary realism than *The New World* or anything [Banks] had written until that time."[31] Used to thinking of Banks as an experimental writer in the Barthelme camp, critics were divided over the conspicuous ordinariness of *Trailerpark*'s style and subject matter. To reviewer Mary Soete the stories were "haunting in their moments of recognition and reversal."[32] Calling *Trailerpark* "a lucid, serious, witty frieze of a book," Anna Shapiro found Banks's characters "impossible to condescend to," despite their "bad grammar and stereotypical poverty."[33] Jonathan Yardley detected "a jaunty, lightly mocking quality" in Banks's prose that he found "entirely engaging" (Yardley, 3). On the other hand, *Kirkus Reviews* felt that Banks made his characters function "as illustrations, as primal types," contriving a "mythic determinism" that replaces "mysterious vertigo with puppetry. Talented work from a special writer, yet somehow it all misses by a hair."[34]

Not long after the publication of *Trailerpark*, Banks entered into a third marriage, with Kathy Walton, then director of the Associated Writing Programs. Intent on working as an editor in Manhattan's publishing district, Walton persuaded Banks to relocate to New York City. After five years at New England College and twelve years of living in New Hampshire, Banks was willing to experience urban life and to "get into a larger pool of writers and intellectuals" (12 August 1993). Walton found work as an editor at Harper & Row, and Banks accepted a combined position, teaching writing at the Columbia University graduate school and at Princeton University.

The next year (1983) Banks finally found a publisher for *The Relation of My Imprisonment*, a novella that he had written in Jamaica in 1977.[35] If critics found *Trailerpark* something of a departure for Banks, they were in for another surprise with *Relation*'s first-person testimony, in mock Puritan dialect, of a coffin maker imprisoned for worshipping the dead. As critic Jodi Daynard notes, "relation" refers to an archaic literary form "first used by jailed Puritan divines in the seventeenth century to relate the tests their faith had endured in prison. Each relation was read aloud to a congregation of their free brethren and framed with selected scriptures and a sermon."[36] Banks generally follows the formal conventions of the genre, but only to convey a message that would have been deeply heretical to the Puritans, who revered God, not death. Indeed, *Relation* struck most reviewers as a bizarre work, but also strangely mesmerizing, as if Banks had set out to repel and fascinate at the same time.

Deirdre Bair calls the novel a "parable, allegory, exemplum, and even scripture of a sort" but demurs from offering any exact explanation as to what Banks's symbolic narrative is about.[37] In Jodi Daynard's opinion, Banks "succeeded in capturing the fundamental paradigm of human worship: the sense of infinity, the awe before something more perfect than oneself, which comes when one has surmounted the worship of desire" (Daynard, 28). Yet the book's rather chilling epigraph, "Remember death," suggests a more primal message: the existential notion that life should be lived in constant awareness of one's mortality, especially in a culture overwhelmingly devoted to the denial of death.[38]

In his 1989 interview with Wesley Brown, Banks used the word "bipolarity" to describe the way his work swings back and forth between New England and the tropics (Brown, 68). The same term can also be applied to questions of style. Until the mid eighties, Banks favored realism for his shorter works, metafiction for his novels. Banks decisively resolved both sets of dichotomies in his fourth novel, *Continental Drift*, published in 1985.[39] Written in a kind of neo-Dreiserian realist idiom that Banks has employed ever since, *Continental Drift* brings together working-class New England and the Caribbean by alternating between two narrative threads.

The main story concerns Bob Dubois, a 30-year-old oil burner repairman from Catamount, New Hampshire, who migrates to central Florida to seek a better life for himself and his family. The other narrative focuses on Vanise Dorsinville, a young black woman who flees the grinding poverty of Haiti for the United States, with infant son and nephew in tow. These symmetrical migrations—one south, the other north—converge off the coast of Florida with horrifyingly tragic results.

At 366 pages, *Continental Drift* was Banks's longest and most ambitious work to date. It is still widely regarded as his best. A strong seller (over 15,000 copies in hard cover, 100,000 in the paperback edition), *Continental Drift* won the John Dos Passos Award and the American Academy of Arts and Letters Award, was nominated for a Pulitzer Prize (which it narrowly missed winning), and was deemed one of "the best books of 1985" by *Library Journal*.[40]

Critics reached an unusual degree of consensus regarding the novel's signal strengths: the vivid, "compulsively readable" prose, the driven intensity of the narrative, Banks's ability to evoke the desperate reality of subaltern lives without condescension or bathos. In an important review for the *Atlantic Monthly*, critic James Atlas praised the novel extravagantly: "*Continental Drift* is the most convincing portrait I know of contemporary America: its greed, its uprootedness, its indifference to the past. This is a novel about the way we live now."[41]

Still, no one claimed the book was flawless. In an otherwise favorable review, James Marcus found Banks's handling of the Haitian chapters less than persuasive: "[S]ome of the lengthier accounts of voodoo ritual ... give off the gentlest whiff of something cooked up from a stack of *National Geographic*s."[42] Conversely, Wendy Lesser accused Banks of "monstrous pretention" for attempting "to tell Vanise's story from the inside."[43] In an interview with Janet Maslin, Banks pleaded guilty to a lesser offense—a certain detachment—in his treatment of Vanise and her culture: "It seems to me that to write about the interior life of a Haitian woman is a presumptuous thing for an American white male to do."[44]

In the end, though, Banks's narrative methods aroused the most controversy. As he had so often done before, Banks bucked convention by deliberately foregrounding the ineluctibly contrived nature of storytelling with an omniscient narrator who sometimes steps in to explicate or comment upon his characters' inner lives.[45] Furthermore, Banks prefaces the body of the novel with an "Invocation" in which he ritualistically summons a narrative voice to conjure Bob DuBois to life. Banks ends the novel with "Envoi," a coda that returns his narrator to center stage, to comment on the significance of all that has transpired.

Mistaking Banks's carefully considered rejection of realist illusionism as mere pomposity, Wendy Lesser found "Envoi," for example, "egomaniacal" and "distressingly arrogant" (Lesser, 468). Less apt to judge, Jean Strouse was filled with questions regarding Banks's authorial asides: "What is the point of these intrusions, which condescend to Bob and lecture the rest of us? It is not that Mr. Banks can't create a character without such assists, since he has done that masterfully both here and in previous work. Maybe he is posing a question about storytelling itself—the process of finding narrative lines that organize, or pretend to organize, experience ... Maybe denying Bob the "magic" coherence of fiction underscores this question precisely by undermining the story—but then, maybe not."[46] To Robert Towers, however, Banks's "intrusive voice provides sweep and momentum, advancing the action rather than impeding it, and this defiance of the conventions of faceless realism does much to make *Continental Drift* a vigorous and original novel."[47]

Winters Tales

However problematic it might have been to some critics, *Continental Drift* was the book that transformed Banks's career. Formerly a respected but little-known writer of "serious" (i.e., academic) fiction, Banks suddenly found himself elevated to mainstream status, extensively reviewed and widely read. Even Hollywood came calling. Director Jonathan Demme bought the screen rights to *Continental Drift* and hired Banks to right the screenplay, a task he says he found "very difficult. In a way, I had already seen the movie" (Wilkie, 27). (The film version has yet to be made.) Another signal of Banks's new status: Robert B. Wyatt, then editor in chief at Ballantine Books, bought the rights to Banks's earlier books and reissued them in a standard format, as yellow-jacketed paperbacks with uniform covers.

The irony of finally becoming a literary success by writing about the failure of the American Dream was not lost on Banks. In a 1987 interview with Trish Reeves, Banks cited his own case to make a distinction between the American Dream of success as spiritual redemption and the reality he had personally experienced.

> I still view myself in the larger world the way I did when I was an adolescent. My view of myself in relation to the larger world is that of a working class family: powerless people who look up from below. I'm unable to escape that. I guess one of my recurrent themes ... is that one can't escape that—how one views oneself in the larger structure is determined at an extremely early age. The great delusion is that if you only can get success then you will shift your view of yourself ... you will become a different person. That's the longing, for success is really not material goods, but in fact to become a whole new person ... The *delusion* is that success

will change you—it's the American Dream—you can kill the old person
and become a new one. (Reeves, 59)

The conviction that American success ideology is predicated upon
wholly fanciful and largely unconscious notions of self-transformation
would form the master theme for Banks's next book, a fourth collection
of short fiction entitled *Success Stories* (1986).

Yet another book that manifests Banks's bipolarity, *Success Stories,* as
Isabel Fonseca has pointed out, "is not a particularly coherent collection—it has the makings of two books (and one of them is a novel)."[48]
Half of the dozen stories contained therein are quasi-autobiographical
narratives; the other six are wholly imagined parables. In one way or
another, though, all 12 stories have to do with success as a decidedly
ironic outcome, devoutly to be wished but, when finally attained,
almost unrecognizable.

The strongest and most haunting of the parables is "Sarah Cole: A
Type of Love Story." The narrator, a divorced young professional named
Ron, self-described as "extremely handsome," even "beautiful," meets
haggard divorcée Sarah Cole in a fern bar in Concord, New Hampshire.
She is, by Ron's reckoning, a woman with a face "homelier than any he
has ever seen or imagined before." Mesmerized by her extraordinary
ugliness, Ron strikes up a conversation with the woman in order to
experience the perverse thrill of gazing at her, perhaps to revel in his
own attractiveness. The two eventually fall in love and begin a very private affair that ends abruptly when Sarah demands that Ron go a step
further and acknowledge her publicly. Committed to his culture's dominant notions of beauty and status, Ron violently rejects Sarah Cole,
repeatedly calling her an "ugly bitch" to ward off his own guilt. Yet the
ending contains a final paradox. By humiliating and reviling her, Ron
transforms the crone with the "dumpy, off-center wreck of a body" into
"the most beautiful woman I've ever seen"; in her dejected vulnerability,
Sarah takes on a delicate, ethereal aspect.

On one level "Sarah Cole" is a deft and scathing attack on the American obsession with physical beauty and the narcissism that skews all
human relationships. But, true to form, Banks deepens the meaning of
his story by taking up the concomitant issue of social class. Ron is, for all
intents and purposes, a "yuppie." Sarah Cole, an overweight, uneducated, divorced mother of three who works in a printing plant, is unmistakably proletarian. Though not conscious of doing so, Ron toys with
his own class identity by involving himself with a woman ordinarily

unacceptable to one of his type and station in life. In the end, he experiences a terrifying epiphany regarding the reality of social class: that it is an unassailable, everyday fact, not merely an uncomfortable abstraction. Furthermore, he learns that the walls separating the classes are virtually impermeable; no sane person of privilege would risk the deep shame of being associated with one's social inferiors.

The quasi-autobiographical stories that comprise the other half of the collection form a loose narrative cycle that deals with Banks's own coming of age. In these stories Banks calls himself "Earl Painter" and changes the names of family, friends, and many other incidentals as well. He does, however, strive to remain true to the emotional reality of the events he is describing. For example, in "Queen for a Day," Banks reprises one of the most painful periods in his life: the immediate aftermath of his father's abandonment of the family in 1952. Desperate to help his struggling mother, 12-year-old Earl writes a series of letters to Jack Bailey, host of *Queen for a Day*, a notoriously maudlin television program that actually awarded prizes to housewives who could summon the worst hard luck stories. Banks subtly suggests that Earl's hope that he can get his mother on the show is tantamount to an equally forlorn hope for his father's return. That Hollywood never calls is a lesson in disillusionment that helps Earl accept the fact that his father is gone forever. Hence, Banks redefines success along deeper lines: as an honest and clear-headed adjustment to the hard facts of life.

After the resounding triumph of *Continental Drift,* the critical response to *Success Stories* was comparatively tepid, indeed a virtual repeat of Banks's handling by reviewers when he brought out *Trailerpark* on the heels of *The Book of Jamaica* five years earlier. And once again, almost predictably, critics refused to accept Banks's Brechtian narrative tactics on their own terms. There were several complaints about the author's tendency "to patly aphorize about characters' feelings and development," as if all good writing must, by definition, preserve the seamless illusion of a text without an author.[49]

Before producing a wholly new work, Banks did something almost unheard of in the literary world; he went back to one of his already-published novels, revised it, and republished it. The novel was, of course, *Family Life,* the one scourged by critics when it was published in 1975. Brought out again, in a deluxe edition by Sun & Moon Press (Los Angeles) in May of 1988, *Family Life* was only a slightly altered rendition of its original version. Yet, this time, the critical response was markedly different. *Publishers Weekly*, which had derided the first edition, noted "a wonderfully funny range of literary styles" and went on to describe the revamped novel as "exuberant and irreverent," baring "a knife-edge of social satire."[50] *Booklist* also offered a similarly glowing evaluation: "Sexually frank, tongue-in-cheek, deliciously humorous, this little novel deserves republication. It's totally original in conception and presentation."[51]

Family Life caricatured the modern nuclear family as a kind of psychosexual circus. With his next novel, *Affliction* (1989), Banks continued to explore issues of family dysfunction, most centrally the curse of male violence that had affected him so directly. The thesis of *Affliction* is a notion that Banks had introduced in his long poem, *Snow*, some 14 years earlier, that the compulsion to do violence is passed down from father to son, "like a secret blood disease."[52] As he later explained in an interview with Laurel Graeber, Banks wrote *Affliction* "to understand my own life, and also my father's and grandfather's. I wanted to know what brought them to be the human beings they were, and why they inflicted so much suffering."[53]

The novel is set in Lawford, New Hampshire, a bleak, impoverished backwoods town "someplace halfway between other places," not unlike Bob DuBois's Catamount. Indeed, Banks's protagonist, Wade White-house, is a more menacing and desperate version of DuBois. Forty-one years of age and uneducated, Whitehouse holds down jobs as a part-time cop, well driller, and snowplow driver, but his "real daily work," in the apt words of Fred Pfeil, "is the management of an unstable and ever-enlarging fund of pain and fear" (Pfeil, 76–77). Mercilessly beaten by his alcoholic father as a boy, Wade has turned into a depressive, rage-filled alcoholic in his middle age, living alone in a trailer in the aftermath of a marriage broken up by his own drunken violence. Predictably, despite desperate, misguided attempts to turn his desolate life around, Wade Whitehouse self-destructs and takes his father and another man with him; the psychic scarring of a brutal upbringing proves too great a force to overcome.

Though "almost unremittingly grim," the spectacle of Wade's steady descent into the abyss is at least partially redeemed through the empathic perspective of his younger brother, Rolfe, Banks's narrator.[54] Rolfe, a high school history teacher in the Boston area, is, like Banks himself, the son who escaped his working-class origins, which also meant escaping the vortex of violence and hopelessness that claimed Wade. Educated, articulate, highly sensitive to the moral nuances of Wade's fate, Rolfe leavens, with pity, the terror of Wade's story. Yet it would be something of an oversimplification to identify Rolfe with Banks himself and to see Wade only as a type for Banks's father, Earl (to whom the book is tellingly dedicated). As Julian Loose has noted, the unmarried "Rolfe can absent himself from the awful tradition of male violence only by cultivating 'an elegiac mode of relatedness,' a drastic kind of emotional withdrawal; but Wade, less fortunate, finds himself doomed to repeat the pattern, and to his horror becomes ever more like his father."[55] In his interview with Wesley Brown, Banks offers a self-description, as reformed and chastened brute, that unmistakably evokes Wade and Rolfe as before-and-after aspects of himself: "When I was much younger, I was a violent man. As I got older, I became a controlled and restrained man who withdrew from any situation where I was vulnerable—especially with women and children. I avoided intimacy, so there was no chance of being caught with my guard down" (Brown, 70). Whatever else it might be, *Affliction* is Banks's most concerted attempt, since *Hamilton Stark*, to exorcise the ghost of his troubled, violent father.

As one commentator noted, *Affliction* "failed to arouse the [almost] unanimous enthusiasm of reviewers, as *Continental Drift* had done." It did, however, confirm Banks's "stature as a major American novelist with access to the mainstream."[56] Elizabeth Tallent termed *Affliction* "psychological portraiture of a high order . . . a beautifully sustained, suspenseful and many-leveled evocation."[57] To Alice Bloom, Banks's sixth novel was "haunting, passionate . . . one of the best I have read for many years."[58] "In its stark intensity and everyday familiarity," wrote Jon Saari, "this superb novel is joltingly disturbing, as all deeply felt personal tragedies can be."[59]

With his next novel, *The Sweet Hereafter* (1991), Banks avoided the omniscient, implicated, editorializing narrator that so many critics have found problematic in his later work.[60] Instead of a single, guiding narrator, Banks employs four consecutive first-person narrators to tell the story of a horrifying schoolbus accident that took the lives of 14 children in the mythical town of Sam Dent in upstate New York. Each narrator embodies a singular and crucial perspective on the events. Dolores Driscoll, the bus driver responsible for the accident, comes to serve, quite naturally, as the town scapegoat. Billy Ansel, a Vietnam veteran who lost two children in the crash, represents all the bereaved parents in Sam Dent trying to cope with the tragedy. Mitchell Stephens, a New York attorney specializing in negligence cases, is corporate society's emissary; his job is to assign legal blame. Finally, Nichole Burnell, a young cheerleader and beauty queen crippled in the accident, embodies the perspective of the victim and survivor.

Banks does not dwell upon the grisy details of the accident itself. As he told an interviewer, he wrote the novel "to explore how a community is both disrupted and unified by a tragedy."[61] An equally important theme is the inexplicable mystery of life and death. Despite what one reviewer nicely described as "the deep-seated human need to fix blame," exhibited by the victims' survivors and their legions of lawyers, the accident was just that: an accident.[62] Yet that critical insight is lost on most of the anguished inhabitants of Sam Dent until Nichole Burnell torpedoes all pending litigation by falsely claiming that she saw Dolores Driscoll driving well over the posted speed limit. Nichole's lie was designed to hurt and repudiate her sexually abusive father, but the overall effect is to liberate Sam Dent from devisive legal battles that distract it from the more subtle and difficult work of healing, of accepting the unacceptable.

Described by critics as "gripping," "beautifully written," "a very good book," "a very accomplished book, well planned and well executed," *The Sweet Hereafter* was less ambitious and more accessible than either *Continental Drift* or *Affliction*.[63] On the other hand, more than one reviewer noted that there was "something disturbingly formulaic about it" (May, 793): "The bus driver is married to a stroke victim; the bereaved father of two is a Vietnam veteran *and* a cancer-widower; the teenaged girl stuck in a wheelchair is *also* a victim of her father's seductions; the lawyer's grown daughter, hopelessly lost to drugs, turns out *also* to have AIDS ... [The story leaves] no topic untouched, as if pleading to become a TV movie."[64] Yet no critic could deny that *The Sweet Hereafter* is a highly readable novel animated by a profound moral vision.

Banks's eighth novel, *Rule of the Bone* (1995), presents the first-person narrative of Chapman ("Chappie") Dorset, a 14-year-old mall rat from upstate New York who bears considerable resemblance to Huck Finn and Holden Caulfield. A product of divorce, Chappie breaks with his mother and abusive stepfather and embarks on a journey of self-discovery that takes him into an underworld of bikers, drugs, child pornography, and homelessness. But, true to the form of the bildungsroman, Chappie, also known as "Bone," eventually achieves a kind of moral redemption through the guidance of a middle-aged Rastafarian mentor figure named I-Man. Though marred by certain improbabilities in plotting, *Bone* received generally favorable reviews for its vivid evocation of the contemporary teenage street

scene, a harrowing world that speaks volumes about the spiritual condition of American society.

As of this writing, Russell Banks, now in his mid fifties and a full professor at Princeton University, is nearing completion of his ninth novel,
on the fiery abolitionist John Brown. Divorced from Kathy Walton in
1988, Banks is now married to poet Chase Twitchell, who also teaches at
Princeton. For the last few years, they've divided their time between a
home in Princeton and a summer house in Keene, New York, in the
Adirondack Mountains—both locations a long way, metaphorically
speaking, from Newton, Massachusetts, or Barnstead, New Hampshire.
Banks himself finds it "hard to believe" he has "come this far," turning
up "alive and more or less coherent" into his middle age: "Yet," he
writes, "year after year, like the proverbial bad penny, I do keep turning
up, and the very persistence of the fact continues to astonish me,
although I've certainly done little else but try to turn up" (Banks, 1991,
33). More than merely "turning up," Banks has already produced a
body of work that will eventually insure his recognition as one of the
most important American writers of the post–Vietnam War period.

Chapter 2
The Poetry

The thing you're after
may lie around the bend.

Charles Olson

Russell Banks started his literary career as an aspiring poet, publishing verse in small press magazines and chapbooks in the late sixties and early seventies. Thereafter, he devoted himself exclusively to fiction writing. Consequently, Banks's poetry is little known now, even among those who admire his fiction. But then Banks has never considered himself much of a poet. In his 1986 interview with Trish Reeves, he spoke of being unable "to write poetry that seems very good or interesting to me ... Faulkner said all fiction writers are failed poets, and he was speaking of himself. But I also think he was speaking of many of us as well" (Reeves, 45). Banks's dour self-appraisal is largely—but, as we shall see, not entirely—true. Certainly his earliest efforts in verse come off as distinctly amateurish, the made-to-order work of a dilletante rushing himself into print without having a great deal to say or knowing how to say it. But there is also verve, precision, and vividness in his writing that bespeak genuine talent.

15 Poems

Among Banks's first publications of any kind are five short, slice-of-life, free-verse poems included in *15 Poems* (1967), the Lillabulero Press chapbook that Banks published with William Matthews and Newton Smith while all three were still at Chapel Hill. Banks's selections begin with "Point of View," an 18-line poem in three uneven stanzas. In the first stanza, the speaker describes the view from his bed: "through three yellow-curtained windows ... twelve Carolina pines / bowing / from half-way down / to just below their tops." The second stanza qualifies the first: "Only when I lie in bed alone, though." Then the final stanza amplifies the one that precedes it: "You will come home / and I will face you; / turning my head / and pressing feet against the wall." What purported to be a matter-of-fact relating of the view from the poet's bed turns out to be something of a love poem, albeit one conspicuously lacking in romantic sentiment.

The deliberate suppression of sentiment that marks "Point of View" becomes the explicit theme of "Old Man in a Bar." A "soft, white-bellied" old man drunkenly sings along with a then-popular Supremes tune on the juke box: "... *what the wurld needs now / is love—Sweet love* ..." Overcome with emotion, the man breaks into tears, a display derided by the younger patrons. Now enraged, the old man "barks" at his tormentors "from across the room," then

> he comes down on their short blond heads
> with his strong silver cane.
> They did not feel the blows.

The crux of the poem is contained in that last line, which literally bespeaks the old man's powerlessness but, on a more metaphoric level, proclaims the world's stubborn impermeability to sentiment of any kind.

Cast in the present tense, the third poem, "Disc," offers a "live" description of the flight of a frisbee in progress:

> Now it crosses the apogee
> dips & now it nears the point
> of a black-haired girl
> carefully shuffling thick legs,
> fixing the point,
> who waits.

The girl misjudges the disc's trajectory, however. She

> shoves out her fat hand
> and before the motion is complete—
> yanks it back,
> still fat,
> and hears the disc
> plop behind her in the grass.

With "Disc" Banks set himself a purely technical problem: to describe an event with maximal accuracy and concision. He mostly succeeds; the poem seems to take place in real time, unfolding at about the same rate as the action it is narrating. The only wrong note is the unnecessary observation that the girl's hand is "still fat" when she "yanks it back."

With his fourth selection, "Lobsters," Banks widens his focus, from the carefully considered moment to an entire day's experience. The poem describes a "3rd of July" excursion, from Boston to the southern Maine coast, "to eat Lobsters & Steamed Clams / in hundred degree heat." Since it is the busiest beach weekend of the year, the poet and his three friends inevitably encounter "baking crowds" everywhere they go. As they proceed further and further north in a vain attempt to find some breathing space, their frustration turns into surly alienation, which just as quickly succumbs to a sense of quiet resignation:

> We 4 told all those fat scarlet people to
> go to hell. *Die! Die!* Sheila cried,
> and we turned back to Ogunquit
> & Kennebunkport.
> We would've had to push too far north,
> way beyond Portland,
> to get away from the crowds.

As so often happens, reality fails to measure up to anticipations, especially for alienated sixties youth. "Lobsters" refers to the edible crustaceans but also to "all those fat scarlet people" who grasp and claw for recreational space by the ocean.

If New England summers can prove oppressively hot and crowded, its winters are to Banks, at least, equally trying. His final offering in *15 Poems* is "Winter Song," a series of eight haiku on a single theme: the vivid feel of cold, snowy weather. A sampling:

> Wet sheets in the wind
> freeze by noon into boards,
> crashing until dark.

> That grey stringy sky
>> pocked by one straggling goose.
> I look to my shoes.

> One leather glove falls,
>> stiffens cold on the numb dirt,
>> While hands warm pockets.

With formal precision and a sense of understated immediacy, haiku are supposed to recreate, and quietly celebrate, luminous moments in nature. Though Banks follows the traditional 5−7−5 syllable form for haiku in English, the overall mood he conjures is one of malaise and blank despair: "Brown dead grasses end / where last spring my wife planted / bulbs in black moist earth." Not exactly what the Zen masters had in mind. In this and in many other poems, there is a sense of New England as a hard, unforgiving place, not at all like the pastoral myth promulgated by L. L. Bean catalog illustrations. Also evident, in these early verse exercises, is Banks's interest in everyday subject matter and an abiding concern for clarity and concision.

30/6

Apart from his ongoing duties as coeditor of *Lillabulero,* Banks's next major venture into poetry publishing was to edit and contribute to *30/6* (1969), special supplement to *The Quest,* a small magazine published in New York City by Thomas T. Beeler and David G. Hartwell.[1] The 35-page pamphlet included five poems each by Banks, Peter Wild, Charles Simic, Robert Morgan, William Matthews, and Doug Collins. Thirty poems, six poets; hence, the austere title, *30/6.*

In his "Introduction" to the collection, Banks rather sheepishly admits that "this is not really a necessary book; it is much more incidental than that" (*30/6,* 3). Acknowledging that he and his five cohorts constitute no "school" of poetry in the accepted sense of that term, Banks nonetheless makes a case for regarding the six "as a unique group, mainly because of their individual seriousness as poets ... the kind of personal seriousness and risk that characterized the best of the 'deep image' poets—[Robert] Bly, [James] Wright and [Louis] Simpson—at the same age, as well as the best of the so-called Black Mountain poets—[Robert] Creeley, [Ed] Dorn and [Denise] Levertov. This is the kind of seriousness lacking in Paul Carroll's under-30 anthology of new poets" (*30/6,* 3).[2]

If, by "seriousness," Banks means a combination of moral gravity, stark objectivism, and elemental imagery, his own contributions to the collection amply qualify as "serious." No doubt inspired by his move back to New Hampshire from North Carolina in 1968, Banks's cryptic lead-off poem, "Waiting to Freeze," is yet another installment in what would come to be a long line of winter laments (30/6, 23–24). The setting and situation is murky, but one gathers that the speaker is a man forced out of doors in the dead of winter by the womenfolk: "Behind windows / women watching / hatchets catching light / fling it to the cold, streak red." While the women "are warm in their homes," the narrator begins to freeze as the "sun falls quickly to the forest, / hisses in hard snow." Though strong on vivid, sombre images—"Blood carries ice / rapidly from the ground / to my face"—the poem, like a nightmare, neither explains nor resolves itself. What we are left with is a mythic sense of male exclusion, loneliness, and doom.

Banks's next offering, "The Poem of the Year of the Bear," is in a decidedly comic key. Banks's subject is the primal allure of sex, demonstrated by bears' cross-species attraction to (in Banks's indelicate phrase) "the smell of teenaged cunt." Catching the scent, the aroused bear, "tongue red and stiffly drooling," follows it "to the very source ... [T]hickened claws sloppily rending taut canvas sides of tents, / bear moaning ... sticking his wagging prick ahead of him." The terrified girls

> stuff their mouths and ears
> with fingers yanked from hot boxes,
> sit on their smells and scream
> for hatchets
> and large barking dogs.

The bear "sprays everything across the bare ground" but does not succeed in getting to his quarry. Instead, "he's got to squat and talk about it / with these serious young ladies from Ohio." Thwarted and repulsed by human females (who "pity" him), the bear has no choice but to drift "slowly back up the mountain ... claws drawn back to elbows, / and prick buried somewhere deep / between his thighs like a womb, / wrinkled and black."

Banks's haplessly amorous bear is a comic figure but not ridiculous. Following his instinctual nature, he embodies the largely frustrated lust

of all teenaged boys. He also reminds human beings that they are animals too. As Banks points out in the opening lines, "You really can't
count on the bastard / to be nice / all the time." Nor can one expect
nature to be merely picturesque; sometimes it threatens to bite back.

This theme of nature as irreducibly other is taken up again in "Early
Snow," a telegraphic 25-line poem in the "Deep Image" manner. The
scene finds the poet tramping New England fields on a balmy day after
an early snow fall. Here, Banks shamelessly indulges the pathetic fallacy
by imaging patches of melting snow in terms of living things, gargan-
tuan and not a little grotesque:

> Shapes like pale blood suckers
> Sated and retreating
> From fields
> Caught thawed
> From last year's freeze.
>
> . . . .
> Saw the snow stiffen
> As I drove up, then
> Go on eating chartreuse grass.

The poet's response to his own, ominous vision is not one of revulsion.
On the contrary, he ends the poem by "beg[ging] for dark / And billow-
ing sheets / Of snow." At a liminal time between seasons, the poet
invokes complete immersion in winter as welcome resolution—exactly
what he seems most to dread in the "Winter Song" haiku and "Waiting
to Freeze."

Thematically, the next selection, "On Acquiring Riches," is something of a departure for Banks. Instead of situating the poem in a particular experience, he engages in general philosophizing. The poem in its
entirety:

> *On Acquiring Riches*
>
> It's best to grow rich at night.
>
> Better than having scales, piled like spilt silver

Coins, auctioned off tables to flashy dressers idling
On fenders—
Sold, for the small price on this man's eyes.

Later in the day, men and women are slain
Driving cars like mad bargains across fields
Of daisies. Racing home to count alone.

When I become rich, O I want it as mushrooms appear—
Suddenly, and in the dark, near bodies of water.

The master trope is a familiar one, really a poetic cliché: that the best things in life are as free, effortless, and magical as dreams conjured by the imagination. Hence, one grows "rich" at night, safely tucked away from the idle, lonely, and sometimes fatal business of acquiring money, a "mad bargain" that trades precious time for material wealth. Indeed, the poem pivots on the word *scales,* which initially suggests trade and commerce but is then recontextualized to refer to the scales on a man's eyes, as in moral blindness and death.

Banks's final and most significant contribution to 30/6 is "Homage to Che Guevara," one of the poet's romantic heroes from his Florida days. Forty-four lines long, divided into a dozen uneven stanzas in three numbered sections, "Homage" begins with an epigraph taken from Curtis Zahn's *American Contemporary*: "All were outnumbered by everybody. / Minorities were an illusion."[3] Like a prism, the Zahn quotation effectively slants one's reading of the poem by suggesting, up front, the sort of world view that Alfred Kazin attributed to John Dos Passos, "that the force of circumstances that is twentieth-century life is too strong for the average man."[4] Granted, there was nothing "average" about Guevara, but the insight still holds; anyone attempting to live a life of heroic stature in the age of the masses is liable to be struck down, especially those individuals selflessly dedicated to "the people."

Implicit, then, in "Homage" is a strong sense of the futility of revolutionary romanticism. Yet, at the same time, Banks makes fun of himself, as something of a gringo tenderfoot playfully captivated by the myth of Che. In the first section of the poem, the poet describes his passage through Customs upon returning to the United States from a trip abroad, probably somewhere in the Caribbean:

I blustered—
wore sunglasses,
a Panama hat,
Puerto Rican shoes,
and held my baggage suspiciously
below the limit.

And when the line's end
turned into the front,
I was arrested
for looking guilty,
and once searched
was discovered
harmless.

That's the sort of thing
can make a man
a Revolutionary,
I decided.

Whether apocryphal or not, the incident, as Banks well knows, is
nothing more than a trivial embarrassment. Any claim for its radicaliz-
ing potential is decidedly tongue-in-cheek. The same sort of self-
deprecatory, absurdist humor marks the second section: " 'In three
years,' I wrote tonight to a friend, 'three more years of this & I will be
thirty.' " Apropos of nothing at all, the poet then compares his own life
to Guevara's: "In one year Che Guevara will be forty." Inevitably, given
the Walter Mitty persona that Banks adopts, the comparison turns silly:

I do not know if he is alive or dead.
If he turns up in Havana alive & well,
I will make myself drunk arguing in barrooms.
If he has been slain and is in fact already dead,
I will make myself drunk arguing in barrooms.

Even though the speaker directs the sarcasm at himself, Banks comes
dangerously close to making a mockery of Guevara by letting the entire
poem devolve into farce.

That danger is narrowly averted at the beginning of the third section, where Banks effects a complete change of mood:

> October 8, 1967. Sunday.
> Che Guevara was shot to pieces
> near Higueras, in the mountains of Bolivia.

Banks's professed reaction to the grim news comes in the form of an apocalyptic vision:

> ... I think of Che Guevara as drowning
> quickly before my eyes in a sea of blood
> while I perch in a two-man liferaft
>
> munching saltines and nipping from a water tap,
> shading my face with a Panama hat,
> and sailing my rubber craft with remarkable skill,
>
> as if I were a Kennedy
> a few miles off Cape Cod.

In sum, Guevara drowns in the blood of a failed Third World revolution while his starry-eyed admirer stays happily afloat, thanks to the metaphoric life raft of North American affluence. And, of course, the reference to "a Kennedy" needs no explication, except to note that the fate of Cuba's special nemesis, JFK, seems to bode ominously for Banks's poet manqué as well.

Waiting to Freeze

Soon after the appearance of *30/6,* Banks published his second Lilla-bulero chapbook (the first exclusively devoted to his own material), *Waiting to Freeze* (1969). Included therein were reprints of "Point of View," "Early Snow," and "Waiting to Freeze," plus eight other short poems, some of which had already been published in little magazines. Far more mature and ambitious a work than either *15 Poems* or *30/6,* *Waiting to Freeze* is also more thoroughly imbued with a sense of the New England landscape as inspiration and subject matter, manifest proof that

Bank's move back to New Hampshire was having a profound effect on his imagination.

The first poem, "Work Song," sets the tone for the entire collection.

Work Song

For building there are
No stones in muskegs,
No rock in a swamp.

Use wood. Use red pine,
Black spruce, and find
One small smooth stone

To keep your blade oblique.
You won't need another,
And it's a damned good thing,

O, it's a damned good thing.

A muskeg is a bog found in northern North America, usually containing sphagnum mosses, sedge, and sometimes stunted black spruce and tamarack trees.[5] Banks argues a commonplace: though the New England soil is strewn with rocks (glacial detritus), such rocks will not be easily yielded from muskegs. Wood will have to do for any sort of building, along with a whetstone "To keep the [axe-]blade oblique." That "it's a damned good thing" the builder "won't need another" is an especially emphatic way of saying that stones are hard to come by in swampy areas.

Deceptively simple, "Work Song" offers pragmatic advice of the sort routinely dispensed in *Yankee* magazine—except that building anything in or near a swamp is an improbable endeavor. Clearly, Banks uses "building" metaphorically, to refer to the exercise of the imagination in poetry. To work the *inner* landscape, to build meaningful images on and out of the murky bog of memory, one must have an "oblique" tool; that is, an acutely-angled yet subtle imagination. Like Melville's "fine hammered steel of woe," the psyche is kept sharp by frictional contact with "one small smooth stone": hard, abrasive experience that has coalesced into the self-conscious point of view we call the ego.

After an appropriately placed reprint of "Point of View," Banks presents "Owls," a short lyric poem that far exceeds "Work Song" in sombre imagery and darkness of mood.[6] In the first and second stanzas, Banks anthropomorphizes owls by characterizing them as "Droop[ing] with sadness / That is vicious" due to severe hunger. The angry birds "bite their branches" with taloned feet "And loathe the creeping hunt . . . as if they themselves / Were the cause." In the third and concluding stanza, the poet identifies with the owls' supposedly stoic desolation by claiming to "know all this" because he himself

> has devoured years
> In dark northern forests
> Searching for the melancholy owls,
> To kiss vicious beaks
> And speak quietly of pride.

Constantly teetering on the edge of credibility, "Owls" slips into the ridiculous with its concluding sentiment. Though probably meant to shock the reader with its assertion of bitter bravura, the speaker's professed desire to "kiss vicious beaks" comes off as rather fatuous nonsense.

More successful is "Place / A Map," an effort free of the reckless overstatement that ultimately ruins "Owls." Banks's imagery is not overly precise, but the poem's main conceit situates a man out of doors, spinning like a child beneath a "sky [that] never moves," and making himself dizzy in the process: "The sky whirls / crazy above me." Standing north but facing south, the poetic "I" images Cape Cod "like a mammoth" who

> peers
> out to sea
> dreams of India
> cannot feel cold winds
> yanking its hairy coat.

The speaker, in turn, hears "mountains piling up / at my back / glaciers shoving uneasily in my sleep." Though it lacks a coherent argument,

"Place" invokes Banks's familiar perils-of-the-North theme while it conveys a feeling that the poet has not fully recovered his New England sense of place. His body is pointed toward Canada but his gaze (like that of Captain Tudor in "The Adjutant Bird") is directed toward the southeast coast and lands beyond.

Rediscovery as a tentative, groping, somewhat disoriented process is a theme further articulated in the next poem, "Stumbling Across Barnstead, N.H., Where I Was Raised." Driving the "coiled dirt" back roads of southeastern New Hampshire on a house hunting expedition, Banks is surprised to suddenly find himself in the town where he spent much of his youth. Rather than rediscovering Barnstead, he considers himself "discovered" in the village of "bewildered women, / of ham-handed men who shove / through crowds of children / waiting patiently in the dark." By "discovered" Banks means revealed, found out, rendered naked, as opposed to merely being found. An overwhelming sense of painful vulnerability ensues: feelings so intense they seem to color basic perceptions. To the poet's memory-stricken consciousness, the slipstream of a passing jet turns into something primal and sinister: "I spot / miles high a silver claw / scraping a thin frosty line / across the sky's blue eye." The poem ends in images of death and suffocation, punctuated by desperate attempts at expression: "The spruce trees all freeze and go black, / and words fly from my mouth like fish / squeezed beneath descending ice."

Banks's next poem, "Purchase," continues the collection's loose narrative thread by describing the buying of the house hunted for in the previous poem. In the first six stanzas Banks admits that his return to New England is, at base, an attempt to "bicker with memories." "Armed with the cool gigantic force / Of dead anger," the poet wants to alter the shape of his past, to remake "everything / In {his} own images." The poem should have ended there, but Banks insists on continuing:

> The house I chose
> Has a slate roof,
>
> Many gables & towers.
> Late-Victorian.
>
> Built at a time
> When nothing was happening

> In families
> Except declines.

These last, anticlimactic lines detract from the strong emotional impact achieved in the first part of the poem. And Banks's final qualification, "Except declines," manages to sound imprecise, banal, and smarmy all at the same time.

"Song (After a 12th Century Irish Song)" is another of Banks's New England winter poems. Loosely based on the Celtic "Song of Cellach," "Song" is divided into four parts.[7] In part I Banks writes of driving on a cold, snowy morning, "Burning dark tunnels / In drifted furls of snow." Reflecting radiance from the winter morning's "Earth, white sky, and sun," the speaker's manuscript (presumably on the seat beside him) "draws light / Reveals the arrogance of my flame." Shaken by the sudden realization that his book is a puny thing compared to nature's brilliance, Banks's speaker feels diminished, vulnerable, and very mortal: "And I see that I am afraid of steel / And the speed in which I'm hurtling."

The sense of foreboding established at the end of part I is both amplified and redefined in part II. Here, "leashed, barking, black dogs" with "slashing teeth" strain against their chains as the poet passes by, apparently now on foot. Like the owls, these desperately hungry dogs would devour the human interloper. Nonetheless, the poet feels some sort of kinship with the ravenous animals, telling them to "Go lurk among the trees / In the end, I'll come." One suspects that, when he does return to feed these angry beasts, the food will be himself.

Yet all is not gloom. The death vision of part II finds its antithesis in part III. Here the poet recounts a dream emanating from his waking encounter with the menacing dogs. Herding him north, the dogs trap him in a muskeg "And lay down in curls and lightly slept / Around the bog on high ground." Their helpless prisoner, the speaker imagines

> That my children came with torches
> And dry clothes and led me,
> Book in hand, home to their mother.
> The torches, blazing light,
> Kept the dogs at bay.

Like a fairy tale, the symbolism here is simple, mythic, and emotionally resonant. The metaphoric meaning of the muskeg, as a murky repository of painful memories, was established in "Work Song." Clearly, then, the hungry black dogs of parts II and III are those ruinous impulses to return to, and be captured by, the darkness of a nightmarish past. The poet's children are not symbols at all but his real rescuers by virtue of the love they bring to, and elicit in, their father: a love is symbolized by blazing torches that keep the wolves of despair at bay.

Part IV serves as a sort of coda. The poet complains about this "blister" of a hard winter day, "Bursting endless clouds of snow on me . . . And these white, hugging winds!" Yet, redeemed by filial love, the poet carries on. His final image is of life and survival: "Seductively, they give way / To my warm, constantly pushing breath."

"Early Snow" (already explicated) is followed by "Trains," Banks's verse eulogy to his brother Christopher, written shortly after Chris's death in a California train wreck in 1968. At 77 lines, averaging only a word or two per line, "Trains" is a long, narrow skein of a poem, appropriately train-like. Indeed, the poem's form is its most recognizable feature; its content is a disjointed series of garbled images that never coalesce into anything concrete. A sampling, in medias res:

> (the housewife
> weeping on her phone
> in Huntsville, Alabama
> —the train
> derailed
> tons of butane
> vaporized
> in her kitchen—
> reached apogee
> at a point
> directly above my head
> my head on the north bank
> of the James
> she plunged—

Typical of the poem as a whole, this passage leaps from one subject and scenario to the next, phantasmagorical transitions sometimes signaled by portentous punctuation. The "housewife" appears to be Banks's mother, learning of her son's death on the telephone. But then the train wreck and explosion seem to overtake her literally and directly in her own kitchen, which in turn engulfs the poet, who is somehow "on the north bank / of the James," but then "she" (?) appears to plunge in the river. Hence, Banks enacts the earth-shattering chaos of the train wreck as a metaphor for the emotional devastation of the victim's survivors. Derailment, however, proves to be a dubious organizing principle. Almost impossible to follow, "Trains" comes off as a febrile mishmash of a poem.

An inexplicably untitled reprint of "Waiting to Freeze" follows "Trains." The chapbook then ends, on a more hopeful note, with a three-part poem entitled "A Dream of Spring." Part I sets the scene in New England's "mud-time," the long weeks in March, April, and May when melting snows turn the ground into a quagmire. Impatient for warm weather and firm ground, the poet "turn[s] off / All machinery / And sit[s] in chairs / Alone in rooms upstairs ... [leaning] to make / The waiting end."

In part II, the season's dreary conditions persist—and sometimes worsen:

> The snow's still thick
> Around, stale, spattered
> With dog turds and ash.
> Mud's slogging its way
> Through, more each day.
> Rain turns to snow by
> Dark and back to rain
> Again by dawn.
> Grey mists breathe
> Vaguely above the fields,
> Shove weakly the low sky.

Yet, much like "Song," the gloomy atmosphere established in the first two thirds of the poem is countered in part III. Here the speaker turns from the depredations of New England weather to thoughts of his wife (whom he addresses directly):

> I dream of you lying
> Beside you sleeping.
>
> Filled with the dreams
> Of you I am as ice
> Is filled with water.

Having hit upon the conceit of dreams as congealed life, as ice is to water, Banks pursues the metaphor in terms of sexual passion:

> Tonight I will burst
> Your belly, a sunburst
> Of icy spears melting
> Down your thighs wetly
> To the warming ground.

In the end, spring is an affair of the inner life, a state of mind freed from an unforgiving landscape.

Snow: Meditations of a Cautious Man in Winter

Six years after the publication of *Waiting to Freeze*, Banks brought out his final effort in verse: *Snow: Meditations of a Cautious Man in Winter* (1975).[8] As already noted in the previous chapter, *Snow* is very much in the mood, style, and tone of the collection that precedes it. And the poetic agenda is much the same: to treat the wintry New England landscape as psychic terrain, a wilderness of repressed childhood memories that need to be sought out and exorcised before the poet can claim a viable sense of identity. Falling snow is, of course, the poem's central metaphor: that swirling, chilling, sometimes blinding substance that threatens to cover all tracks and leave the seeker of self lost and stranded. Indeed, much of *Snow* is taken up with navigational crises in a countryside where the landmarks have been erased by the snows of time, change, emotional repression, and psychic scarring:

> What do you
> see? Nothing!
> Nothing! The

innocent
crashing of
shapes in space . . .
There is no
way
to tell
outside from inside . . .
Yet there is no end
to huge corners, there is no
horizon's barred threat . . .
A point
expands infinitely . . .
In this space,
I cannot locate
myself . . .
No clues to mysteries,
no cryptic messages
in unknown tongues
lapping in waves at his feet.

In order to make some definable progress, the speaker eventually resolves on a first law: *"I cannot refuse to be simple."* But even that resolution dissolves in the endless complexities that arise when the self seeks immediacy in some irreducible definition. In the end, Banks's speaker—much like his favorite poet, Walt Whitman, in "Song of Myself"—concludes that he is a myriad of shifting selves:

I am a batch
of egos—a field
of grasses
and large dogs
in changing
weather.

At least momentarily freed from narcissistic self-absorption, the poet realizes, not unhappily, that "Nothing / will in / deed / save me." He therefore resolves to go outside himself and "save / the others."

A mercurial, skittish, hit-or-miss quality is often evident in the work of young writers struggling to master their craft. In Banks's poetry, these traits are particularly pronounced. As already noted, some poems are unmitigated failures. Others are well fashioned. Still others, though obviously flawed, contain striking lines and images. Restlessly inventive by temperament, Banks never quite succeeded in finding his own voice as a poet; the form, which requires the steady intensity of a miniaturist, proved inimical to his nature. Looking back over his initial efforts at poetry, Banks admits "Everybody has his apprentice work or juvenilia, and the trouble with being a writer is that you sort of have to grow up in public. I cringe a little over some of the early poems, and I make every attempt I can to destroy those when I come across them."[9]

Chapter 3
Apprentice Fiction:
Searching for Survivors

Nobody had enough imagination.

John Barth, "Lost in the Funhouse"

With the short stories that eventually comprised his first collection, *Searching for Survivors* (1975), Banks continued to use his writing to process the traumas of his youth and young manhood.[1] Yet, unlike the poetry, *Searching for Survivors* goes well beyond the autobiographical impulse. Though Banks does not classify them as such, these 14 stories lend themselves to three general groupings: (1) five moral-political parables; (2) a trilogy of stories that feature the slain Cuban revolutionary Che Guevara as a kind of icon or informing presence; (3) a half dozen quasi-autobiographical tales set in New England. While many of these carefully crafted stories are presented in a relatively straightforward realist style, in more than a few, Banks parodies the illusionist conventions of literary realism. He also conducts the kinds of experiments with narrative style, structure, and point of view that were then all the rage among young writers avid to ally themselves with John Barth, Donald Barthelme, and other practitioners of the metafiction vogue. Moreover, *Searching for Survivors* manifests an abiding concern with questions of psychological displacement and alienation, or, as reviewer Carll Tucker put it, "the dissociation of the ratiocinative and the feeling self."[2]

Parables

If Banks's theme is, indeed, the modern divorce between cognition and feeling, his parables stylistically enact that schism with a vengeance. Almost all are solemn in mood, cerebral in tone, and written in a detached, clinically descriptive style that tends toward the cryptic, somewhat in the manner of the fiction of Jorge Luis Borges or Julio Cortazar.

"The Investiture"

Even after repeated, careful readings of "The Investiture," one is not entirely certain what has happened or to whom. Yet the plot seems simple enough. The charismatic "Sweet Prince" of some unnamed kingdom ventures out among his subjects "alone and unarmed," only to be run down and killed by a "little Japanese truck." The incident is narrated by a commoner who describes following the prince, witnessing the accident, and holding the royal body until a Cardinal arrives on the scene, interrogates him, and has the corpse removed to the palace. Then the story takes a surprising turn. The narrator-witness speaks of getting up out of the street and "walk[ing] straight home to the palace" where he "washed, shaved, dressed gorgeously in black and made a sombre, perfunctory appearance at breakfast. No one seemed to suspect a thing" (20). Apparently, then, the narrator was the real prince and the man who was run down was an imposter.

Such a closure raises more questions than it resolves. Why have a double venture out among the people? And who employed him? Scheming ministers or the real prince himself? A hint at an answer is supplied in the narrator's last lines, after the accident victim is honored as the prince and buried:

> As for me, I never go outside the outer walls anymore. Once in a lifetime is enough. When you become Leader, you're suddenly the only person left who is still interested in imagining the pain of your own death. For everyone else, it's history. (20)

Though too ambiguous for its own good, "The Investiture" still manages to problematize political fame and power. Banks suggests that a charismatic head of state is depersonalized by the mystical aura that surrounds him, a paradoxical condition brought into stark relief by his death, especially if that death is sudden and violent. In the public mind the leader qua person doesn't die; a mythic image is shattered. Hence the *human* tragedy of the man's demise is lost in the larger sociopolitical fallout of his assassination.[3]

"The Nap"

"The Nap" is less than a page in length but every bit as cryptic as "The Investiture." On a lazy Sunday afternoon at home with his wife and kids, an ordinary family man is reading "a recently published novel ...

about a spy for the CIA, a Jew who, stumbling across an ex-Gestapo officer living incognito in the Bronx, [is] forced to confront his own life as a spy by choosing whether to blow his own cover by turning the ex-Nazi over to the Israelis or to maintain his identity as an American spy and thereby violate his Jewishness" (34). Falling asleep before he finishes his potboiler, Banks's reader expects "to awaken to a difference," any difference; it's "a private tradition" with him to feel somehow transformed by the fiction he's reading. But this time he perceives no difference. The man's wife "is still the nice, very same wife with the wiry hair," scolding one of his daughters, a son is still reading the comics, another daughter still visiting a friend, and the family dog is being called outside the house "because [it bears] the smell of a dead skunk." Bewildered, if not horror-stricken, the man begins "that period of his life when he trusted nothing and no one and greeted sleep with a wariness that bordered on hysteria" (34).

The question here, of course, is why Banks's protagonist is so deeply shaken by a nap that fails to live up to expectations. The spy novel appears to be the culprit, inasmuch as it has a disastrous effect on its reader's psyche—for the paradoxical reason that it has no effect at all. The man drifts into the world of his own unconscious not knowing how the spy will resolve *his* dilemma, whether patriotism or racial loyalties will win out in the end. Falling asleep trusting that he'll dream up a refreshing solution for a man whose moral, political, and psychological identity is in limbo, Banks's reader awakens to discover that, this time, his imagination has failed him. The chilling truth is that there is no readily apparent answer; conflicting political claims on one's sense of self may all be equally valid or too complex to sort out. At any rate, the inner life matters. Mental and moral health may have little to do with material circumstances, a fact Banks stresses by describing the comfortable ordinariness of the afternoon. Despite the Norman Rockwell milieu, Banks's reader is vexed for reasons as real to him as they are intangible to any casual observer.

"The Neighbor"

"The Neighbor" involves a different sort of epiphany on the part of the title character. Intent on "living off the land," a black man "in his fifties," his white wife, and four teenaged children from previous marriages, move to a farm in an all-white area of the country (55). "Incompetent and, in various ways, a little mad," the man and his family do not prosper; "the climate prove[s] harsh, the ground stoney and in hills, the neighbors more or less uncooperative—and of course there was that incompetence," which angers the people around them (56). Indeed, the family's one immediate neighbor, "a dour young man in his late twenties," is outraged to discover one of their chickens, loose for the 10th time, scratching in his own back yard. He rushes into his house, gets his .45, and fires "eight bullets into the chicken, making a feathered, bloody mess of it" (55).

Some weeks later, the neighbor's tolerance is put to the supreme test. The black man buys Jenny Lind, an 18-year-old mare, so that his wife can drive "her frail-wheeled sulky" the half-mile to the country store, an image of genteel respectability that sends the man's mind "reeling with delight." But while he and his wife are away from the farm to buy a hitherto elusive used sulky, their four teenagers decide to race "the old horse full-speed along that half-mile route" (56). After a "hundred" passes, a terminally exhausted Jenny Lind drops dead on the front lawn of the neighbor.

Returning home that evening, the black man and his wife spot the dead horse in their headlights, get out of their pick-up, and sit "stroking the mare's forehead" (57). The spectacle of their profound grief moves their otherwise irascible neighbor:

> The neighbor was a young man, and while a dead animal was nothing new to him, the sight of a grown man with black skin, weeping, and a white woman sitting next to him, also weeping, both of them slowly stroking the cold nose of a horse ridden to death—that was something he'd never seen before. (57)

Shaken out of his harsh attitude toward the hapless family, an attitude undoubtedly tinged with racism, the neighbor pats the woman and man on their heads and, "without judging the children," quietly tells their parents how the animal died. He then offers to help bury the stricken beast. In that moment of pity, the neighbor is able to go beyond his own mental caricature of the black man and white woman as miscegenetic fools. Seeing them in their full, suffering humanity, he becomes human himself. Thus "The Neighbor" suggests that some mishaps are so pathetic, so redolent of human misery, disappointment, and failure that they cancel out petty judgments. In situations of real extremity, social prejudices are apt to melt away, and even the smug are sometimes inclined to act compassionately.

"The Lie"

Considerably more depressing in its handling of the vagaries of human nature is "The Lie." Perhaps the best, certainly the most haunting of Banks's *Survivors* fables, "The Lie" bears an oblique resemblance to *Family Life* inasmuch as it explores the same intriguing questions that lie at the heart of the novella: how are a man's character and personal ethos transmitted to the next generation and beyond? And, more crucially, how are they transformed and redefined in the process?

"The Lie" begins with an accidental killing. Playing spies on a roof parking lot in Waltham, Massachusetts, circa the mid fifties, 10-year-old Nicholas LeBrun stabs his playmate, Alfred Coburn, in the heart with a penknife. Horror stricken, LeBrun runs home and tells his father, Robert LeBrun.[4] He also tells his father that, as he was running away, he glanced back and saw Toni Scott, a known homosexual, walking to his car, coincidentally parked at the scene of the killing. Instantly hatching a lie to cover for his son, Robert LeBrun calls the police and tells them that

> his son and another neighborhood kid have just been sexually molested by the neighborhood fag and his son broke away from the guy but the other kid is still with the sonofabitch in his car which is parked in the Transilex parking lot ... and he (LeBrun) is leaving right now to kill that filthy sonofabitch with his bare hands so if they want Toni Scott alive they have about three minutes to get to him. (61)

Despite his protestations of innocence, Toni Scott is arrested, deemed "a scorned and therefore outraged deviate," convicted of murder, and sentenced to "life plus ninety-nine years" (62).

Although Toni Scott's "absurd fate" points up the extreme social vulnerability of homosexuals in American society, Banks's main concern is to explain why Robert LeBrun chose to lie rather than submit his son to the authorities. The paradoxical answer to that enigma is found in the character of Robert LeBrun's father, Ernest "Red" LeBrun. "A French Protestant and native New Englander," the late Ernest LeBrun was "thrifty, prudent, implacably stable, high-minded and honorable, incorruptible, intelligent, organized, [and] good-humored" (59). Ironically, these impeccable character traits have a devastating effect on Ernest's son, Robert. By virtue of his ironclad and unselfconscious moral certainty, "Ernest [unwittingly] gave to his young son [Robert] an absolute truth and an absolute falsity and for that reason Robert was forever a child" (64). So when Robert's son, Nicholas, brings news of the killing, Robert "attributes to his son the overwhelming quantity of fear that he knows would have to be his were *he* ten or nine or eleven years old and faced with something 'really awful' " (63). Conditioned by his upbringing to feel guiltily inadequate, Robert Lebrun lies "not to save his son but rather to save himself" (64). To round out this complex moral paradox, Robert's neurotic self-absorption has the opposite effect on *his* son, Nicholas: "Robert to his son gave relative truth and relative falsity and for that reason Nicholas was never a child" (64). Banks's dispassionate narrator concludes that the "question of responsibility then seems not to have been raised in at least three generations" (64).

A finely nuanced and convoluted examination of an extremely subtle ethical question, "The Lie" is apt to leave the casual reader in its wake. Those not given to jesuitical ruminations might be interested to know that this story has biographical underpinnings. Perhaps an amalgam of both grandfathers, Ernest (Red) Lebrun is almost certainly based on Banks's maternal grandfather, Ernest Taylor, a Waltham clockmaker. Described by Banks as "taciturn" and "with a highly developed sense of his own significance" (Banks, 1993, 39), Taylor seems to have had an intimidating effect on Banks's parents not unlike the effect that Ernest Lebrun had on his son, Robert. Accordingly, Nicholas Lebrun can be thought of as a fictional type for Banks himself, who freely admits that he was, emotionally, "never a child," which would, on one level, make the catastrophe in the Transilex parking lot symbolic of Banks's traumatic childhood. According to Banks, our grandparents "are the people who may have affected us the most, who may be our true psychological, if not strictly genetic, origins" (Banks, 1993, 39).

"The Masquerade"

In marked contrast to the tragic filial determinism of "The Lie" is the gleefully comic tone of "The Masquerade," an offbeat revision of Hamlet. The story's first-person narrator (the young monarch of some unspecified European kingdom) tells how he and his brother, Paris, outwitted his scheming mother and her coconspirator, his uncle, the cardinal, for the throne left vacant by his father's death six months earlier. In the first part of the story, the then crown prince informs his mother and the cardinal of his intention to select a date for his coronation. To the prince's surprise, the cardinal receives the news "with a disgust and violence [he] had not thought him capable of" (77). The young man's mother is more crafty;

she proposes a grand masquerade as "the occasion to announce the coronation" (77). Still unsuspecting, the crown prince agrees, and "the plans for such a shindig" are put into motion (78).

The prince's suspicions are aroused, however, when his gay brother, "gorgeous" Paris, informs him of an alarming piece of intelligence supplied by Regis, the court sculptor, in a moment of drunken indiscretion. At the masquerade, the queen will be disguised as Paris and the cardinal will be disguised as the crown prince; apparently they plan to steal the throne before the real prince can make his coronation announcement.

Together, the two brothers come up with a plan of their own, which they execute flawlessly the night of the masquerade. Dressed in drag, as "a perfect imitation" of his mother ("sable, ermine, and fox, royal blue velvet with hammered gold trim, white taffeta ruffles and cuffs" etc.), Paris ascends the throne in full view of "the awe-struck multitude" (83). Mistakenly thinking he's been betrayed by the queen "at the last minute," the cardinal (disguised as Paris, of course) "stumble[s] over his [own] feet" and falls down, "losing all remaining composure and temper simultaneously, stamping his heels against the floor in a tantrum as he lay there" (83). Stricken "with shock and fear," the cardinal sees no choice but to throw himself at the mercy of the real crown prince, who orders him to change his "costume" and "present himself as quickly as possible in his usual clerical garb" (84). In place of the horrific bloodletting that marks the denouement of Hamlet, Banks supplies a happily farcical ending, with the crown prince triumphantly joining his brother, still in queenly drag, on the dais of the ballroom, as faux mother and son. "With a wave of my hand, I ordered the dancing to begin, and immediately it began" (84).

The Che Stories

Though he had written an ironic elegy for Ernesto "Che" Guevara, Banks seems to have been unable to resolve something inside himself about the fallen guerrilla leader. More than likely, Banks's quixotic and easily frustrated attempt to join Castro's revolution in 1959 came back to haunt him as a painfully absurd confusion of the personal with the political. In the early seventies Banks wrote three stories that invoke the ghost of Che as an ironic counterpoint to his own Walter Mitty-like aspirations as a "revolutionary." In a larger sense, Che's shadow haunts the depoliticized vacuity of American life, quietly chastizing our obsession with the privatized experience of the self-interested individual.

"With Che in New Hampshire"

The story's incongruous title is, of course, ironic; Banks's first-person narrator is not, and never has been, with Che in New Hampshire, or anywhere else, for that matter.[5] Banks's *real* subject is the complex recollective, imaginative, and cognitive processes by which a writer creates a story loosely based on an experience from his own life. The conceit here is decidedly postmodern: to pretend to let the reader witness the story being dreamed up, in fits and starts, as it is being written.

In keeping with the self-mocking tone of "Homage to Che Guevara," "With Che in New Hampshire" frustrates its "author" by stubbornly refusing to assume satisfactory form as an authorial wish-fulfillment narrative. In a comically cliché-ridden opening, the narrator fabricates a wildly romantic identity for himself, as a battle-scarred revolutionary traveling the world incognito, one step ahead of the CIA. The story proper begins with the narrator's alter ego returning to his hometown of Crawford, New Hampshire (a mythical version of Banks's Barnstable). That a sleepy community in ultraconservative New Hampshire could have produced a world-class leftist firebrand or that he'd ever return there are underlying absurdities that help to give the tale its parodic thrust.

Almost as soon the author-narrator imagines himself stepping off the bus in Crawford, his romantic imagination begins to run afoul of what he actually remembers about the denizens of his hometown. Picturing some of the town's old-timers observing his arrival from McAllister's Gulf station and general store, the narrator tries to conjure their reactions to his alter ego but cannot quite get it right. At first he has Bob McAllister remark to Doc Cotton that he hopes "the boy's come home for good, 'cause the family'll be needin' him up there." Doc would supposedly reply: "They sure as hell do, Bob. And by gawd, we need him down here, too" (12). But then the narrator thinks better of such dialogue: "*No. Erase that remark.* Wipe it out. Doc would never think such a thing, let alone say it, and Bob McAllister hates and distrusts me, I'm sure" (12).

Another try at picturing his protagonist's arrival in Crawford bogs the narrator down in a mire of complicated, interconnected logistical details. How should he arrive? By car or by bus? And what would he have in his duffle bag? Would he have a gun? And if he does have a gun, how would he get into the country? How old is he? What is he wearing? What is his physical condition? Once again, the story founders on such questions because their answers are, to a large extent, arbitrary.

In a last attempt at an arrival scenario, Banks's narrator approaches his subject matter from an entirely different angle. He imagines the man's *internal* state and finally achieves the creative breakthrough he sought:

> I stand next to the idling bus for a few moments, gazing passively at the scene before me, and upon receiving simultaneously the blows of so much that is familiar and so much that has subtly grown strange to me, I become immobilized. Seeing them, I remember things that I didn't know that I had forgotten, and thus I experience everything that comes into my sight as if it were characterized both as brand new, virginally so, and yet also as clearly, reassuringly, familiar. (15)

When he shifts perspective, it becomes clear to Banks's would-be narrator that the story he is trying to create is not a heroic wish-fulfillment fantasy but rather an oblique attempt to reconstruct a younger version of himself, when he was still a product of his hometown—an imaginative exercise that clarifies his present identity, or at least throws it into stark relief.

"With Che at Kitty Hawk"[6]

Having just left her husband, Roger, after eight years of marriage, Janet is visiting her parents at the family cottage near Kitty Hawk, North Carolina, where she vacationed when she was a child. Now 30 years old and the mother of two girls (Laura, aged seven, and Eva, four), Janet had hoped that she could begin her life anew, with a "new man, a new place to live, a new way of life, a profession even" (49). But even after a scant few days, the lonely, fractured reality of her situation generates a feeling of newness that is "a mockery, a sad, lame reaction to the failure of the old" (49). Furthermore, the experience of bringing her children to the haunts of her own youth under such circumstances plunges her into "anger and revulsion for her own life, for the entrapment it offered her" (43). For it occurs to Janet "that she [is] trapping her own children [as well]. The terms of her life had become the terms of their lives now, and thus they too would spend the rest of their lives in relentless, unchanging reaction to patterns she could not stop establishing for them" (49).

Janet's overwhelming sense of her life's suffocating cyclicity is unexpectedly broken when she takes her children to visit the Wright brothers memorial. "[P]eering down at the slope the two bicycle mechanics had

used for flying their strange machine," Janet has an epiphany about the
Wright brothers:

> Then, as if a wonder were unfolding before her eyes, filling her with awe,
> she saw a large, clear image of the two men from the midwest, their
> clumsy wire, wood and cloth aircraft, the sustained passion, the obses-
> sion, which was their work, their love for it and for each other ... They
> did not permit themselves (she decided) to live as she had feared she was
> condemned to live—curled up inside a self that did not really exist,
> slowly dying inside that shell, no matter how many additional whorls of
> shell she managed to extrude, each new whorl no more than a dumb
> reaction to the limits of the previous one, spun by anger or bitterness or
> despair. (53)

In a characteristically Banksian ending (though perhaps more pat and
preachy than usual), Janet, released from her glum self-absorption,
resolves to "go to work, pitching herself into the task of making a
machine that could fly, making it out of wires and shreds of cloth and
odd remainders of wood and rough pieces of other machinery—the junk
of her life so far" (54).

"With Che at the Plaza"

The close companion to "With Che in New Hampshire," "With Che at
the Plaza" once again involves the metafictional conceit of the storyteller
transparently creating his narrative as he goes along. In both stories the
narrative is self-flattering in the Walter Mitty style, but Banks's coy sat-
irization of his day-dreaming narrator is funnier in this instance because
it eschews elaborate, repetitive technical ruminations that make "With
Che in New Hampshire" somewhat tedious.

While staying at the Plaza Hotel in New York City, Banks's first-
person narrator, "an American businessman," thinks he recognizes an
elegantly dressed Che Guevara having breakfast in the hotel's Green
Tulip Room—despite the fact that Che was widely reported to have
been killed by counterrevolutionary forces in the mountains of Bolivia
five years earlier (68).

His imagination fully engaged, the narrator proceeds to sketch out
the details of Che's clandestine life at the hotel. He also posits a friendship between himself and Che that gives the Cuban exile "some pleasure
and, indeed, even comfort" (68). Banks's narrator even imagines Che
writing a letter to his mother in which he rather rapturously describes

his new American friend as "deep, compassionate, with an imaginative relation to men who happen to be radically different from him, whether they be peasants or men like myself" (68).

The narrator's imaginative self-aggrandizement reaches a kind of crescendo when he fantasizes a dream in which he is playing poker with an unlikely assortment of sixties notables—Robert Kennedy, Lyndon Johnson, Perry Como, and Frank Sinatra—at Sinatra's Palm Beach home (70). Beating his formidable poker companions with four aces, Banks's narrator gets up to depart with his winnings when he is forced to remain seated at gunpoint by Sinatra. Imagining himself "ripping away from the dream" at that point, the narrator then imagines himself being surprised by Che in his room at the Plaza (72). After demanding the man's poker winnings, Che shoots his friend in the chest (72)—an imaginary turn of events that prompts Banks's hero *manque* to note that, "[T]his Guevara thing was getting out of hand. I was beginning to wish I had never met the man" (73).

A rollicking farce that pretends to no great purport, "With Che at the Plaza" implicitly suggests that the human imagination is a volatile creative force that can never be completely guided or controlled.

Stories from Life

"Searching for Survivors (I)"

Banks's regional stories combine autobiographical elements with a flare for the vivid evocation of the New England landscape that Banks had already demonstrated in his poetry. Yet the synthesis of these two concerns is never straightforward. "Searching for Survivors (I)" is, for example, a complex hybrid. Part historical parable, part fictionalized autobiography, the story's meandering narrative structure is determined by the mercurial logic of free association.

Banks's first-person narrator begins his tale by identifying with the Arctic explorer Henry Hudson, who was deposed by a mutinous crew on a 1611 voyage and subsequently disappeared. The narrator decides that, if he had been in that actual situation, he "would have stuck with the [the mutineers in the] bigger boat" (1). He nonetheless feels tremendous empathy for the "darkly iron-willed" Hudson (1).

"[R]eminded of Hudson," the narrator notes that he is "always reminded in turn of other things, mainly automobiles," particularly the 1949 Hudson Hornet owned by the father of his boyhood friend, Daryl:

The car was deep green ... and the restrained stabs of chrome on the grill
and bumpers and around the headlights and taillights merely deepened
the sense of wellbeing that one took from such huge expanses of color.
Shaped more or less like an Indian burial mound ... whether stilled or in
motion, the vehicle expressed permanence and stability, blocky arrogant
pacts with eternity. (3)

In its absurd but somehow elegant massiveness, the Hudson is more
than the embodiment of American technological grandiosity. For
Banks's speaker in his youth, the Hudson epitomizes a kind of timeless
serenity; more specifically, the "permanence and stability" of his friendship with Daryl.

The illusory nature of that ideal is dramatized in the third phase of
the story. Here, the narrator recounts a chance meeting with Daryl
when both are about 19 and haven't seen each other in "five or six years
at least." Both men quickly perceive that they stand on opposite sides of
the great divide of social class. The narrator is decidedly blue-collar,
working as a timekeeper at the Boston naval shipyard.[7] Daryl, on the
other hand, is an apprentice stockbroker "in an expensive-looking char-
coal grey, pinstripe suit with a vest and a black wool overcoat with a silver fur collar" (3). During the brief chat that follows, Daryl discloses
that his father, loving custodian of the green Hudson, died of a heart
attack two years before. After uttering platitudes about getting in touch
again, the two rush off "in opposite directions" (4). Struck by the realization that the seemingly endless days of his youth are over, Banks's
speaker feels "lonelier" than he'd ever felt before.

In the fourth and final phase of the story, Banks's narrator speaks of
buying a Norwegian elkhound puppy whom he has named Hudson Fro-
bisher, "so that I could be sure I was naming him after the explorers of
the Arctic seas" (4). Fantasizing about acquiring other elkhounds,
putting together a team, and entering the National Sled Dog Champi-
onship Races in Laconia, New Hampshire, Banks's speaker imagines
that he "would pull off the course after a while" and "light out for the
back country" until he reached Hudson Bay. When spring came he
would circle "the muddied edge of Hudson Bay on foot, looking at the
wet ground for pieces of old iron or charred wood, or maybe a yellowed,
half-rotted journal—signs that Hudson had made it to shore" (5).
Hence the title of the story and the collection. The figurative "search for
survivors" is, at base, a search for enduring continuities between past
and present: memories, lessons, articles of faith that can withstand the

depredations of time and life's chaos. Such patterns, if they can be discerned, might add up to a stable sense of self.

"The Blizzard"

The sometimes harrowing instability of the self is sharply rendered in "The Blizzard." Appropriately arranged in nonlinear fashion, "The Blizzard" also alternates between the first and third persons, as Banks's protagonist fades in and out of his own skin. The man sees his derangement as a perennial event, triggered by the onset of winter in New Hampshire: "First, I lose my hold on my sense of self, then of my life as some kind of continuing history. Then of my wife, and finally, of my children ... by the time, the first trickles of spring appear, I am like a vaguely discolored fluid floating on the surface of a stagnant sea" (22). Haunted by a generalized "and rather extreme sense of personal guilt," the man sinks into "silence and detachment," a mood that drives his long-suffering wife to distraction (26–27). To make matters worse, his wife knows that he's made a pass at her friend, Rose, a woman he's attracted to because of her own tendency toward silence.

Tensions come to a head when the narrator castigates his wife in front of her friends for letting the well-water pump run on. She responds in kind, by telling him to shut his "god-damned mouth." In a fit of anger the man drives 40 miles to Portsmouth in a raging snowstorm, intent on spiting his wife by finding a woman to seduce. His plan quickly founders; due to the storm, all the Portsmouth bars are closed. His car buried in rapidly accumulating snow, Banks's protagonist, "hatless and without gloves," finds himself walking the five miles back to his motel in a blizzard that has virtually obliterated the landscape (33). Both awed and disarmed by the fury of the blowing snow, this wayward, egocentric man begins to come back to himself:

> At that time, as he stumbled, walked, and finally jogged happily through the streets of Portsmouth in the middle of a blizzard, I could not believe that I was anyone other than that man with the icicles in his moustache. I was on both side of his eyes, inside and outside as well ... It occurred to me the man might die ... that he was insane. It occurred to me that he was not insane. (33)

Winter being the protagonist's bête noire, it is more than a little ironic that a blizzard should succeed in quelling his destructive willfulness.

Reduced to his unaccommodated essence by the snows, this troubled man is, at least temporarily, made whole again. He reaches the motel, stays the night, then drives home the next day, not necessarily chastened but certainly in possession of a renewed sense of proportion.

"Impasse"

"Impasse" describes the critical moment in another deeply troubled marriage.[8] Having foolishly married a woman he has never loved, a young Boston bookstore clerk named Ham finds himself in a moral dilemma: "Leaving her now, telling her the truth and walking out, seemed to him as loathsome as its opposite act, marrying her in the first place" (89). Unable "to choose one of two kinds of guilt," Ham has latched onto a third alternative. He has become deeply infatuated with Rosa, an alluring, mysterious music student he met at a party.

Visiting Rosa at her apartment for the first time, Ham has spent hours telling her "mainly of his [marital] dilemma, little else" (90). Agreeing with him, that he has indeed reached an "impasse," she disappears into her bedroom for cigarettes. When she reemerges, Ham is faced with a critical decision. Will he try to seduce her or just go home to his wife? Banks offers no real closure, only Ham's prurient wish-fulfillment fantasy. He imagines Rosa seducing *him,* an act, he hopes, that will produce the "clarity" his life so sorely lacks (91).

"The Drive Home"

"The Drive Home," a long, meandering story, features yet another Banks protagonist enduring not-so-quiet desperation. Like Ham and the errant husband in "The Blizzard," Fletcher Bass is a young man suffocating on the constrictions of his life, "dying"

> Of being a father. A husband. A Caucasian. A Ph.D. A twenty-five year old American male. A high school teacher of American history ... Of being the husband of a nineteen-year-old blonde from Hartford, Connecticut. Of being the only child of parents dying silently, slowly, in Crawford, New Hampshire. Of being an insomniac who dreams. An adulterer. A wife-beater ... A formal man. A cold man. A stingy man. Of being a ridiculous man ... full of pity for himself. (95)

Bass's surfeit of corrosive self-awareness produces recurring nightmares (indeed, the whole story may or may not be a series of dreams within dreams). In one anxiety-ridden dream, he finds himself shooting a "creature" with a high-powered rifle. In another, he kills a young girl who catches him stealing her "Daddy's whiskey" (98). Convinced that he is the moral equivalent of "a murderer and a thief," Bass is fully cognizant of the danger of obsessing on his pain: "For the truth is that I cannot need to know these kinds of things, if I also need to exist" (95). Predictably, he broods on "these kinds of things" anyway, laying waste to an already fragile ego.

To bolster his self-esteem, Bass cheats on his wife, an act that only engenders more guilt and anxiety—and brings the marriage to an apparently terminal crisis. In the midst of an angry confrontation, Bass's wife, Dagmar, declares the marriage "over" and "dead" and accuses Fletcher of having "killed it." With their young daughter, Linda, in tow, Dagmar departs for her parents' house in Hartford. Her parting shot is to declare her husband "insane" (101).

Left to his own devices, Bass gets on a bus to seek some solace from *his* parents in Crawford, New Hampshire, a "drive home" that mirrors his wife's drive home to hers. On the bus, Bass attempts to flirt with a young and attractive but not very bright "Christian lady" named Cynthia. A more likely candidate for Cynthia's attentions is Buzz, a garrulous, "big, blond, crewcut boy of twenty or so," who wields a guitar and invites everyone to join him at the back of the bus for a "sing-along" (103). In Buzz, Fletcher Bass senses a kindred soul: another preening narcissist, "whose thoughts can drown out the very voices of the others, whose pride is greater than all their vanities and whose guilt is greater than their trivial shames" (105). Deciding that "he is the one to be encountered," Bass follows Buzz and Cynthia to the rear of the bus and then proceeds to disrupt Buzz's hootenanny by plucking out one of his guitar strings in mid song. Angry and confused, Buzz tries to ward off Bass, but to no avail. Taunting the younger man with sadistic glee, Bass ends up putting his foot through Buzz's guitar, then orders him off the bus.

On the face of it, Bass's psychic demolition of Buzz is nothing more than a mean-spirited act of displaced aggression, both funny and gruesome. But there's more to it than that; by humiliating Buzz (his mirror image), Bass is able to repudiate a measure of his own narcissism, an emotional catharsis that allows for a significant breakthrough.

Such a breakthrough *seems* to occur in the final phase of the story. Bass arrives at his parents' home in Crawford, only to discover that they are in the midst of moving and don't even notice his presence. Rushing into the now "cold" and "stripped" house, Bass desperately hopes "To see if *anything* has been left me. Anything at all!" (110). Until the business with Buzz, Fletcher Bass's every attempt to conquer the demons of self-doubt had only resulted in further regression because he had failed to perceive the real source of his neurosis: an emotionally desolate childhood. At story's end, Bass seems to confront that painful reality. Whether or not the experience will prove illuminating or merely traumatic is left open to conjecture.

"The Defenseman"

In a decidedly milder and more nostalgic key is "The Defenseman," the first-person narrative of a grown man looking back on his childhood initiation into ice skating and hockey. Though he is not sure why he "should happen to seize onto" the remembrance, the narrator suspects that his reverie has its sources in a half dozen ice-skating sessions the previous winter (112–13). When he is skating alone on a small meadow pond in his front yard, the narrator finds that his "physical responses" and "fantasies" of hockey heroics come "straight out of childhood" (113). In Proustian fashion, physically reenacting an activity of one's youth effects "a brief slip backwards into the consciousness of one's ordinarily objectified past" (113). As Banks's narrator later notes, "The conditions surrounding an event, the textures, physically, emotionally, spiritually, these remain uniquely our own; the particulars of an event, what we use to name it for strangers, are no more ours than our dates of birth. Perhaps this is why so much of the act of remembering is an act of the body" (120). Experiencing a renewed connection to his childhood, Banks's narrator also feels reconnected to his father, who patiently and lovingly taught him how to skate.

"Searching for Survivors (II)"

Searching for Survivors ends with "Searching for Survivors (II)." The collection's longest (10,000 words), most complex, and poignant story, "Searching" is Banks's fictionalized account of the aftermath of his brother Christopher's death in a train accident in California. A study in the psychology of grief, the story is more fundamentally about the emotional repression—and resulting fragmentation—that plagues the contemporary American family. To evoke the sense that the family is broken up and hopelessly dispersed, Banks segments his narrative into 11 distinct sections or scenes (each transition clearly marked by a line across the page) then rearranges those sections to deliberately violate chronological order.

Hence, "Searching" begins with Reed (Banks) flying home from the West Coast after a futile search for Allen's (Christopher's) body. The next section finds Reed at home in New Hampshire, preparing to visit his father with news about the death and memorial service. Banks then flashes back to California, with Reed at his grieving mother's house after the search. The fourth section reverts to the beginning of the previous summer, with Reed picking up Allen from Boston's South Station for a summer-long visit. Banks jumps ahead to a recounting of the wrenching memorial service for Allen in California, then jumps ahead again to Reed's visit to his father in New Hampshire. The eighth section reverts to Reed's mother's house in California, after the memorial service. The next section flashes back to Reed dropping Allen off at the bus station in New Hampshire for his return trip to California at the end of the previous summer. The ninth section jumps ahead to Reed's leaving his numb father's house after the visit, a scene complemented by the next section, which focuses on Reed's leaving home at the age of 17. The story's final section is set at the site of the train wreck, south of Santa Monica, with Reed and his brother, Gerry (Steve Banks), scouring the wreckage for some sign of Allen's remains. Reed finds nothing except the torn half of a sock that might have been Allen's. As Reed puts it earlier, "My brother wasn't just killed here ... He was destroyed. Decimated, and then incinerated. Poof. Gone" (151).

What Banks has very deliberately created is a disjointed series of arrival and departure scenarios. Geographic distance equals emotional distance and vice versa. Split by divorce and divided between the East and the West Coast, Reed's family is unable to sustain viable emotional ties. But it never could, even when its members were in close proximity. Banks attributes the underlying cause of so much distancing to the emotional repression that typifies American life. This, Banks implies, is every bit as tragic as Allen's senseless death. Reflecting on the emotional sclerosis that has crippled his family, Reed thinks that it is

> pathetic that we surviving children, we survivors, loved Allen only in secret and never had the pleasure ... of uttering it full-faced to him. Pathetic that his death didn't free us to do for each other now what we were unable to do for him then ... I can't believe that we have been so incredibly stupid and weak, that we go on doing it!" (140).

This, then, is the final emphasis of *Searching for Survivors:* a plea for genuineness of feeling and direct expressiveness that is sadly lacking in contemporary American life.

Chapter 4

Experiments in Metafiction:
Family Life, Hamilton Stark, and
The Relation of My Imprisonment

Henceforth, it was necessary to begin thinking that there was no center, that the center could not be thought [of] in the form of present-being, that the center had no natural site, that it was not a fixed locus but a function, a sort of non-locus in which an infinite number of sign-substitutions came into play.

Jacques Derrida, "Structure, Sign, and
Play in the Discourse of the Human Sciences"

The first three novels that Banks wrote (which are not the first three he published) form a kind of literary triptych.[1] Though highly distinctive works, all three—*Family Life, Hamilton Stark,* and *The Relation of My Imprisonment*—readily fall under the aegis of seventies metafiction. In creating these works, Banks eschews conventional storytelling, characterization, and scene-painting in favor of narrative styles that would have to be described as ratiocinative in content, protean in form, and self-reflexive in their treatment of the relationship between individual identity and language. The net effect of these postmodern literary strategies is to deliberately foreground the artificial nature of writing. In the manner of Brechtian theater, Banks is avid to remind his readers that they are, indeed, reading imaginative constructions, not mimetic transcriptions of "reality." At the same time, Banks presents equally compelling reasons for reader involvement—cognitive, moral, and philosophical conundrums and complexities that are sometimes baffling, sometimes amusing, but never shallow or facile. As one reviewer noted, "Banks is a writer who has a mind."[2]

Family Life

The peculiar mixture of angst, confusion, and exuberance that animates Banks's verse and early short fiction is equally evident in his first novel,

Family Life (1975). A short book (only 134 pages), consisting of a dozen brief chapters further divided into a dozen numbered sections each, *Family Life* looks and reads something like a long prose poem consisting of 108 installments, each one no more than a paragraph or two in length. Content aside, the very form of the book blurs genre distinctions between fiction and poetry, a blurring presumably designed to disarm reader preconceptions about fiction narratives.

The fragmented look of *Family Life* is misleading, however; like all of Banks's prose work, his first novel is scrupulously logical and orderly in its layout. Banks begins with mock-heroic fanfare, self-consciously comparing his opening scene with that of Hector Berlioz's opera, *The Trojans* (which was itself modeled on "The Sacking of Troy" chapter from Virgil's *Aeneid*, as Banks delights in noting). What immediately follows is a passage of catalog verse typical of epic poetry, in this case a list of some 70 writers, from Boccaccio to Ed Sanders, that *Family Life* somehow hearkens after "*in time* . . . if not in manner" (4).

Despite an initial flurry of classical references, *Family Life* is set in what appears to be contemporary America; its main characters are a not atypical modern family consisting of unhappy, self-absorbed parents and three sons who are "lolling through their extended adolescences" (3). The twist is that Banks casts all of these characters as fairy tale royalty with absurd names: King Egress, the Hearty (perhaps after the deviously worded sign in P. T. Barnum's museum, "This way to the Egress"); his wife, Naomi Ruth (Sunder); their three sons, the crown princes Dread, Orgone (the Wrestler), and Egress (the Wild). Other characters include a mysterious Green Man, and King Egress's drinking buddy (and gay lover), Loon, a hashish-smoking, hippie bon vivant who lives in a tree house.

The action proper gets under way when "a handsome youth" who wears "slick green suits and strangely decorated hats" goes to King Egress and expresses "a passionate desire" to have one of the king's three sons for his lover. The king is amused by the request, so much so that in the midst of making love to his queen, Naomi Ruth, Egress mutters to himself, "I like a plucky faggot" (8). The remark arouses Naomi Ruth's suspicions about her husband's sexual proclivities. Likewise, Egress's macho sons are much "disturbed" by news of their gay suitor.

Largely ignored by her husband, Naomi Ruth becomes a closet alcoholic, "languish[ing] alone among the gin-and-tonics afternoon after afternoon" (13). To escape her desolation she enters into an empty liaison with the "slender, hard muscled" wine steward in order to exact revenge on her husband. Banks's narrator reports that, after lovemaking, "Naomi Ruth felt no guilt. Anger. Only anger. Mainly at the king but also at Loon, whoever that one was" (17).

For his part, Egress is as strange a monarch as Austria's notorious King Ludwig II—giddy, lonely, whining, petulant, cruel, and philosophical by turns. Egress is not, however, a mystery. Banks supplies the key to the king's psychological makeup by establishing his character as the product of a brutal upbringing. Egress's father, Donald the Flailer, beat Egress "mercilessly, constantly, while never touching the boy's five brothers, except to caress them affectionately" (27). Driven to the end of his wits "after a particularly bad beating, Egress, then twelve years old, crie[s] out, 'Why, Papa? *Why? Why?*' " In the exchange that follows, Donald the Flailer explains that the beatings will toughen his son enough to make him a ruthless wielder of power in his own right: " 'You're going to be king, goddammit, and a king has to know that a man [who beats women and children] must be *killed!* When you know that, I'll stop beating you,' he promised his son" (27–28).

Donald the Flailer's confusion of paternal love with sadistic violence is inexorably transmitted from one generation to the next, as Banks notes with understated gallows humor: "Egress the Hearty loved his sons no less than his own father had loved his. It was a family tradition. So many things cannot be helped" (28). Indeed, the king's three sons take after their grandfather (and, to a lesser extent, their father). All three are boisterous, thrill-seeking, fiercely competitive, and brutally arrogant in their pursuit of hypermasculine identities. The consequences are predictable. Dread accidentally kills himself by mishandling his rifle during a hunting expedition (48). Young Egress dies after eating a wine glass in the midst of a wild drinking bout with a group of Abenakis (61–62). Orgone, obsessed with physical fitness, ironically dies of blood poisoning contracted after he cuts his foot in the shower room of a gym (73).

"Mad with grief" for their sons' deaths, Naomi Ruth blames King Egress (84). Plagued by his own feelings of grief and guilt, Egress deals with the pain in a typically male way: he escapes by going on a seven-year pilgrimage with his best friend and consort, Loon (89–97). Traversing jungle, desert, plains, and mountains, Egress eventually begins to "come out of his grim withdrawal" (94). He also manages to slough off every trace of guilt, a change of heart evidenced by the fact that he "screw[s] the Loon at least once a night" during a fourteen-week ocean voyage" (95). "But after all," Egress protests, "isn't that what a pilgrimage is *for?*" (96).

Presumably more typical of her gender, Naomi Ruth's coping strategy is to delve within. While Egress is away she writes "Remember Me to Camelot," a wish-fulfillment fantasy in the form of a short novel (i.e., Banks's chapter 10) whose plot and characters mirror Banks's own. Naomi Ruth's first person narrative features Kay, a Sarasota, Florida, housewife married to Rex, a Korean War fighter pilot turned plumber in civilian life. In the twelve-year interregnum between Korea and Vietnam, the couple bring up three sons, Rex Jr. (also known as "Biff"), Rory, and Hunter. As the boys get older, Kay begins to notice that her husband's harsher traits—his "fierce competitive pride, his love of sports and danger, and his occasional dark fascination with solitude"—in one way or another become manifest in their sons, crowding out "the milder, sweeter traits" that made her love Rex in the first place. When Rex is recalled to active duty in Vietnam, Kay is surprised to find herself experiencing "a wave of relief" as he drives away, an emotion that only deepens when she is later informed that Rex has been shot down over North Vietnam and made a prisoner of war. With Rex on ice, Kay begins to come into her own, doing all the things he would have forbidden. She gets her G.E.D. (high school general equivalency diploma), goes on a diet and exercise program, studies yoga, cooks exotic dishes, and learns how to drive. When he is repatriated, Kay hopes that they both "can sit down and cry for what has been lost." "If he can't do that," she vows to leave him.

Resuming the narrative proper, when Egress returns from his long sabbatical, he is surprised to find that Naomi Ruth, backed by a troop of Abenaki, has taken over command of the kingdom and will not relinquish power. Arrested, Egress soon escapes and forms a huge army of loyalists to regain his throne. In the end, though, he attains a victory of the Pyrrhic variety. The queen has left his city-state destroyed and deserted; there is no longer a kingdom to regain. Viewing the devastation, "Egress was at first astonished, and then when he had begun to piece together what had happened ... he was deeply depressed. One might say broken" (113). Thus Banks creates a fitting metaphor for the emotional carnage caused by the patriarchal will to power. Appropriately, in the closing chapter of *Family Life,* Egress and Naomi Ruth, now divorced, are featured in a series of chance encounters at a variety of public venues—encounters that are banal, awkward, and poignant all at the same time. After all is said and done, there are no victors, only an estranged couple in the throes of moral exhaustion manifest in a pervasive sense of emptiness and loss.

As is probably evident from the foregoing synopsis, *Family Life* is a free-wheeling combination of tall tale, fable, and social satire. Hard pressed to define the book according to received categories, at least one reviewer resorted to the vague label "experimental novel."[3] Banks himself rejects the term, observing that "all fiction is an experiment."[4]

Whatever else it might be, *Family Life* is decidedly not in the naturalist tradition that Banks would soon revive on his own, postmodernist terms. Nothing in the novel is meant to ring true to life or have even the smallest scintilla of credibility, at least on the surface level of the narrative—quite the opposite. In place of a story that would persuade the reader to willingly suspend disbelief, Banks deliberately foregrounds the artificiality of his narrative by offering fast pacing, smart-aleck humor, and wildly imaginative inventiveness—essentially, metafiction as screwball comedy, yet not quite. As more than one critic noted, the almost hysterically jocular mood created by so much high-octane foolishness comes across as decidedly unfunny. If *Family Life* had been intended as a comic novel, it would have to be deemed an abject failure.

For his part, Banks has recently observed that "the novel seems to me apprentice work, more useful to the writer, perhaps, than the reader" (Banks, 5 November 1993). Technically useful as another opportunity to hone his craft, *Family Life* was equally useful to Banks for private, therapeutic purposes. He identifies "the book's personal sources" in his parents' divorce and his own "onrushing breakup" with his second wife, Mary Gunst, to whom the book is dedicated. A quasi-feminist critique of the resounding emotional devastation caused by a domineering, violence-prone patriarch, *Family Life* is clearly inspired by the grim legacy of Banks's father, Earl. "As for its literary sources," Banks notes that "because of the force of my personal connections to the material, I felt the need to work with it at a considerable distance, which led me to the high artifice of mock fairy tale" (Banks, 5 November 1993). In another context, Banks has noted that he has written "formalistic, allegorical, sometimes satirical" fiction when he has been "most angry and disoriented. I reach . . . for high artifice in times of disarray."[5] Clearly the mid seventies were such times for Banks.

Hamilton Stark

For several years prior to writing his second novel, *Hamilton Stark* (1978), Banks had been reading "with great enthusiasm, tempered by occasional seizures of skepticism," objectivist poet Charles Olson and other Black

Mountain poets and writers, among them Paul Metcalf, Robert Creeley, and Ed Dorn.[6] He also read Olson's principal "sources and mentors": Carl Sauer, William Carlos Williams, and the New England Transcendentalists. Looking back on that period, Banks notes that

> one positive result of this [kind of reading] was that it invited a deep investigation into the "local," a vertical look into the surround rather than a horizontal one. By keeping things local, I could also keep them personal, without actually being "autobiographical," which was anathema to me, a kind of fatal narcissism (New England Puritanism at work here). The particulars of the local—that was my route to the personal, the only one I could morally justify. And I did need a route to the personal; it was the only source of the writing's emotional power, I knew that much. This conflict (a need for the personal vs. an aversion to it), it seemed to me ... could only be resolved by means of my immersing myself in New England (specifically New Hampshire) history, geology, economics, geography etc. (Banks, 4 February 1995)

Having hit upon a suitably objective "route to the personal," Banks inevitably invoked another, and perhaps more daunting, question: how does one structure a novel that rejects the conventional narrative approaches (pseudohistory or pseudobiography) in favor of an in-depth examination of "the local"?

This question of structure was not easily resolved. Banks recalls having to "re-organize and re-write *Hamilton Stark* several times" over a number of years before he was satisfied with its overall form: "It was pretty much hit-or-miss until I began to see a pattern emerge that seemed to work for me; working out of the principles of collage ... one has to intuit [an organizing principle] and can only really apply [it] usefully after you have something to work with, i.e., long patches of narrative" (Banks, 4 February 1995).

The structure that finally emerged was a complex amalgam of various perspectives and modes of narration. Neither whimsical nor arbitrary, the ultimate shape of the novel was dictated by its ostensible purpose: to present materials toward an intensive character study of "A.," a mysterious, misanthropic Yankee dubbed "Hamilton Stark" for narrative purposes by an unnamed friend who serves as the novel's main narrator and editor of its other narrative strands. These other narratives include geological, economic, and political histories of northern New England; anecdotes from Stark's childhood; excerpts from an unpublished novel about Stark by his daughter, Rochelle; transcriptions of interviews with his first and second of five wives, Trudy and Jenny; family incidents and the histories of his other marriages; philosophical digressions, reactions, and interpretations by the narrator, and a male confidant referred to only as "C." In sum, *Hamilton Stark* is less a "novel" than a fictive journal about the entire cognitive, emotional, and investigative process of novel writing. Rather than merely recounting Stark's life story as a fait accompli, Banks's narrator brings in his imaginary source material as it was supposedly made available to him. Thus, readers witness the fitful evolution of the narrator's thinking about his subject and experience their own perceptual evolution as well.

While *Hamilton Stark* goes a long way toward a rich and nuanced evocation of its title character in all of his contrariness, its patchwork form rejects the mimetic authority of a single, seamless, chronological narrative. Implicitly, *Stark* asserts that life is chaotic, complex, and multifarious. Furthermore, the book's sutured quality materially enacts the notion that there is no "whole truth" of individual identity because there is no unified or coherent identity to know. Ultimately, there are only viewpoints on the self, a mass of data to be collated after the fact, as each perceiver sees fit. Epistemologically daunting, the novel's structure also presents its readers with a moral challenge. As its narrator notes in passing, "An orderly progression of perceptions makes the moral life easier to accomplish. When a flood of perceptions washes over one, however, one's moral certainty gets swept violently away" (146).

In order to call into question philosophical and moral sureties, the book opens by preempting any direct access to its subject. Invited to Stark's house in rural New Hampshire for a drinking bout on a winter day in 1974, his friend finds the place deserted and, more ominously, discovers three bullet holes in the windshield of Stark's car. The mystery of Stark's fate acts as a powerful catalyst on his friend's already enlivened imagination:

> [At the time of his disappearance] I had reached a point in my relation to him where almost anything could happen and where whatever did happen would be believable. It would seem "natural," "right," consistent with all I had known of him before. In other words, the man had become sufficiently real to me that I could and, therefore, should write a novel about him. (17–18)

The nature of the narrator's quasi-mystical attraction to Stark grows more apparent as Stark's character is gradually fleshed out. As everyone who knows him attests, Hamilton Stark is undeniably larger than life. An expert pipe fitter by trade, Stark is physically huge, fearless, highly intelligent, and emotionally impenetrable—an imposing, some would say, intimidating presence. An unrepentant individualist, Stark hearkens back to ideals of brash, rugged American masculinity and independence embodied in such figures as Davy Crockett, Daniel Boone, and the mythical Paul Bunyan. Apparently conventional and mild-mannered himself, the narrator looks up to Stark as "a man who had gained control of his life without suppressing his life" (162). He celebrates his friend unreservedly, in Whitmanesque terms, as "my Roarer, my Crank, my Colossal and Cosmic Grouch and Bully Boy, my Man Who Hated Everything so as to Love Anything, my Man Obsessed with a Demon so as to Avoid Being Possessed by One—my one last possibility for a self-transcendent ego in a secular age!" (162).

Stark's former friends and intimates hold markedly different views. Speaking to her daughter, Rochelle, Stark's first wife, Trudy Brewer Stark, calls him "a despicable man," a thief, liar, drunkard, and bigot who "hated people of all races, creeds, and colors" (84). She goes on to describe their brief marriage as having been utterly disastrous for her: "Life with your father was horrible for me right from the start. First there was the affair ... Then there was the drinking. And after that there was all the violence, the fighting, the times he actually hit me. Then came the silence. He went silent on me" (78). While Rochelle was still an infant, Stark abandoned his young family altogether. Trudy notes that she "did hear from him again, numerous times ... [but] was lucky enough never to have to see him again" (80).

Despite ample evidence that Hamilton Stark has always been a reprehensible lout, Rochelle Stark (now in her 20s) is just as fascinated with him as is the novel's narrator. Anxious to reclaim the father who had abandoned her, she researches and writes *The Plumber's Apprentice*, her own (unpublished) novel about Stark. The experience is a harrowing one. While conducting the necessary interviews, she is "literally overwhelmed with tales of [Stark's] selfishness, of rage, drunkenness, lust, greed, of eccentric violence and destructive manipulation, of betrayal, disloyalty and deceit" (130). Thrown into a crisis of faith, Rochelle undergoes a year of Jungian psychoanalysis (131). Still unable to fully confront her father's dark nature, she later contrives the bizarre belief that Stark is not inherently evil but has been the victim of possession by the ancient Semitic demon Asmodeus, "a figure who combined rage with lust and loosed these emotions onto the institution of marriage" (133).

Though the narrator rejects Rochelle's thesis as a desperate "superstition," their shared obsession with Stark leads them into a passionate sexual relationship. In love with Rochelle's character, intelligence, and physical beauty, the narrator also finds her to be a more skillful writer than himself. Offered unlimited use of "the voluminous materials and several texts of *The Plumber's Apprentice*" for his own book, he cannot resist the temptation to include whole chapters verbatim from Rochelle's novel: a practice that precipitates a turning point in their relationship (235).

At first, Rochelle claims to be flattered that her lover is "able to take so *much* ... [and] change so *little!*" (236). Priding himself as sensitive to women's emotions, the narrator interprets Rochelle's exclamations as "whimpers of pain, a woman's pain," caused "by man himself, or rather, that aspect of himself that is characterized by gender" (236). What follows is an elaborate ritual of mutual concern that only results in further misunderstandings. The narrator, "bearing a typically heavy burden of typical male guilt," repeatedly apologizes for taking too much; Rochelle, bearing "a typically heavy burden of typical female pain," repeatedly counters by refusing to acknowledge any hurt (239–40). The narrator soon reaches the sort of communicative impasse with Rochelle that Banks had described in some of the *Searching for Survivors* stories. No matter what he says to soothe her, her demure reactions to his pleadings only foster greater amounts of guilt and frustration on his part.

Based upon thousands of years of male dominance, the dynamic is deeply ingrained in human relations. Forbidden civil power, women have learned to derive some measure of control over men by inducing guilt in them. Stark contends that "it's one of the very few routes to power for ... wives and mothers, which naturally invites them to specialize in it, and through disuse, all the alternative routes gradually get broken up or overgrown, until soon they are impassable altogether" (227). Until there is a revolution in gender relations, a man still has two choices. He can relieve the guilt arising from male privilege by accepting the validity of "woman's pain," or he can repudiate his guilt by dehumanizing her altogether, treating her as a sexual plaything or domestic slave. The ethical choice is abundantly clear, but Hamilton Stark seems to feel that there is a paradox here for the male concerned about questions of existential autonomy and freedom. To his way of thinking, doing the right thing by women involves paying further homage to a rotten social system by succumbing to the coercive power of guilt. Refusing to behave civilly at least constitutes a principled aversion to emotional manipulation.

Stark's elaborately rationalized misogyny seems to have come out of his relationship with his mother, Alma, whom he sees as the archetype of the manipulative woman, gaining power over the men in her life by turning "suffering into a virtue":

> She converts the one into the other, completely. She makes a condition of being female—and a wife and mother—an ethical feat, which feat we as men have no choice but to reinforce. Most men don't understand this conversion ... and that's why most men, rather than reinforce this conversion, deny that it's even taken place. They treat their women as if they were still suffering. But what we're *supposed* to do, what they *want* us to do, is to reinforce the conversion by acknowledging it and making it possible for the process to continue. So, naturally, what they want is for us to increase their suffering, to build their supply of it back up at least to where it was before they managed the difficult task of converting it into something that gave them power, the power of possessing virtue. (230)

Having grown up under the aegis of "smotherhood," that is, a mother with a gendered martyr complex, Stark has come to believe that male-female relationships are inherently sadomasochistic. In his view, any attempt to assuage women's suffering not only impedes their quest for power through accrued virtue but also feeds male guilt. Accordingly, Stark reasons that he is doing women a favor by mistreating them. To "honor" his mother's "conversion of generalized suffering into particularized forbearance," Stark goes so far as to legally maneuver her out of her own house: a brutal gambit that supposedly earns her all the virtue she will ever need while earning him a house and the permanent enmity of his family and neighbors (232). He compounds that outrage by having a gravestone for both parents quietly installed at the family plot while his mother is still alive, as if to invite her death. When she finally does die, he refuses to attend her funeral and burial.

Hesitant to match Stark's level of brutality, the narrator has "grown feeble and confused" trying to negotiate his increasingly tortured relationship with Rochelle, both as lover and colleague. But, "one afternoon following a particularly vicious turn of the wheel" that he and Rochelle are locked into, the narrator opts to follow "Hamilton's advice and example" (240). In a flurry of destructive will, he gathers up all of Rochelle's drafts and research materials and mails them back to her, along with a stilted, insulting letter, declaring that her "manuscript fails to interest or amuse" (241).

Having emulated his hero by needlessly alienating the woman he loves, the narrator suddenly suffers his own crisis of faith in Stark as a Nietzschean role model. With Rochelle's love and support lost to him, he is compelled to rethink his lofty image of Stark as a "holy man, the man outside all social prescriptions for meaningful behavior" (241). This occurs at a time when the image has already suffered severe deflation as evidence of Stark's cruelty has reached grotesque proportions.

Another resounding blow to the narrator's mythic construction of Stark is delivered by his friend, C. With the benefit of greater objectivity, C. interprets Stark's behavior as not willed at all but hopelessly neurotic and reactive:

> In Hamilton's case, by becoming conscious of his attraction to women who wanted to "smother" him, and his resultant revulsion at the indebtedness incurred, that is, his "guilt," his only recourse seems to have been to introduce "wrath," so as to speed up the process, to spin the wheel a little faster, hoping thereby . . . that the pain for the woman and the confusion for himself would be lessened. (240)

To counter Rochelle's image of Asmodeus, and the narrator's image of the holy man, C. invokes his own image, that of the Uroboros (the serpent eating its own tail) as an appropriate "image of closure, a frightening image of compulsive, ritualistic repetition" (240). To C., with no personal stake in the affair, Stark is neither possessed nor heroic; only a tragic figure, doomed to play out his defeat and desolation over and over again.

The narrator functions as Banks's mouthpiece when he notes that we are "the only creature that must perceive itself through the use of images. The limits implied by those images are the limits and possibilities for our perceptions of ourselves" (241). Having imagined Stark as the archetypal embodiment of masculine strength and dignity, the man he would be if he had the resolve, the narrator must come to terms with Stark's disappearance at precisely the moment when his image of the man is in crisis and dissolution.

The final chapter (aptly titled "*An* End" as opposed to "*The* End") finds an "extremely distressed" narrator returning to Stark's house the day after he turns up missing, desperate to find a clue to his whereabouts, knowing that this errand is a "final test of [his] faith" (277). In the blowing snow of a February storm, the narrator picks up what he believes are Stark's boot tracks, leading up to Blue Job Mountain nearby. They vanish in the snow near the summit, and the narrator is ultimately left "alone, completely alone" on the mountaintop (288). He has no choice but to turn around and begin his descent. Thus the search for an exalted other ends in the most instructive way possible: in utter futility and confusion.

A brief critical rendering of *Hamilton Stark* cannot do justice to the intricacy and originality of its structure or the depth of its moral vision. It is safe to say, however, that the novel is remarkably coherent, that its key themes enhance and echo one another. Nominally an investigation into a mysterious personality, *Stark* is more essentially concerned with the construction of male identity within a patriarchal social order. As is readily apparent from the early stories and *Family Life,* Banks is fascinated by gender politics within the nuclear family: how men deal with mothers, wives, and daughters; how women deal with fathers, husbands, and sons. The question of Hamilton Stark's true character is not only unresolvable but finally tangential. As Terence Winch puts it, "The answers aren't there because the relationship between the novel's 'I' and Hamilton Stark is meant to be an insoluble puzzle, just as the more conventional battle of selves in all of us remains a mystery."[7] The moral crux of *Hamilton Stark* is the narrator's quest for self through a passionate and committed involvement in the life of another person. Though clearly misguided in some ways, his obsession with Stark is ultimately enlightening because it leads away from the trap of self-absorption. The novel also suggests, by default, that a bona fide partnership, with all its strife and ambivalence, is always superior to hero worship—which is, after all, the purview of adolescent boys. In the end, the transcendence of the ego is effected by empathy, not by an ornery defense of one's autonomy.

The Relation of My Imprisonment

When Banks's novella *The Relation of My Imprisonment* was published in late 1983, critics assumed that it was his latest book. Actually, Banks had written *Relation* some seven years earlier, while on his Jamaican sabbatical in 1976 to 1977. A publisher had not been easy to find, probably because *Relation,* though brief and straightforward in diction, is such an odd and puzzling work, perhaps Banks's most difficult.

Having experimented with the mock fairy tale and a quirky offshoot of the detective novel, Banks tried his hand at an equally peculiar literary form: the Relation. A genre of personal narrative first introduced by jailed seventeenth-century Puritan divines "to relate the tests their faith had endured in prison," the Relation was read aloud to "a congregation of their free brethren" for religious inspiration and instruction.[8] Deirdre Bair explains that in "its usual form it was recounted by those who had been imprisoned for their deviation from rigid religious orthodoxy, and it was often a literal account of the actual details of the sinful or criminal act, told within certain literary conventions or typologies."[9] Typically, the prisoner would recount his fall into despair and faithlessness, sometimes even debauchery, before undergoing a conversion experience that would culminate in a sweeping and joyous spiritual regeneration.

In broad terms Banks follows the generic structure of the Relation. He also manages to imitate the dry, scrupulous formality of seventeenth-century English prose with a generally unfailing ear for authentic-sounding diction, syntax, and speech rhythms. Banks does not adhere to the Relation's traditional religious values, however. His unnamed, first-person narrator is no Puritan. Rather than worshipping the God of Martin Luther, Banks's protagonist worships the dead. A coffin maker by trade, he builds coffins not only for the disposal of the dead but for himself and other living members of his cult, who use them to lie in for prayer, worship, and meditative solace from worldly woes.

Suddenly and without explanation, the state decrees that the building of coffins, or any kind of memorializing activity for the dead, constitutes "the crime of heresy" and will be "prosecuted to the fullest extent of the laws" (2). A well-meaning friend urges the coffin maker to turn his talents toward the manufacture of "high wooden cabinets with glass doors for the purpose of exhibiting fragile and expensive possessions," an item then all the rage among "the better-off families" (3). Fanatical in his religious devotion, the coffin maker naturally refuses the order to cease and desist. As a result, he is arrested and imprisoned for the next 12 years.

An event early in the coffin maker's incarceration shapes the spiritual character of the years that follow. Although he is repeatedly refused a fair hearing from the court (probably to keep the case hushed up), the coffin maker is befriended by his jailer, John Bethel, who converts to his "faith." Bethel attempts to aid his friend by adding his name to the court calender so that he can be tried expeditiously: an act that earns Bethel the death penalty when he confesses it before the justices in order to save the coffin maker. "Lashed by regret and shame" that the jailer has died in his place, the coffin maker gives up his "own personal coffin"

for Bethel's "journey unto the dead" (29). More importantly, he decides
to atone for the "sin" of conspiring to alter the court calender by more
systematically withdrawing from the world of time while also "resisting
death" (30).

Total self-purgation proves to be a long and extremely arduous
process, even for a man so deeply dedicated to the renunciation of
worldly concerns. The endless hours of confinement in a small, damp
cell conjure ferocious sensual desires, the strongest of which is that
"abominable longing," lust. Visited in his cell by his wife every afternoon, the coffin maker finally succumbs to his desire for her. One act of
copulation leads to a daily round of sexual intercourse. After a time, he
begins to "vary from one day to the next the modes and positions of
[their] interpenetration" (40). Jacob Moon, the coffin maker's second
jailer, discovers the tryst and is allowed to join in, making it a three-
some. The following week, the wife's young cousin, Gina, also joins the
debauch.

In the meantime, the coffin maker, now an utterly "fallen man," suffers a precipitous disintegration of personality. His mind "swiftly divides
itself into segments, boxes of thought, attitude and activity with no necessary and discernible link, consistency or communication between
them" (45). Bereft of his "old forthright self," he becomes "that pathetic
and sorrowful figure, the man of time," a self-conscious chameleon of a
man who, like T. S. Eliot's Prufrock, instantly arranges his own face into
"a matching mask" of the person he is encountering (45–47). Having
forfeited "self-unity," the coffin-maker succumbs to other weaknesses. In
the ensuing months he obsesses about food, ransacking his memory in
order to imagine all manner of gourmet fare. Vividly realized food fantasies are replaced by equally elaborate fantasies of drink. These, in turn,
are supplanted by obsessive daydreams of money. Eventually, though,
the coffin maker, through intensive meditation and self-analysis, manages to free himself from "the bondage of the finite, the chain of life, the
links of the desire that springs from memory" (85). Reconfirmed in his
worship of the dead, the coffin maker is able to deal with a series of later
trials. These involve the death of his wife, threats of violence by other
prisoners, and a host of painful physical ailments that bring him to the
brink of death.

Though the *Relation* closes with its narrator still sick, alone, and in
prison, he has once again come into possession of an all-important coffin
and is fully recovered from the spiritual ravages of the time-bound. Like
Job, King Lear, and countless other examples from the literary and

homiletic traditions, the coffin maker is systematically and thoroughly reduced in this finite world of time, *in order* to be exalted in the world of the infinite. The hero's spiritual apotheosis does not just happen; he chooses it, surrenders to it, and is thus "saved."

In formal terms *The Relation of My Imprisonment* resembles a conventional Protestant sermon; it advises a discipline of sensual abnegation as the only means to the life of the spirit. Yet Banks's strange parable radically differs from religious orthodoxy in one key respect: rather than worshipping an all-powerful deity, his narrator worships the dead. Thus, the tenor of *The Relation* is deeply existentialist, not religious. The book's real emphasis is on the ineluctable burden of mortality, a burden that Christianity acknowledges but also wishes to efface by the promise of another life beyond this one. Rather than salve the human ego by foregrounding some animating, intelligent, and benevolent power behind this life in time, Banks offers the stark inevitability of death. Indeed, the novella's epigraph, "Remember death," perfectly encapsulates its meaning. With sly, postmodernist irony, Banks uses the very form of the religious tract in order to subvert conventional religiosity. One may dismiss the coffin maker as perverted or insane, but there is a profound wisdom contained in his view of things.

Chapter 5
The New World: Tales

To allegorize life as a masquerade, and represent mankind generally as masquers. Here and there, a natural face may appear.

> Nathaniel Hawthorne,
> Journals

Seemingly disparate works, *Hamilton Stark* and *The Relation of My Imprisonment* actually have a great deal in common; both books center on what Banks was then fond of calling "self-transcendence," that is, the willed struggle to tame and focus the self. With savage recklessness, Hamilton Stark gropes toward a new kind of self by flaunting social conventions at every turn. Conversely, the coffin maker sets out to transform the self by systematically sloughing off all worldly desires and attachments. Though they approach the problem of self-transcendence in markedly different ways, both men are ultimately alike in their single-minded pursuit of a unique identity. Both seek a self that is fully resolved, disciplined, and free of guilt, a self that inevitably comes into conflict with societal norms because it does not partake of the predominant values of the age.

With his second collection of short fiction, *The New World* (1978), Banks continued to explore issues of self-fashioning. Indeed, he describes the collection, somewhat grandiloquently, as "a carefully structured gathering of ten tales that dramatize and explore the process and progress of self-transcendence, tales that ... embrace the spiritual limits and possibilities of life in the New World."

Banks's evocation of the New World as his figurative setting is a complicated trope, both straightforward and ironic in its implications. Of course, in the literal sense, Banks's "New World" refers to the Americas that were "discovered" by Columbus; more specifically, the already inhabited Caribbean islands where the Italian explorer first made landfall. Banks's choice of title is more than metaphorical; he wrote and assembled most of *The New World* tales during his 18-month sabbatical on the island of Jamaica in 1976 and 1977, and the collection's title story is set there. In the largest sense, though, "New World" refers to those moral, psychological, and spiritual territories broached by the self as it undergoes radical transformation.

Renunciation

Banks divides the collection into two parts. Part I, entitled "Renunciation," is the more conventional half of the book. The five parabolic stories contained therein are all vaguely set in New England, are written in a quasi-realist idiom, and deal almost exclusively with sexual issues: coming-of-age, lust, marital relations, and infidelity.

"The Custodian"

"The Custodian" features Rubin, a 43-year-old virgin bachelor who is left to his own devices after his father dies. Alone for the first time in a house he has lived in for the past 27 years, Rubin begins to succumb to vivid libidinal fantasies. Shaken by recurring images of "slender necks," "graceful calves," and "plum-shaped breasts with coffee-colored nipples," he curses his parents "for having waited until they were in their fifties before having a child, curse[s] them for being so old that they themselves had become the object of his custodial mission" (4–5).

Ashamed of himself for cursing his parents, Rubin decides that the only way to cope with his sexual longings is to find a wife. With impeccable but grossly naive logic, he reasons that a woman who is already a wife would make the best candidate for one! He approaches Deidre, Mame, and Molly, the wives of three of his friends, discreetly proposes marriage to them, and is "astonished by the alacrity of the wives' responses, their apparent urgency to become his wife" (6). As the narrator notes, Rubin does not realize it, but "in some crucial way, he was the perfect husband, for he was the son who was willing to be the father, the custodial waif, a lodestone which, when touched, converted unconscious or barely conscious needs and desires into precious possibilities" (6).

Their dormant imaginations suddenly inflamed, all three wives make aggressive sexual demands on their husbands, who shrink from them in surprise, confusion, and, finally, rage. The story ends with the narrator speculating that Rubin "will retreat back into his night of solitude" after having discovered, upon a second visit to each of the three wives, that married couples are incurably miserable with each other (8).

Though he at first appears to be the tale's protagonist, Rubin is only a catalyst figure. Essentially about the three wives, "The Custodian" is an ironic commentary on the emotional and sexual frustrations that married women have to suppress to stay married. Beneath placid bourgeois exteriors, these women harbor deep "discontent with their lives, their husbands, their children, their homes," discontent that needs only the right stimulus to bring it to the surface (5). In this context, the story cycle's title, "Renunciation," takes on a host of ironic significances. Rubin attempts to renounce bachelorhood only to renounce marriage in the end. But the wives have renounced much more, perhaps without realizing it until Rubin comes along: independence, dreams of fulfillment, a sense of possibility and adventure. Briefly awakened to a glimpse of an alternative life, they have to renounce that, too.

"The Perfect Couple"

As another tale of naive hope come to grief, "The Perfect Couple" bears some likeness to "The Custodian." It bears greater resemblance, however, to a Hawthorne parable titled "The Maypole of Merry Mount." Based on a clash between the New England Puritans and a renegade settler named Thomas Morton, Hawthorne's tale of love soured by religious zealotry dramatizes a fundamental split in the American psyche, a schizoid ambivalence between repressiveness and sensuality that remains unresolved to this day. Written in mock-Hawthornean style, "The Perfect Couple" revisits and reinterprets the same dilemma.

Saul and Gavin, ex-army buddies turned bachelor farmers, buy farms adjacent to each other. No one in town ever learns much about the two men. The only thing that is readily apparent is the uncanny complementarity between them:

> What one man lacked, the other possessed. Saul was the tall, thin one, Gavin, the short, portly one. Saul was fair and hawk faced, Gavin was dark and moon faced. Saul was somber, soft spoken, measured, and in all ways restrained. Gavin was gay, brash, elaborate, and in all ways unrestrained. (12)

The stark symmetry of the passage fairly shouts allegory. Saul clearly embodies the dour Puritan seriousness of a Jonathan Edwards. Gavin conjures the easygoing American garrulousness of a Benjamin Franklin.

After their first harvest, both men lock up their farms and disappear. Much to the town's amazement, when they return a month later, each man—apparently still unmarried—is carrying a two-year old child.

Saul's child is a girl named Sally; Gavin's child is a boy named Glenn. Ironically, each child bears far greater resemblance to the other parent. As they grow and mature, everyone in town constantly remarks upon the exquisite complementarity between them. Dubbed "the perfect couple," Sally and Glenn are widely expected to marry when the time comes.

Paralleling the growing affinity of the children for each other, Saul and Gavin's farms are quite literally coming closer together with each passing season. Both farmers have gradually encroached on a strip of rich bottom land that separates their two properties (land owned by a wandering singer named Oakes, who pays taxes on it but has never returned to it).[1]

Coincidentally, Sally and Glenn reach maturity the same season that Oakes's land finally disappears into the farms owned by Saul and Gavin. Although there is no cause-and-effect connection between the two events, the couple and a large number of townspeople tend to think otherwise; when the last furrow is being plowed, they go out to the field to celebrate the symbolic conjunction of lands and hearts (17–18).

Unfortunately, Saul and Gavin refuse to cooperate with this fairy tale scenario. When Sally and Glenn stand at the end of that last furrow and declare their intention to marry each other, their fathers remain silent for a moment, then drive off, "snarling" (19). Though crestfallen, the couple refuse to leave the spot. Later that day, Saul and Gavin return to drag them home. The ensuing scuffle is interrupted by Oakes, the itinerant singer, who appears upon the scene deus ex machina and "forthwith" offers Sally and Glenn "the land upon which they were fighting" (20). At this, Saul suffers a stroke and Gavin goes mad. The couple flee, like Adam and Eve out of Eden, and are condemned to a life of wandering. Rumor even has it that they eventually commit suicide. Now frail, Saul and Gavin retire to town and refuse to speak of their children. As for the townspeople, events prompt them to contradict their earlier opinions. With no hint of embarrassment, the parson explains that it "does no good to take coincidence too far" (21).

An allegorical interpretation of "The Perfect Couple" might start with the observation that the farmers and their children occupy vastly different worlds. As for Saul and Gavin, they dwell in the public realm of work and commerce, embodying opposite poles of the human psyche, Thanatos and Eros, respectively. In a business civilization, these polarities must remain parallel but separate; too much melding would undermine a social order that remorselessly divides work from leisure, intellect

from imagination. Interestingly, the farmers' growing proximity involves the usurpation of Oakes's land, suggesting that a tendency to
narrow the gap between thought and feeling naturally leads into the
world of art and creativity embodied in the figure of Oakes, the wandering singer.

Like Romeo and Juliet, Glenn and Sally occupy the private sphere of
romance. Their coming together represents a threat to their father's
order, where all polarities must remain separate and partitioned, lest
property relations and the Protestant work ethic be threatened. As in
Hawthorne's tale, the young lovers are deprived of their nuptial bliss by
their stern fathers. But Banks's version adds a crucial element: the
attempted intervention of the artist figure. Oakes is willing to sacrifice
his property for the happiness of the couple, a selfless act that inadvertently crushes the fathers. The fact that Oakes's well-meaning intervention fails, that the lovers are exiled and the fathers broken, suggests the
limits of the Western imagination. Likewise, the populace is not dis-
abused of its naive confusion of commerce and romance; it is merely
reduced to a torporous mixture of cynicism and despair.

"A Sentimental Education"

Veronica Stetson is "the only and pampered child of big-in-oil Earl Stetson" (23). "Blonde and blue-eyed, long and tanned of limb," she is a
product of the best schools, fluent in five languages, "a concert-level
pianist and an Olympic-quality freestyle swimmer" (23). Despite—or
because of—such blessings, Veronica, two years out of college, suffers
from the *"colossal* boredom" that comes of "being able to predict practi-
cally every word and act of every person that [she] meet[s]" (26). Insu-
lated from life by "her parents, her class, her wealth and education, her
good looks and charm," Veronica despairs of finding innocence or
romance; she is beginning to understand that a world without contin-
gency or real peril is a world without hope (27).

In a desperate attempt to stave off the cynicism that she fears will
some day overwhelm her, Veronica transforms herself into Martha, an
impoverished divorcée with a mythical four-year-old daughter named
Pearl. Appropriately dressed down, Martha enters Wink's Bar & Grill,
a working-class dive. There she meets Vic, a "tall, hawkfaced" auto
mechanic with an ominous tattoo that reads "Remember Death." They
flirt, dance, go on to other bars, and end up at Vic's house trailer, where
they have sex. The next morning, a Sunday, Martha accompanies Vic to

his job at the garage. They make love again, in the bed of his truck. An hour later, on her hands and knees in the garage's grease pit, with Vic "bang[ing] against her from behind," Veronica wonders how she "could have been such a fool" (23).

For protagonist and reader alike, the coupling in the grease pit is too raw, too grotesque to be comical. Enjoying her wild ride up to that point, Veronica suddenly wonders if "all her connections—to her true self and where and what she came from—[are] broken, sundered, lost" (24). She even questions her own sanity. The proletariat she had stereo- typed as spontaneous, realistic, and physically overdeveloped, turns out to be more than she bargained for. Their world and their ways are often ugly and crude: not an antidote to "the coldly glittering sanctity of her parents' home" but an object lesson in the proper appreciation of com- fort and privilege (26).

As Vic ejaculates inside her, Veronica imagines that she has been impregnated. Envisioning a daughter, whom she (like Hawthorne's Hester Prynne) will call Pearl, Veronica vows that Pearl

> will be rich, advantaged, educated, comforted, and though her life would
> be different than this, no grease pits, no ominous tattoos, no house trail-
> ers, no convertible sofas, it would neverthless be a life with many alterna-
> tives at every moment. It would be a life of romance, innocence, and
> hope. (30)

Now fully apprised of the enormous gap that separates wealth from the working class, Veronica despairs of her own escape from a sheltered, stultifying life. The practical consequences of such a renunciation are horrifying, unthinkable. In a larger sense, "A Sentimental Education" traces the huge split in American experience between the smug, blood- less comfort of affluence and the raw, wounded intensity of the plebeian classes.

"About the Late Zimma (Penny) Cate: Selections from Her Loving Husband's Memory Hoard"

No woman could have been less like Veronica Stetson than the late Penny Cate. Devout, scrupulously moral, and hardworking, Penny lived her life doing "God's work" (36). Her husband's reminiscences take place a couple of days after her death at age 63, after 45 years of mar- riage. Mr. Cate speaks to assuage his grief and to stave off the realization that she is, in fact, dead.

His brief narrative centers on an incident that took place in July of 1931. Falsely arrested by the Crawford, New Hampshire, police chief for "taking a hurt man to the doctor so he would not bleed to death," Cate is fined $55 for some unspecified offense (33–34).[2] Ordered by the judge to chop the equivalent in firewood or go to jail, Cate asks his wife if he should appeal. "Without a moment's hesitation, she replied in a loud voice that everyone could hear. 'Call their bluff!' " (34). Working around the clock for three days ("the three days of my harrowing"), Cate manages the superhuman feat of cutting and stacking 38 cords of wood, an achievement he attributes to Penny's devotion and their shared faith in God.

With its deliberately corny title and rather unctuous and sentimental diction, Cate's eulogy exhibits all the conservative conventionality of a dyed-in-the-wool New England yeoman. No matter; whatever the metaphysical limitations of their religious views, those views clearly work for the Cates. Like the coffin maker in *Relation,* their unwavering commitment to a well-defined belief system gives them the strength not only to defy the government but to sustain a happy and loving marriage for nearly half a century. The secret to a meaningful life lies not in the content of one's belief but rather in the act of believing.

"The Conversion"

Some 14,000 words in length, "The Conversion" is by far the longest and most ambitious of the *New World* stories. It is also the most autobiographical. Banks draws heavily on the traumatic experiences of his own youth to produce an intimate, thoroughgoing, and funny character study of an obsessive-compulsive 16-year-old named Alvin Stock.

Coming of age in the repressive fifties under the tutelage of a cold, judgmental father, Alvin has had to develop two very different kinds of masks. The public persona he shows to his parents and other authority figures is bland, innocuous, and suitably compliant. Adults consider him "peaceable, sober, disciplined, a hard-working credit to his 'poor but honest' parents" (55). Among his peers, however, Alvin is a markedly different sort of boy: tough-talking, hard-drinking, and quick to pick a fight. Unable to reconcile these two selves into a coherent identity, Alvin feels "bisected, or worse, as if he were two separate human beings" (50). To add immeasurably to his inner torment, Alvin's dour New England upbringing makes no allowances for the hormonal rages of puberty that prompt him to masturbate every chance he gets. Dogged by guilt, though still a virgin and ashamed of that as well, Alvin often considers himself "slime, a bug, an animal lower than carrion eaters ... a soulless bag of appetites, a disease, a corruption of lusts" (37).

After a particularly miserable Friday night outing punctuated by masturbation, excessive drinking, a senseless fistfight, housebreaking, and defecating in an empty bathtub, Alvin is so filled with remorse that he vows to "turn over a new leaf" by making a series of private resolutions at the breakfast table: never to masturbate again; never to drink alcoholic beverages again; never to strike another human being; always to respect women; always to respect private property (47).

The one resolution Alvin neglects to make is to curb his incessantly wandering imagination. Assigned by his father, a plumber, to inventory hundreds of pipe fittings in the storage barn behind the house, Alvin concocts elaborate fantasies to while away the time. Initially, his thoughts turn to escape. He daydreams of migrating to New Orleans, where he visualizes himself working on a shrimp boat, bonding with his Cajun mates, being loved by a dusky beauty named Mantilla, and then vanishing without a trace, in the tradition of all romantic heroes (52–53). Chilled by the cold of the barn, Alvin decides that "his dream of 'a new life' was just that, a dream, nothing more, useless to him, a trick he was playing on himself" (53).

Wish-fulfillment having failed, Alvin's thoughts return to his woefully divided self, a condition he blames on the people around him. In a desperate bid for firm ground, Alvin decides to punish his friends and family by reversing all the pious resolutions he made at the breakfast table. Rather than rectify his behavior, he vows to "jack off every chance I get, drink myself drunk every chance I get, screw everything that'll let me, beat the shit out of anyone who gets in my way—in short, become in public the very person I already am in private" (54).

After a sullen lunch with his mother, Alvin returns to work in the afternoon and finds his anger gradually dissipating into maudlin feelings for his friends and parents "that approached sorrow, sorrow for their ignorance of him, for their apparent affection, respect, and, even, in some cases, their admiration for him" (56). Filled with remorse that he will never fulfill the high hopes they have for him, Alvin contemplates suicide.

Ironically, Alvin's morbid brooding results in a distinctly prosaic outcome: he loses track of his plumbing inventory. Subjected to a fierce tongue-lashing by his father, Alvin is only reconfirmed in his desire to do away with himself. Now utterly disconsolate, he spends the rest of the afternoon counting pipe fittings, composing suicide notes in his head, and pondering the best methods of self-destruction before settling on hanging.

Fully intending to hang himself in the barn after a school dance that evening, Alvin begins to "feel physically strange ... as if the decision had altered his metabolism":

> He was shaking, shivering with cold. The small of his back felt knitted and icy. His limbs felt cumbersome, sodden, thick and graceless, and his whole head felt swollen, puffed out around his eyes and mouth, so that it seemed he was looking and talking, when he talked, down a tunnel. He felt trapped inside his skin, but only tentatively, and explosively, the way a smoldering volcano is trapped by the earth's crust just before it erupts. (63)

Having worked himself into an altered state of consciousness, Alvin suffers through the dance in a kind of spiritual vertigo.

What happens next effects a sudden and radical change in the mood of the story, from grim to fancifully comic. In the parking lot outside the dance hall, Alvin Stock comes face to face with none other than the angel Raphael! Dressed in the stereotypical "white robe that glistened," the longhaired, barefoot angel is holding a staff in one hand and, less characteristically, "a fish about the size of a three-pound bass" in the other (68). "Smiling sympathetically," he identifies himself as "the healer" before floating up into the heavens. Whether an occult experience or, more likely, a hallucination, the mystical encounter prompts Alvin to abandon thoughts of suicide and decide to become a minister, an intention he announces to all comers.

Soon after his alleged run-in with a supernatural being, Alvin moves toward a religious vocation by applying for a summer job at a Presbyterian boys camp on Lake Winnipesaukee. Alvin's mother, his English teacher, Miss Waite, and his football coach, Mr. Plumley, all want him to take the job at the camp. They tacitly agree that it "would give him a chance to associate with a better class of people than his parents" (79). Only his father is displeased, partly because he expected his son to help him with the plumbing business and partly because he suspects that Alvin is selling out his working-class identity by associating himself with a bourgeois profession.

Though Alvin is put off by the exaggerated sincerity of the minister who interviews him, he is offered a job in the camp kitchen and accepts it "with outspoken enthusiasm and endless gratitude" (78). On the drive home, however, Alvin wavers and finally buckles "under the weight of deep misgivings and waves of unexplainable depression" (78). He phones the minister and says his father is going to need him this summer after all.

That evening when Alvin and his friend, Chub Feeney, double-date a pair of sisters, Alvin finally loses his virginity to the younger sister, Mary Buck. Feeney later informs Alvin that Mary will be residing near the Presbyterian boys camp all summer, proximity that will allow him to "knock off a piece of ass" any time he feels like it (77). Duly informed, Alvin changes his mind again about the job he just turned down. Ironically, in the end, it is sex in the guise of religion that compels Alvin to pull out of his father's working-class orbit.

In many respects, Alvin Stock comes off as a despicable young man—dithering, egoless, a moral coward and hypocrite. But Banks also takes pains to detail the excruciating environmental pressures under which Alvin labors to find himself. Much like Banks in his youth, Alvin is torn between the promise of upward mobility and loyalty to his father's proletarian ethos. Caught in a double bind, Alvin oscillates between middle-class conformity and underclass alienation and nihilism. His vision of Raphael no doubt emanates from his own unconscious, an inner reassurance that seemingly impossible contradictions can be lived through if not overcome. The "conversion" to which the story's title refers is not so much a conversion to Christianity, which proves to be merely opportunistic, but rather a conversion from childish autoeroticism to the beginnings of psychosexual maturity. Following Freud and his epigones, Banks affirms that identity formation is inextricably tied to sexual development.

Transformation

Unified, overall, by a consistently detailed style and uniformly laconic tone, the *New World* tales are also marked by a set of very deliberate bifurcations. The five "Renunciation" stories are pure fictions dealing with domestic themes, told in the third person, and set (vaguely) in contemporary New England. By contrast, the "Transformation" stories are based on historical events and persons, range over a variety of settings, and sometimes employ unusual modes of narration (e.g., the first three are told in the second person). Overall, *The New World* is carefully structured to underscore a series of interrelated dualities: religion and commerce; present and past; interpersonal relationships and social politics; North America and South America; and Old World and New.

"The Rise of the Middle Class"

Told in the second person, "Rise" fictionalizes a day in the life of South American revolutionary and statesman, Simón Bolívar (1783–1830). Banks bases his setting and principal action on verified historical facts. From May to September 1815, "El Libertador" was in exile in Jamaica, having been defeated by the Spanish in Venezuela and repudiated by his own subordinates. As J. B. Trend records, an attempt was made on Bolívar's life during that period that only failed because he "suddenly and unexpectedly chang[ed] his lodgings. A friend who was expecting him, and had gone to sleep in the hammock while he was waiting, received the death blows meant for the Liberator himself."[3]

In his quasi-mythical account, Banks correctly places Bolívar in Jamaica on 7 June 1815 and, also true to history, describes an attempt on his life. The rest, however, is pure invention. In Banks's decidedly more melodramatic version of the assassination attempt, Bolívar is at his desk, writing a letter, when he is attacked by a crazed, knife-wielding assailant who has entered his quarters by climbing a drain pipe up to the balcony. After a desperate struggle the intruder is vanquished, reduced to an inert "chunk of meat with a mouth shuddering with flies" (85).

After the near-fatal attack, Bolívar stands on his balcony, gazes down at a slave in the courtyard below, and ruminates on the peculiar existential burden of world historical figures: "He is a slave, a man wholly outside history, you reflect. No one will assassinate him. He can only be murdered. To be assassinated you must first step outside history; have to be guilty of trying to affect history from the outside. Like God" (85). The crux of the story is that Bolívar actually envies the slave his unimportance, in which there is, at least, a certain kind of personal safety and innocence.

"Indisposed"

With "Indisposed" Banks shifts from the world of international politics to the confines of the early-modern bourgeois marriage. A story that manifests a strong feminist sensibility, "Indisposed" posits a fictive turning point in the married life of Jane Hogarth (1710–1790), wife of William Hogarth (1697–1764), the English painter and engraver famous for his satiric portraits of eighteenth-century London social life.

Because of a paucity of documentation, very little is actually known about Jane Hogarth or the nature of the Hogarths' marriage. Biographer Peter Quennell admits that "Jane Hogarth's character is difficult to invoke" but hazards the guess that it was "exceptionally simple and straightforward."[4] Inevitably, much more is known about the personality and character of William Hogarth. Barely five feet tall, he was, in the words of a contemporary, " 'a strutting, consequential little man,' " proud, blustering, and excitable (Quennell, 185–86).

One can only speculate as to the quality of the Hogarths' 35-year marriage, but certain things stand out. Hogarth was a worldly, ambitious man of 31 when he married Jane Thornhill in 1729, apparently to augment his social standing.[5] She was only 19, reputedly rather large-limbed and homely, and still under her parents' roof when Jane Thornhill eloped to marry Hogarth; a sure sign of the genuineness of her feeling for him. The considerable difference in their ages, circumstances, and motivations may have made the Hogarths' marriage even more unequal than the norm for its day. Nonetheless, Peter Quennell deduces that the marriage must have been "singularly happy—so happy that it was destined to run its course without scandal or commotion, almost without friendly record" (Quennell, 72).

Banks has other ideas. Extrapolating from the known facts, he imagines that the diminutive, egotistical Hogarth must have been a bantam rooster of a husband—inattentive, unfaithful, and selfish in the extreme. Indeed, Banks's Hogarth treats his wife like a live-in whore, using her body for sex but otherwise hardly acknowledging her existence.

"Indisposed" chronicles that wholly speculative moment when Jane Hogarth reaches the limit of her endurance. Initially her rebellion manifests itself as profound lethargy, no doubt induced by depression. She tells her younger cousin (and housekeeper), Ellen, that she is "indisposed," the era's euphemism for an undetermined female malady. Around midday Hogarth comes to his wife's room, "barks" irritable questions at her regarding her inertia, then promptly leaves (91). At dusk, Hogarth returns with an elderly, decrepit physician who procedes to "examine" the stricken woman. All the while, William Hogarth, Ellen, and the doctor tellingly refer to Jane Hogarth as nothing more than a mindless body: "Indisposed. *It* said *it* was indisposed, the girl tells the man … I've given *it* a purgative, he says to your husband. By morning *it* should be back to normal again" (93; emphasis added). Satisfied that the problem has been identified and is being corrected, the three depart.

The ensuing hours constitute both the nadir of Jane Hogarth's life and the beginning of her spiritual salvation. Her bowels violently evacuated by the laxative, she lies torporously in her own wastes, pitying her "large, slow body ... for its very presence in the world, its large and pathetic demands on space, the way it tries and constantly fails to avoid being seen" (94). Faced with the stark and undeniable reality of her body, which "has at last agreed to be seen, to be wholly present," Jane Hogarth finally accepts its sheer size and power (95). At that moment she moves beyond pitying it to understanding it: a transformation that allows her to inhabit her body fully and without shame, thus reclaiming herself.

So when she hears her husband sneak up the attic stairs to make love to Ellen, Jane Hogarth finally has the strength to assert her rights as a human being. She ascends the stairs, enters the room, pulls the lovers apart, throws her husband against the wall, smashes him in the face, and then "slaps the girl powerfully across the side of her small head" (96). In so doing, she grasps an identity that had been nearly obliterated. As the narrator notes in conclusion, "[N]ever again, for as long as you live, will you be indisposed. You will live in your body as if it were a perfect mate, the adoring father, the admiring handmaiden, the devoted child of your devotions. You will live in your body as if it were your own" (96).

"The Caul"

After years of passively colluding in her own demoralization, Jane Hogarth accepts her less-than-ideal body, an affirmation of nature over patriarchal ideology that enables her to liberate herself with a vengeance. With "The Caul" Banks describes no such breakthrough. Quite the opposite. His subject is the great poet of psychic repression, solipsism, and neurotic ratiocination, Edgar Allan Poe (1809–1849).

"The Caul" is set in Richmond, Virginia. No specific dates are mentioned, but textual clues indicate that the action takes place on 24–25 September 1849.[6] Banks's choice of timing is quite deliberate. On the evening of the 24th, Poe gave the second of two lectures that summer in Richmond on "The Philosophy of Composition." He concluded his program by reciting "The Raven." This particular lecture is noteworthy as Poe's last public appearance; he died in Baltimore two weeks later, on 7 October.

The setting of the story is equally significant. Throughout his short life Poe was haunted by an idealized image of his mother, Eliza Arnold Poe, who died of tuberculosis in Richmond in 1811, when her son was only two years old—too young to remember her. During his stay in Richmond in the summer of 1849, Edgar Poe courted a rich widow named Elmira Shelton. Coincidentally (or not), Mrs. Shelton lived in a house on Church Hill, directly opposite the small cemetery of St. John's Church, where Poe's mother, Eliza, lay buried in an unmarked grave (Silverman, 427). More than likely, Poe thought of his mother every time he went to call on the widow Shelton.

In his imaginative rendering of Poe's last days in Richmond, Banks skews or otherwise embellishes the biographical facts in order to emphasize a primal connection between Poe's art and his mother's early demise.[7] Banks does this in several ways. Though Poe's final public appearance was more of a lecture on his aesthetic method, Banks puts equal if not greater emphasis on Poe's recitation of "The Raven," a poem that despairs of reunion in the afterlife with his beloved "Lenore" (doubtless a figure for his mother, Eliza, but also for his foster mother, Frances Allan, and his late wife, Virginia Clemm Poe). To further emphasize the connection between these deaths and "The Raven," Banks has a woman in the audience cough throughout Poe's recitation of the poem, thus reminding him of his mother's (and wife's) consumptive, dying cough. Banks also excises all mention of Elmira Shelton in order to foreground Poe's attraction to his mother's grave.

While biographers might rightfully object to Banks's flagrant use of poetic license, it may be said in his defense that he is not presuming to write biography but rather a canny hybrid of biography and fiction that attempts to dramatize certain psychological truths. Implicit in "The Caul" is the highly plausible notion that Poe's mental life was haunted by a guilty belief that he had somehow caused his mother's premature death ("You were bad, a bad boy, bad little boy. She died" [97]). In Banks's account, Edgar Poe's chronic anxiety is amplified by his inability to remember anything about his mother, a natural failing Poe judges to be tantamount to heresy:

> To aspire to purge one's mind and all its manifestations of every taint of un-reason—such an aspiration must be *blasphemy!* For to be pure reason, to be self-generating, to be unable to remember your mother—is to be a *god!* Is that why you can't remember your mother's face, her smell, her touch, her voice? (101)

To try to resolve his tortured feelings about his mother (and himself), Poe supposedly made "hundreds" of visits to her grave over the years (103).

As depicted in Banks's story, what will be Poe's last visit to St. John's cemetery results in a transformative moment. Poe's usual response to the gravesite has been one of unbridled terror, "a feeling painful and frightening, of falling, as if down a well that reaches to the center of the earth" (103). Accompanying the panic is a claustral sense of being "wrapped in silence, as if in a caul" (103). A part of the mother's amnion that sometimes happens to get stuck to the newborn's head like a skull cap, the caul makes a fitting metaphor for Poe's unconscious and deeply conflicted obsession with his mother's memory, like a membrane around his mind that blocks out the world. This time, though, Poe is somehow able to imagine an image of his mother's eye, a "beautiful" eye that "stare[s] peacefully back" at him when he stares at it (104). Finally possessed of a concrete image of his mother's love, Banks's Poe is able to leave Richmond—and the world—forever.

"The New World"

The most ponderous and, therefore, least successful of the *New World* tales is its culminating title story. Set in early seventeenth-century Jamaica, "The New World" juxtaposes the life and work of an obscure Catholic prelate and poet, Bernardo de Balbuena (1562–1627), with that of an even more obscure Sephardic goldsmith by the name of Mosseh Alvares. Though the Spanish cleric and Jewish merchant occupied wholly different worlds in the "stagnating backwater" that was then Jamaica, Banks detects a number of telling similarities between the two figures:

> The two were approximately the same age, and both felt themselves to be cultured men who, because of the provinciality of the place they were obliged to live in, were not properly appreciated by their culture. Also, they were both, in the ways of their respective worlds, ambitious, the abbot as churchman and literary figure, the Jew as artisan and articulate member of the Jewish community.
>
> Alvares, as much as Balbuena, believed that what we make of our lives is merely the fleshly expression of our idea of what's possible. (121)

Furthermore, both Balbuena and Alvares managed to achieve a slight vestige of immortality by leaving literary traces behind. Alvares was the author of what Banks describes as "a rather shapeless and morose version of a medieval tale" entitled "The Patriarch" (135). Balbuena labored for years over *El Bernardo,* in Banks's words, a "bizarrely mediocre epic poem" more than 40,000 tedious lines long. As Banks proves by unduly elaborate synopsis, both works were uninspired efforts, now only occasionally read and studied by only the most avid scholars of the Spanish Renaissance.

One may well ask why Banks bothers to write about Balbuena and Alvares; surviving records indicate that their lives were ordinary, arduous, and banal. And their pretentious literary efforts speak for themselves. But it is precisely that contrast between the life and the art that interests Banks. He argues that a failure to grasp "the tactile facticities of Balbuena's daily life ... its lifelong patterns" results in a failure to understand "the spark that during his life flew between it and the other pole, the poem" (135). Missing that spark, "one would have missed *everything*. That spark was everything. It's how one forgives oneself and others" (135).

Likewise, Banks sees Alvares's intellectual life as a means "to inflate his sense of social worth," his only escape from an "oppressed and depressing daily life ... in a colony of exiles at the end of the known world" (135). One's refusal to acknowledge the validity of such psychic survival strategies results in a failure to "perceive how that life makes another, more lucid life possible, and perhaps even necessary" (136). While admitting that it is easy to scoff at their mediocre literary efforts, Banks finds it admirable that Balbuena and Alvares spent their lives "puttering away at signs of self that are larger than the self" (136). In some ultimate sense the quality of the work they left behind is irrelevant. What really matters is the perennial impulse they manifested, an impulse to transcend the spatiotemporal confines of the mortal self, confines that condemn the vast majority of the human race to utter and final oblivion in death.

Chapter 6

Caribbean Odysseys: *The Book of Jamaica* and *Continental Drift*

Everything struggles to change, except the outworn systems.

Pablo Neruda, *Memoirs*

As would become increasingly evident in the 1980s, Russell Banks's stay on the island of Jamaica in 1976 and 1977 fostered enormous changes in his outlook and the nature of his writing. Because he was there for a year and a half and was willing to participate in the day-to-day life of the island, Banks's Jamaican sojourn opened his eyes to things that harried white tourists never experience. Nonetheless, Banks's time there left him somewhat frustrated and troubled. As he later told interviewer Curtis Wilkie, "I found myself absolutely fascinated by the people who surrounded me. The carpenters, pipe fitters, the storekeepers. Just the average Joes and their wives, and I brought a quality of care and attention that I had not brought to anybody. Yet I found I couldn't penetrate. I couldn't eliminate my white-ness, my American-ness, my middle-class-ness."[1]

In order to grapple with the alienation he felt, Banks undertook a novel that would eventually become *The Book of Jamaica* (1980). To do justice to his subject, Banks had to widen his scope as a writer. His early experiments in metafiction, with their privatistic focus on moral growth in the context of family and marital strife, gave over to a new idiom, still "experimental" and deeply personal but with a pronounced emphasis on social themes. In ways both obvious and subtle, Banks's Jamaican interlude decisively turned him into a practitioner of neorealism. The shift toward realism was inevitable anyway; Banks remembers becoming "bored" with formal experimentation at this point in his writing life: "I wasn't endlessly fascinated by infinite regress ... How many times can you prove over and over to yourself that you're making it up?"[2]

A combination of fictionalized memoir, travel book, and sociopolitical allegory, *The Book of Jamaica* can be viewed as an important transitional work, a bridge between Banks's early forays into metafiction and the full flowering of the working-class realism represented by his best novel, *Continental Drift* (1985).

The Book of Jamaica

Though utterly dissimilar in style, setting, tone, and subject matter, *The Book of Jamaica* has something essential in common with *Hamilton Stark*. At base, both books can be thought of as existentialist detective stories that feature sensitive, morally scrupulous narrators struggling to define their identities through obsessive immersion in concerns outside the self. Indeed, *The Book of Jamaica* can be seen as a logical extension of the novel that precedes it: a journey of self-discovery that carries the narrator-protagonist well beyond an adolescent fixation with heroes and hero worship and into the wider world of realpolitik, where the fate of peoples takes precedence over the concerns of any individual.

Much like the author himself at the time of his Jamaican adventure, Banks's unnamed narrator is a 36-year-old New Hampshire college professor, visiting the island on a foundation grant to study the Maroons; that is, "the direct descendants of [Ashanti] slaves who had escaped from their Spanish and then British masters in the seventeenth and eighteenth centuries and who afterward from their inaccessible mountain enclaves had successfully conducted a hundred-year guerilla war against the British" (3). The narrator never explains the precise nature of his fascination with the Maroons, but his attraction no doubt stems from their inherent exoticism and larger-than-life heroism. Wrenched away from their African homeland to a strange island in another part of the world, the Maroons displayed enormous courage, tenacity, and resourcefulness in successfully defying their would-be colonial overlords. Such a people are worthy of any thinking man's respect, especially if that man is still in the midst of his own moral, intellectual, and political evolution, as is Banks's narrator.

In the course of the novel, the Maroons come to symbolize and embody the heart of Jamaican culture, but many and varied digressions intervene. *The Book of Jamaica* is leisurely paced, almost desultory, as Banks allows his narrator-protagonist to range freely over the island, absorb its exotic influences, and gradually modify his views and perceptions as he gathers more data. As in *Hamilton Stark,* learning how to see and interpret is much more important than active intervention, at least initially.

With some justification a reviewer characterized the early sections of the novel as having the qualities of "a book *about* Jamaica, a brilliant

travel book that's passing itself off as fiction."[3] Charges of plotlessness
are far from accurate, but the impression is understandable enough.
Eschewing conventionally lineal plot construction, Banks tends to proceed discursively. The key to his method is to be found in one of the
book's two epigraphs, a quotation from Octavio Paz's *Laughter and Peni-
tence.* Paz contrasts the role that causality plays in Western culture with
"the role played by analogy among the Meso-Americans":

> Causality is open, successive, and more or less infinite: a cause produces
> an effect, which in turn, engenders another. Analogy or correspondence,
> by contrast, is close and cyclical: the phenomena evolve and are repeated
> as in a play of mirrors. Each image changes, fuses with its contrary, dis-
> engages itself, forms another image, and in the end returns to the start-
> ing point. Rhythm is the agent of change in this case. The key expres-
> sions of change are, as in poetry, metamorphosis and mask.

His subject being a tiny island nation—the ultimate example of a world
unto itself—Banks fits form to content by moving his story forward
through reiterative "analogy" and "correspondence" rather than the
"open, successive" causal dynamic better suited to the sprawling matri-
ces that characterize the landscapes of modern industrial states.

"Captain Blood"

The book begins with "Captain Blood," an elaborate and chilling anecdote that establishes a symbolic image and pole of reference diametri-
cally opposite the anticolonialist history of the Maroons. With grisly
irony, Banks uses Captain Blood to refer to Jamaica's most famous white
resident, Errol Flynn (1909–1959). Michael Curtiz's 1935 swashbuck-
ler, *Captain Blood,* made the dashing Tasmania-born actor a major Hollywood film star, but Banks's narrator comes to suspect that the title
might be an accurate label for Flynn himself. Nearly 20 years after his
death, rumors persist on the island that Flynn and two cohorts (an abortion doctor named Menotti and his son) were involved in the murder
and dismemberment of a young Jamaican woman—despite the fact that
the woman's husband, DeVries, was tried, convicted, and executed for
the killing.

The more Banks's narrator investigates Errol Flynn, the more troubled he becomes. His Jamaican friend and guide, a young Rastafarian
named Terron Musgrave, sees Flynn in mythic terms, as "Captain Blood,

obeah man, a proud, laughing prince of Darkness" (23). Another
Jamaican acquaintance, Evan Smith, sees Flynn in social terms, as "an
elegant mafioso don, a wealthy and famous land baron, a possible CIA
agent" (23). The narrator himself prefers to understand Flynn in psychological terms, as "a sybaritic debauchee, an aging and decadent
movie star" (23). The apparent irreconcilability of these views leaves the
narrator with "an irritated grasping after certainty, an insecurity that
was distinctly unsettling" (24). The obvious solution is to fall back on
the dominant "assumption of the age, the convention of rational analysis" that establishes a causal hierarchy between mythic, social, and psychological categories: "It was presumed that [Flynn's] psychology
caused his social identity which then caused his mythic function. Each
stage is impossible without the previous stage as underpinning" (24).
But what depresses the narrator is that, "for Smith and Terron, the social
and mythic levels, respectively, seemed sufficient, as if they were self-
determined. For Smith and Terron, there was no irritated grasping after
certainty" (24). Whatever their inherent truth value, their views had
"clarity and certitude." The narrator's arguably more sophisticated
vision only brings him "anxiety, mistrust, [and] depression."

The undecidability of Flynn's character is mirrored by the ambigui-
ties of the murder case. Presented with a welter of sketchy and often
contradictory accounts, some insisting on Flynn's involvment in the
death of Waila DeVries, some denying it, the narrator is ultimately
unable to solve the mystery. All he is left with are unremarkable sites of
alleged occurrences, half-forgotten traces of stories, and his own mus-
ings. The "Captain Blood" section ends with the narrator finding the
cliff hole where part of the victim's body was supposedly deposited. He
peers into the abyss for a long time, listens to the sea crashing below,
and seems to wait for some sign. But nothing is revealed. Like the investigative narrator in *Hamilton Stark,* the American professor has no
choice, in the end, but to turn around and go home empty-handed.

Though the DeVries case has no bearing on the larger history of the
island and is never taken up again, Banks has good reasons for devoting
some 20,000 words to the incident. As already noted, "Captain Blood"
serves as a symbolic counterpoint to the saga of the Maroons. The modern epitome of the colonial ruling class in terms of masculine arrogance,
power, and invulnerability, Errol Flynn possesses a mythic stature that
underscores the tremendous divide that separates the rich from the
poor: "he who had wealth was truly a magician, was outside the powers
that controlled the lives of ordinary men and women" (54).

On a more subjective level, Banks's account of his narrator's dogged but perhaps pointless investigation into the DeVries slaying emphasizes the man's obsessive desire for certitude, a potentially dangerous trait in a culture that operates along entirely different cognitive lines. Animating "Captain Blood" is the notion that fervent curiosity is not enough; the participant-observer must be willing to forsake an inculcated point of view, perhaps all points of view, in order to really *see*. Appropriately enough, Banks prefaces the book's second and longest section, "Nyamkopong," with an epigraph from the Marxist theorist Walter Benjamin: "Only he who has made his dialectical peace with the world can grasp the concrete."

"Nyamkopong"

"Nyamkopong" opens with the narrator settling himself and his family into a rented villa on a hillside overlooking Montego Bay at the north-west corner of the island. The narrator's account of the early days of his sabbatical is laced with self-caricature for the man he was then. Naive, selfish, and self-deluded as to his own considerable privilege as a white American, Banks's punctiliously liberal professor envisions a stay ideal for its political correctness:

> This time, I told my wife and children, we will not be tourists. This time we will not even have to *see* any tourists! We will see only the *natives!* They will be black, of course, and mostly slender, smiling, and poor— but when they learn that we are not tourists, they will be honest, and they will like us, because even though we are rich and white, we are hon-est and like them. (68)

Laughably optimistic regarding his chances of integrating into the real Jamaica, the narrator is, likewise, willfully obtuse about his accommo-dations. The time is January 1976, just months into the socialist regime of Michael Manley, "whose government had determined to eliminate . . . by gradual and democratic procedures, capital and capitalists" (69). Banks's narrator is given a huge discount on his villa's rent when he agrees to mail the rent checks to the owner's son at his Canadian address, a ploy that keeps the money out of the confiscatory hands of Manley's government. With witty irony the narrator recalls his having turned a blind eye to the illegality of the scheme: "Naturally [the owner's] cutting the rent in half was something of an aid to my not see-ing anything wrong or unusual. I merely felt lucky. It's amazing, I thought, how lucky I am" (70).

The narrator's disingenuous sense of good fortune quickly wears off once he gets to know his landlords, Preston Church and his wife, Abbie, and other affluent white Jamaicans. At their social gatherings, "the conversation seem[s] to turn obsessively to the subject of imminent racial war" as Manley's economic policies begin to destabilize a 300-year-old status quo based on, in the narrator's words, "relentless racial oppression and economic exploitation" (76). Constantly exposed to the alarmist thinking of the racist white minority, the narrator is not shocked to find himself at a party, listening to "an elegantly dressed and manicured physician . . . recommend forced sterilization [of poor black people] as a solution to the problem of 'overpopulation,' " a "solution" the narrator quite rightly terms "a kind of genocide" (77).

Matters of conscience come to a head for the narrator at a dinner party hosted by Captain and Mrs. West (parents of a close friend), when Mrs. West shrieks angrily at a young black servant for pouring water from the wrong side: "From the *right!* Serve from the *right,* you idiot!" (106). Although the other guests ignore the interruption as if it "had been no more than a phone call for someone else," the narrator is appalled by his hostess's unself-conscious display of racist bile (107). Feigning illness, he excuses himself and is escorted to his car by Captain West, who proceeds to rant and rave about Manley's regime opening the door to "Looting! Rape! Murder! Economic collapse!" (108).

Finally overwhelmed by the ugly spectacle of white racist hatred and fear, the narrator drives home but is too upset to go inside. As he walks hastily, "in a kind of tantrum," along a crumbling road near his home, the narrator's anger at the Wests quickly surges into a generalized rage. He finds himself bitterly angry at "the tourists whose prosperity and innocence protected them from knowing the reasons behind the obsequious questions and politeness of the 'natives,' " at "the full-bellied black Jamaicans that run the country, the corrupt bureaucrats and cops and petty officials who never took off their sunglasses," at "the British-educated intellectuals, white and black, who condescended to their own history" (110). Most of all, the narrator is furious at himself for his own weak-willed detachment, a timid moral neutrality that isolates him from blacks and whites alike.

Arriving at a decaying villa abandoned by whites on an opposite hillside, the narrator makes his way to its terrace facing the sea. There, in the moonlight, he gazes down on "the glistening black Caribbean" and decides, once and for all, "to despise the Wests and the Churches and all the people who resembled them, and to love a people I might never understand and definitely would never become" (112). The narrator's moral epiphany is an important turning point in the novel; from that moment on, his involvement with the "natives" steadily becomes more intense and obsessive.

The second half of the novel largely focuses on the narrator's investigative forays into the Maroon town of Nyamkopong, in "Cockpit Country," a rugged, remote section of the interior. Nyamkopong is presided over by Colonel Martin Luther Phelps, an unctuous petty bureaucrat the narrator finds annoying. More to his liking is Phelps's social and political nemesis, Wendell O. Mann, the gregarious tribal secretary who manifests a strong sense of his Maroon roots. Taking a liking to the narrator in the course of countless rounds of cigarettes and brimming glasses of rum, Mr. Mann regales his guest with a fanciful history of the Maroons that makes contemporaries of Christopher Columbus, Queen Elizabeth, Winston Churchill, and Julius Caesar (101–4).

Exactly opposite in temperament and outlook, Colonel Phelps and Mr. Mann serve to embody a fundamental split in the Maroon psyche, a gap the narrator traces back to the 1790s, when the Nyamkopong Maroons refused to join the Maroons of St. James in a war against the British "because of flagrant violations of the treaty of 1738" (119). The narrator quickly comes to understand that there are two kinds of Maroon descendants: those like Mr. Mann, "who saw the Maroon people as a separate polity in Jamaica," and those like Colonel Phelps, "who wished to accommodate themselves with the larger, national entity by assimilating into it" (119). Not surprisingly, the two men loathe each other. Phelps tries to pretend that Mann does not exist; Mann dismisses Phelps in the harshest possible terms, as a "monkey" cleverly imitating a real human being (134).

Divided by their views on Maroon independence, the townspeople also fall into opposing camps regarding the Rastafarians among them. Some believe "the brethren" to be religious people; others see them only as dope-smoking thieves (135). Those in the former group—Mr. Mann, "a surprisingly large number of the older mothers, and most of the children in town"—resent the occasional Jamaican police raids into Nyamkopong to arrest, beat, and jail Rastafarians suspected of dealing in the marijuana trade (136). Such raids are considered violations of the 1739 treaty, which supposedly guarantees the Maroons full legal jurisdiction over their own people (except in capital murder cases). As the town's chief official, Colonel Phelps is blamed for police incursions. Yet, as the narrator astutely points out, popular antipathy toward Phelps is misplaced. As it slowly modernizes, Jamaica is inevitably becoming a more unified and integrated polity. In the process, the Maroons are being "swallowed by the nation, hard edges, inconsistencies, contradictions and all" (137). Phelps allows the police raids not only because he has been bribed to do so but also because "the raids were the compromise that had been worked out all over the island between police control and local, tribal autonomy, and the young Rastas were the sacrifices that made it work" (136). Whatever their suspicions, no one is selling out the Maroons; the collectivist pulses of modernity are simply overtaking them.

The uneasy relations between assimilationist Maroons and their more traditional counterparts begin to disintegrate when Colonel Phelps requests the treaty from Mr. Mann (its custodian) so that it can be handed over to a government official in Kingston for copying. Suspecting a plot to alter or destroy the treaty, or, at best, to exchange what he *thinks* is the original in his possession for a copy, Mann angrily refuses (140).[4]

As intrigue concerning the treaty simmers, the narrator and Terron embark on a tour of the other Maroon towns in Jamaica—Gordon Hall, Moore Town, and Charles Town—all near Port Antonio in the southeast. At this point in the narrative (the third and last chapter of the "Nyamkopong" section), Banks switches to the second person, to signify a dramatic transformation in his narrator's identity (177–91).[5] Living among the Maroons for days and weeks at a time, the narrator bonds closely with Terron and Mr. Mann and his "growing obsession" with the island begins to eclipse his habituated sense of self: "Who is this white American traveling with you and your friend Terron in Jamaica? Because of that question you are [no longer] a tourist" (182).

Fittingly, the final stage in the narrator's metamorphosis, from "tourist" to committed partisan, occurs in Gordon Hall, the most "independent, suspicious, scornful, and proud" of the Maroon villages, which still employs "Ashanti passwords, rites, songs, gestures [and] lore" (182). Though unnerved by the stark otherness of what he encounters there, the narrator agrees to act as liaison between Gordon Hall and Nyamkopong, so that the Maroons "can make themselves stronger against the government than they are alone" (185).

"Obi" and "Dread"

The protagonist's decision to commit fully to the Maroons' cause is indicated by yet another carefully contrived shift in narrative perspective, from second to third person. Having cast his American professor as an utterly subjective first-person narrator, then, briefly, as an intersubjective second-person narrator, Banks renders him entirely from the outside, as "Johnny" (the Jamaican sobriquet for a trusted foreigner), in the book's final sections, "Obi" and "Dread." By gradually shifting his narrative personae outward, toward the world, Banks inverts the traditional, ego-based perspective of the bourgeois individual, an inversion that suggests his protagonist is being absorbed into the culture of the island, a fate not unlike that of the Maroons.

For the reader, however, the situation is more complex and paradoxical. Having come to identify with the novel's first-person narrator, one is apt to forge an even closer identification with the protagonist when the story switches to the second person. Though Banks's professor is conversing with his alter ego, the reader can scarcely avoid being interpolated into the narrative by the force of the direct address, *you.* Then, just as suddenly, the narrative devolves into the third-person, leaving the reader distanced from the narrator with whom he or she had come to identify. By altering the terms and degrees of reader engagement, Banks underscores the hazards inherent in attempting to really *know* anything or anyone, especially one's self. The closer one gets to one's object, the more problematic and elusive it seems to become.

Inevitably, given the novel's rather pessimistic premises, "Johnny's" passionate involvement with the Maroons comes to grief. Things start to go wrong when Johnny transports Colonel Bowra of Gordon Hall and his entourage across the island to Nyamkopong, to meet with Colonel Phelps and participate in an important Maroon festival. Phelps is not ready for them when they arrive: a social blunder that sets off irritable grumbling among Bowra's group. To make matters infinitely worse, a Land Cruiser full of burly Jamaican policemen suddenly roars into Nyamkopong. With brutal swiftness, the police drag a young Rasta named Rubber out of his hut, beat him, and take him away—a show of force that sends a clear message: "Behave yourselves in the next few days. We are in charge" (234). Then, with outrageous nonchalance, the police help themselves to the food that Phelps had prepared for his Gordon Hall guests.

Disgusted by the entire incident, Bowra and his people conclude that Colonel Phelps is a traitor, "a whore to Babylon," and must die (240). Soon thereafter Johnny hears the grim but unsurprising news: Phelps has been found dead, a bullet in each eye. The killer is unknown, but the gun belonged to Benjie, a partner with Terron Musgrave in the marijuana business. Shortly after Phelps's murder, Benjie is also found dead, with five bullets in his body and his dreadlocks shorn: undoubtedly the work of the police. Having facilitated the meeting between Bowra and Phelps, Johnny understands that he is more than a little culpable for Phelps's demise and for Benjie's as well. The killings not only leave him badly shaken but deeply implicated and endangered.

Things are no more sanguine on the domestic front. Johnny's wife (who is not named and barely mentioned throughout most of the novel) decides to take the children and return home early, to "figure out what to do with this thing we're still in the habit of calling a marriage" (283). Bereft of his family *and* a sense of purpose on the island, Johnny next loses the comfort of his well-appointed rental home. The Churches, eager to cut their losses and flee Manley's Jamaica, offer to sell Johnny the house he is renting. When he refuses to buy or to be evicted, Mrs. Church derisively declares him a "squatter" and simply begins to sell all the furniture out from under him (273–77). Conversing with his friend, Yvonne (a barmaid in Anchovy), Johnny admits that his life "is coming apart" and that he does not "know how to stop it from coming apart" (285). No longer able to trust his own judgment, Johnny fears that "unless I'm really careful from now on ... I'm likely to get myself killed" (286).

Indeed, Johnny's guilty paranoia nearly proves to be his undoing. Sent to Gordon Hall to deliver messages from Mann (the new Colonel of Nyamkopong) to Colonel Bowra, Johnny is accosted by a "large, muscular youth" who is "extremely angry" at his presence in town. Fearing for his life, Johnny lashes out at the man with a machete and cuts off his right hand (307). Hustled away from the screaming crowd by Harris, one of Bowra's lieutenants, Johnny delivers his messages. Ironically, every one of them is stale news to Bowra. His absurd, futile mission completed, Johnny is spirited out of town in the back of a pickup truck by a visiting politico who wants it made clear that the white pariah "does not work for me and he is not my friend" (309). The novel ends with Johnny, one step ahead of retribution, hurriedly boarding an Air Jamaica jetliner bound for Miami.

Lessons

Contrary to prevailing American ideology, which affirms "the essential sameness among people [rather] than ... their difference," Banks's liberal academician has learned the hard way that there are, indeed, *essen-*

tial differences between Americans and Jamaicans (25). The particularities of race, culture, and economics function as insurmountable barriers between the likes of "Johnny" and the Third World's poor. No amount of personal empathy or good will can change the real structures that keep the world locked into a pitiless hierarchy of wealthy exploiter nations and their penurious client states. Politically and morally awakened, "Johnny" has renounced the entitlements of his whiteness, only to discover that he can never really cross over; black Jamaicans live in another world. As Banks put it many years later, the lesson he had learned from *his own* Jamaica experience was that "in a racialized society, I couldn't avoid being implicated by race and that's one of the themes in [*The Book of Jamaica*]: you can't escape your skin color in a racialized society, even if you're white" (20 August 1995).

Continental Drift

While *The Book of Jamaica* limned the disillusionment of a bourgeois, liberal intellectual regarding racial matters, Banks's next book, a third collection of short stories entitled *Trailerpark* (1981), completed his transformation into a writer of working-class fiction in the naturalist mode. Racial concerns are not absent from these new stories, but they take a back seat to Banks's primary aim: to evoke the harsh conditions under which New England's predominately white working-class carries on its struggle for survival. With his next novel, *Continental Drift* (1985), Banks moved to consolidate the gains in depth and breadth of treatment he had managed on these hitherto separate fronts of race and class. Indeed, *Continental Drift* can be considered a deliberate synthesis of the two novels that precede it, *Hamilton Stark* and *The Book of Jamaica,* in that it melds the class concerns of New England with the racial politics of the Caribbean, forming a synergistic whole that is much more powerful than the sum of its parts.

Linking such culturally disparate locales and themes would seem to present enormous challenges to the unity and coherence of a novel in terms of structure, tone, narrative voice, and the like. Banks's formal solutions are brilliantly economical and pragmatic. He creates two very different but ultimately complementary protagonists—Bob Dubois, a white working-class American male, and Vanise Dorsinville, a destitute black Haitian female—as *types* to exemplify issues of class and race (and gender), and then proceeds to tell their respective stories in alternating chapters. If such a structure sounds grindingly mechanical and contrived, the book does not read that way. Both characters are types, but they are also drawn as distinct, highly specified, and "rounded" characters in narratives that are fast paced, gripping, and rife with convincingly realistic detail.

Banks also avoids predictability by not giving Bob's and Vanise's narrative strands equal weight. Bob Dubois' story occupies the lion's share of the book, but the interchapters devoted to Vanise serve important functions in their own right. By periodically interrupting his primary narrative with interludes from what amounts to another world (and vice versa), Banks keeps on deconstructing the realist illusion that he so carefully nurtures within each chapter. The effect is to keep the reader engaged but not so mesmerized by the overall flow of the narrative as to lose sight of the fact that it is, after all, a fiction. As noted in other contexts, Banks's aesthetic is Brechtian in the sense that he deliberately constructs distancing devices to preserve the reader's ability to judge the story critically, as opposed to merely "taking it in" as harmless entertainment. Correspondingly, on a thematic level, Vanise Dorsinville's far more dire story of a poor woman's deprivation and helplessness serves as a dramatic corrective to Bob Dubois's tale of American working-class male angst; a necessary reminder that the United States proletariat, though certainly battered, exploited, and demoralized, is still a privileged class in global terms.

Furthermore, Vanise's religion, voodoo, provides the novel with much of its symbolic iconography. A talented visual artist, Banks researched, adapted, and drew voudon ceremonial symbols called *vevers* for his chapter heads.[6] Banks also borrows from voodoo to frame the novel with an "Invocation" and "Envoi," a kind of author's preface and afterword that enable him to step outside of his work by invoking the *loa* or "mouthman" (the voudon spirit of the dead that speaks through the mouth of the living). In these brief sections the *loa* is conjured not only for inspiration but also as a model for the author's self-appointed role as medium, giving voice to the voiceless, whether living or dead.

"This Stupid Life"

As already noted, the novel's main character, Robert Raymond Dubois, a 30-year-old oil burner repairman from Catamount, New Hampshire, is Banks's exemplar for the Anglo-American working-class male.[7] As such, Bob Dubois is "basically an inarticulate man."[8] In order to make Dubois a distinct individual with a suitably vivid emotional life, Banks chooses to adopt a "dual voice," as Ralph B. Sipper puts it, by interposing "his authorial omniscience with the character's unspoken feelings" (Sipper, 95). As Banks well knows, this device, sometimes referred to as *indirect discourse,* is yet another, albeit slight, departure from the traditionally seamless illusionism of naturalist fiction, whose conventions dictate that a character never think anything he is not capable of saying aloud.[9] Nonetheless, Banks is willing to incur some slight risk to narrative congruity in order to delve deeply into Bob Dubois's troubled inner life. The operant theory is that a man's feelings and perceptions, no matter how sketchy or deluded, often have more of an effect on shaping his destiny than actual circumstances.

Though "there is nothing dramatically or even apparently wrong with his life"—he holds a steady job, is married, is a homeowner, and is the father of two young children—Bob Dubois is haunted by the sense that he has no real future (14):

> The trouble with his life, if he were to say it honestly ... is that his life is over. *He's alive, but his life has died.* He's thirty years old, and if for the next thirty-five years he works as hard as he has so far, he will be able to stay exactly where he is now, materially, personally. (14, emphasis added)

A job that pays "chump change," endless boredom, and a sense of stagnation are bad enough, but Bob's lot is made even worse, psychologically, by the American Dream ideology that bombards him on a daily basis. The message is everywhere, "in store windows or on TV, everything he reads in magazines and newspapers and everyone he knows" reinforces "the old life-as-ladder metaphor" that condemns mere survival as insufficient (14–15). The glaring contrast between Bob's actual life and the advertised life contributes to his desperation.[10] Lacking an informed political perspective that would put the blame where it belongs—on an exploitative class system—Bob Dubois tends to blame himself. Consequently, he harbors intense, impotent feelings of anxiety, rage, frustration, and confusion: feelings pent up by a working-class ethic of emotional repression to which Bob unthinkingly subscribes. Rather than admit his pain and deal with it openly, Bob expresses it obliquely, through drinking, philandering, and sporadic bouts of violence.

Given the suffocating way that Bob Dubois lives his life, matters inevitably come to crisis. Departing from a tryst with his girlfriend,

Doris Cleeve, on a snowy night in late December of 1979, Bob arrives,
half drunk, at a Sears store just before closing, to buy his daughter ice
skates for Christmas. After a quarrel with a surly clerk, Bob finally snaps
and smashes all the windows of his own station wagon with his fist
(20–21). That violent, self-defeating but cathartic outburst signals the
end of his old life and the start of a new one. Later that night Bob is able
to confess his troubles to his wife, Elaine:

> Listen to me. It's this place. This goddamned place. It stinks. And it's my
> job at Abenaki [Oil Co.], that fucking job. And it's this whole fucking
> life. This stupid life. All of a sudden, this whole life came to me, showed
> me itself. (27)

Listening sympathetically, Elaine suggests they move to Florida, where
Bob's older brother, Eddie, has promised him a job in his liquor retail
business. Bob readily agrees. Thus begins Bob's migration in search of
the American Dream, a migration propelled less by economic necessity
than by psychological compulsion. He is pushed, on the one hand, by a
desire to escape his stagnated existence and pulled, on the other, by the
opportunistic, status-conscious culture that bears down on him.

"A Moral Imperative"

At this juncture Banks interrupts Bob Dubois' story in order to intro-
duce his secondary protagonist, Vanise Dorsinville, a young, unmarried
mother who lives in Haiti in circumstances that make Bob Dubois's
hard life look like a miracle of material comfort and abundance. But
before he focuses on Vanise, Banks includes a long and elaborate digression on human migration as a kind of natural, global process, "a subsys-
tem inside the larger system of currents and tides, of winds and weather,
of drifting continents and shifting, uplifting, grinding, cracking land-
masses" (39). A fundamental thesis of the novel is that it is almost "a
moral imperative" for millions of human beings to "keep moving" across
the planet in flight from war, poverty, famine, drought, and political
oppression, in search of a better life (45). As Banks's narrator puts it,
"It's the only argument we have against entropy" (45).

The digression on migration serves two purposes: to link the migra-
tory journeys of Bob Dubois and Vanise Dorsinville, and to place them in
the largest possible context: that of nature itself. But general similarities
must give over to particular differences. Indeed, it would be hard to

imagine someone less like Bob Dubois than Vanise Dorsinville. While Bob embodies the plight of the American blue-collar worker, Vanise typifies a new, international lumpen proletariat: young, nonwhite, female, and disenfranchised and uprooted not by status shame and anomie but by rank poverty and brutal political repression. While Bob is indeed "pissed," and rightfully so, Vanise is "on the further side of resignation, where people, especially women, laugh and cry too much and too often, where nothing matters and a second later everything matters" (58). Nor does Vanise freely choose to leave her home, as does Bob. She is forced to flee Haiti with her nephew, Claude, and her infant, Charles, when Claude steals a ham from a delivery truck overturned in a mudslide: a transgression against the island's ruling class that will probably result in some horrible retribution for Claude, Vanise, and their village neighbors, all of whom partook of the purloined ham because they were starving.

"Making a Killing"

Having established Vanise's character and situation, Banks switches back to Bob in a chapter entitled "Making a Killing" (61–121). For the veve at the head of the chapter, Banks has chosen a representation of Azacca (otherwise known as Azaka Médé or simply Zaka).[11] The loa who is the younger brother of Ghede, the loa of death and resurrection, Zaka is characterized with a straw sack and a machete about his waist. A farmer's hero, not as glamorous or eccentric as his brother, Ghede, whom he tries unsuccessfully to emulate, Zaka is an apt emblem for Bob Dubois, a man who has always resided in the shadow of his flamboyant older brother, Eddie.[12]

As the chapter opens, Bob and his family have already "done a terrible and frightening thing: they have traded one life for another, and this new life is the only one they have" (62). Arriving in central Florida, they see more "people of color" in one day than they have seen in their entire lives in New England: a sudden and jarring plunge into a racialized society that echoes Johnny's equally frightening immersion in Jamaican culture in *The Book of Jamaica*. And Banks's point is much the same; that white people, regardless of class affiliation, do not think of themselves as *having* a color until they are confronted by masses of "colored" people. Fully apprised of the relative strangeness of the world he has opted into, Bob feels "embarrassed—that is, exposed, revealed to the world for what he is [i.e., a white, Northern interloper]—and perhaps for the first time in his life, his entire body fills with fear" (64).

In marked contrast to Bob's frightened reaction to Florida's multira-
cial character, his older brother Eddie, who has lived there for many
years, is simply and virulently racist:

> You bet your ass things are different here. We got niggers with guns and
> razors here ... We got Cubans who cut your balls off. We got Haitians
> with their fucking voodoo sacrifices and Jamaicans with machetes as long
> as your fucking arm. We got dark skinned crazies of all kinds, all hopped
> up on their fucking pot and cocaine, riding around in brand-new Mer-
> cedes-Benzes without enough pocket money to put gas in the tanks. We
> got Colombians, for Christ's sake, with fucking *machine guns!* (67–68)

Though, on an interpersonal level, Eddie's venemous rant is a self-
dramatizing way to scare and humble his brother, it is, in the largest
sense, a hideously authentic rendition of the deep-seated racist paranoia
that permeates so much of American society. In sum, Eddie is Bob's
demonic alter ego, Banks's type for the unregenerate white yahoo who
takes perverse pride in his ignorance and cruelty.

That Eddie is the almost cartoonish villain of the novel is further
manifested by his mindless worship of the crudest form of American
Dream ideology. Accordingly, his analysis of life is thoroughly cynical
and aggressively materialistic. Firmly believing in the hoary but ever
popular shibboleth that "money makes the world go round," Eddie
avers that there are

> only three things you can do in this life, which happen to be making
> things, selling things and buying things ... If you do at least two of those
> things, and one of them happens to be selling, then your ass is golden.
> Simple. It came to me when I was eighteen, and it's been my guiding
> light ever since. My philosophy of life. My religion. I buy things and I sell
> things. (76)

Having absorbed the not unjustified but narrow notion that society is a
Hobbesian war of all against all, Eddie is openly contemptuous of his
younger brother's lack of business acumen. For his part, Bob does not
know "what in hell" Eddie is talking about when he champions bucca-
neer-style capitalism and speaks of "making yourself a fucking killing,
man. A killing" (77).

To his further chagrin, Bob Dubois soon learns that he is not exempt
from Eddie's exploitative creed when he finds himself working behind
the counter at one of Eddie's liquor stores twelve hours a day, six days a

week, for a paltry $200 "under the table," on Eddie's vague promise
that he will make Bob a partner in the business once he "catch[es] hold
of the system" (77). If anything, Bob Dubois's new employment is even
more tedious and poorly paid than the job he left behind in New Hampshire. To add to Bob's increasingly suffocating sense of entrapment, his
family is now ensconced in a cramped house trailer at Oleander Park;
his daughter, Ruthie, is diagnosed as having a learning disability; and
his wife, Elaine, is pregnant again.[13]

Inasmuch as Bob's character and identity have been shaped mostly
by life's exigencies rather than by conscious choice, his solution to his
mounting troubles is characteristically passive, escapist, and unconscious. He quickly develops an overpowering infatuation for Marguerite
Dill, the adult daughter of a black coworker at the store. Single and
lonely herself, Marguerite soon reciprocates Bob's attentions, and the
two embark on a love affair that threatens to destroy Bob's already
shaky marriage.

Whatever his private wishes, Bob's intimacy with a black woman can
never result in a separate peace with America's de facto apartheid system. Part of Bob's tragedy is that racial divisions are too powerful for
any one individual to overcome, especially one as naive and marginalized as Bob Dubois. Banks dramatizes this state of affairs with a particularly harrowing incident. After a motel rendezvous with Marguerite one
evening, Bob has car trouble in front of the liquor store. Going in the
store after hours to phone her for help, he discovers an armed burglary
in progress. Humiliated, threatened with death—and then shot at—by
the robbers (both of whom are black), Bob pulls out the .38 that Eddie
gave him for protection and shoots one of the intruders dead. The other
man, whom Bob dubs "Cornrow," escapes while Bob is phoning the
police. Eddie's fatuous promise to Bob, that he would "make a killing"
has indeed come true, but with chilling irony.

"A Man's Man"

Though clearly an unavoidable instance of self-defense, the shooting is,
nonetheless, a monstrous act of violence that pitches Bob into a severe
emotional and moral crisis. Accordingly, the veve Banks chose for this
crucial chapter is Ogoun (also known as Ogun or Ogou) Badagris (Kristos, 20). Ogoun, a Nigerian deity creolized by Haitians during the colonial period, is "the suffering general," a loa often depicted as well-armed
but mortally wounded, held up by his supporters as tears roll down his

cheeks: an apt figure for Bob's state of psychic shock and confusion in the aftermath of the shooting (Desmangles, 145–47).

Deciding that he no longer loves Elaine, Bob continues his affair with Marguerite—until he misses the birth of his third child (a son) because he was with his mistress at a motel. Racked by guilt and remorse, Bob tries to rectify his furtive, chaotic life by breaking off with Marguerite (171–73). Immediately thereafter, though, Bob stumbles into another emotional and moral crisis when he *thinks* he recognizes the passenger in Marguerite's car as Cornrow, one of the men who tried to rob the liquor store three months before. At this point, Bob is possessed by the more sinister persona of Ogoun, the hunter and fanatical god of war whose "fierce nature is one of violence and destruction" (Desmangles, 147). Madly intent on vengeance and the recuperation of his wounded manhood, Bob loses all control of himself. He grabs Eddie's .38 and gives chase, but loses the man. Still enraged, he returns to Marguerite and confronts her about her companion, ranting that he "wants" him (180–81). Marguerite calmly informs Bob that the mystery man is her cousin's husband, and that the papers reported that the robbers were from New York anyhow. She then pronounces Bob "crazy" and ejects him from her house (181).

In a searing but typically belated moment of enlightenment, Bob reverts to Ogoun Badagris's more beneficent aspect when he realizes that he has disastrously mishandled the situation:

> Bob look[ed] stonily into Marguerite's brown eyes for a few seconds. Then he sigh[ed] heavily, and as if he'[d] taken off a mask, his gaze soften[ed]. "Oh, God," he says. "Oh God damn everything. I fucked it up. I fucked it all up, didn't I? Everything. Everything. All of it. Done." (182)

Deflated, deeply ashamed, and finally terrified at having lost himself so completely, Bob subsequently tries to regain some sense of stability and self-respect by at least renouncing the gun once and for all. (Interestingly, Ogoun is also the god of metal tools and instruments.) But even that desperate attempt at moral redemption only results in further trouble. When Eddie, typically hectoring and abusive, insists that the gun be kept at the store, Bob feels he has no choice but to quit his job (191). The break between brothers could not come at a worse time. With a new baby in his life, Bob is suddenly without a source of income. Eddie's situation is even more dire; his debts to loan sharks are mounting so rapidly he fears that "one of these mornings you're gonna find me sleeping in the trunk of my car and my car'll be in Tampa Bay" (186). The unbearable stress is destroying his marriage and his health: "I got holes in my stomach and a bleeding asshole. And now my epilepsy is coming back. I had two fucking seizures this month" (188). Though still thoroughly detestable, Eddie is somewhat humanized by his terrible trouble; like Bob's, his situation begins to take on tragic overtones, as does the brothers' relationship. Neither man can afford to lose the support of the other, but both subscribe to a working-class code of sullen, stoic independence that stifles genuine fraternity and closeness.

Always clumsily reactive, even when he thinks he is taking some initiative, Bob has not managed to build a new life; he has only succeeded in systematically narrowing his chances. By this point in the narrative (if not earlier), the downward spiral of Bob's life has taken on an aura of ironclad determinism. Every honest attempt he makes to extricate himself from the mire only results in more floundering. Indeed, after the break with his brother, Bob is virtually at the mercy of the fates.

With startling swiftness, the fates intervene. When Bob returns home from his disastrous confrontation with Eddie, he finds that his best friend from high school, Avery Boone (and Boone's current girlfriend, "Honduras," also known as Joan Greenberg), has suddenly appeared on the scene, rather like a buzzard at the site of a fresh kill (191). Bob tells Avery all about his recent troubles. Avery, in turn, offers Bob work, as the skipper of his charter fishing boat, the *Belinda Blue* (201). Little does Bob know that Avery is every bit as corrupt as Eddie.

Dark Passage

As shattering as they are, Bob's travails in Florida pale in comparison to Vanise Dorsinville's struggles after she, Claude, and her infant, Charles, flee Haiti. Using her life savings to book passage on a boat that will supposedly smuggle the three of them to Florida and a new life, Vanise soon learns that she has been duped. After taking hundreds of dollars in fares, the smugglers strand their passengers on North Caicos Island, some 575 miles southeast of Miami (130). To avoid inevitable deportation back to Haiti, Vanise and her charges split off from the other refugees and set off for the interior of the island. They eventually arrive at the farm of one George McKissick, a scrofulous marijuana grower who offers the trio food and shelter (i.e., incarceration in a dark, filthy shed) in exchange for Vanise's sexual favors (145).

The sexual exploitation of Vanise Dorsinville becomes even more horrific after she, Claude, and her infant, Charles, obtain passage in the
dark hold of the *Kattina,* a rusty freighter plying the 300 miles of sea
between North Caicos Island and the Bahamas. Vanise is savagely raped
by the ship's crew at the outset of the voyage (209). Then she and
Claude are raped repeatedly during the two-day passage, a nightmarish
transit also marked by a fierce and terrifying storm (214). Arriving in
Nassau in the dead of night, Vanise and kin make their way to nearby
Elizabeth Town, where they are discovered sleeping in an alley the next
morning by an unsavory shopkeeper named Jimmy Grabow. Immediately realizing that they are illegal aliens, Grabow takes custody of them
(225). Sensing that Grabow "is bad, *a gros neg,*" Claude escapes, but not
before begging Vanise to join him (226). In a state of psychic shock, "her
mind an utterly silent, burned-out charnel-house by now," she refuses to
leave Grabow's house (228). She spends the next few weeks there as
Grabow's sex slave and prostitute, beaten and degraded so relentlessly
that the last vestiges of her tattered sanity slip away, "as if the dark, hard
thing, like a piece of coal, that had always been at the center of her mind
had been heated with too hot a flame and had become a cinder that had
crumbled to ash" (235). When Claude finally returns to rescue her and
Charles, Vanise again refuses to go; she believes that she must stay
because the loas are angry with her (236). Of a less superstitious temperament, Claude kills Grabow with a machete, takes his money, and
leads Vanise and her baby on a renewed quest for freedom.

"Selling Out"

Meanwhile, Bob Dubois is pulled inexorably deeper into the American
underworld. At least initially unbeknownst to Bob, Ave Boone's fishing
business is actually a front for the smuggling of drugs and illegal aliens
into the country from the Caribbean. Bob soon makes another unpleas-
ant discovery: that the seemingly romantic profession of fishing boat
captain is more of a tourist diversion than a seafaring adventure. Not
gregarious by nature, he finds his patrons "self-centered and arrogant"
and cannot bring himself to fraternize with them (254–57). Consequently, his boat does poor business, his income languishes, his partnership with Avery Boone becomes strained, and his home life continues to
deteriorate.
    True to form, Bob attempts to at least temporarily evade his troubles
by flirting with another woman. This time the object of his attention is

Allie Hubbell, his next-door neighbor at the trailer park who reminds him of Doris Cleeve. She invites Bob in, but he uncharacteristically turns her down. In the process he hits upon a vital insight that represents a nascent, halting step toward moral redemption: "Jesus, he thinks, if you can control what a man wants, you can control everything he does" (265).

Bob returns to his trailer, takes a nap, and dreams he is inside a smouldering airplane that everyone else has abandoned. Just as suddenly he finds himself at his mother's funeral. He puts out the fire on the plane, then wakes up to discover that, indeed, something has been burning: a pan left unattended on the stove (267). At that moment Elaine returns and chastises Bob for his carelessness, but her anger has deeper roots: "She is lonely, overworked, without money, she hasn't lost the weight she gained during the pregnancy, and both she and Bob know that everything, all of it, is Bob's fault" (269).

On the way back to the boat that afternoon, Bob mulls over the dream, remembering not so much its content but

the emotions it carried, conflicting emotions that Bob can't imagine resolved: shame and pride; solitude, desertion, being left behind—a child's horrified view of these conditions—and social acceptance, the security of rite and family affection; fear of death, pure terror of it, and an uncontrollable longing to confront it, an obsessive curiosity almost. (272)

It is clear from the foregoing passage that Bob's is a woefully divided psyche: part lonely, frightened child; part adult, who is strong, even heroic, in some respects. But the two identities refuse to merge and coalesce into an integrated whole. Banks's omniscient narrator offers a plausible reason for this failure: "[n]either parent . . . treated [their sons'] futures as something the boys themselves had any control over" (273). This was especially true for Bob's emotionally unresponsive father, whose every word and gesture imparted one lesson: "Life is grudging in what it gives, so take whatever it gives as if that's all you're ever going to get" (273). Such an upbringing, so typically working-class in its grim, Malthusian view of things, has imbued Bob with a kind of siege mentality toward life, a passive, resigned fatalism that amounts to a self-fulfilling prophecy.

After a chance encounter with one of the great heroes of his youth, aging Red Sox legend Ted Williams, Bob goes from nostalgic euphoria to rank despair when Elaine informs him that their daughter, Ruthie, has been diagnosed as "emotionally disturbed" (282).[14] Shattered by the news, Bob goes berserk, smashes some furniture, and stalks off in a daze (283–85).

From this point on, Bob's already blighted life spins wildly out of control. After a casual, degrading sexual encounter with Ave's girlfriend, Honduras (payback for Ave's once having slept with Elaine), Bob returns home to find Elaine hostile, alienated, and giving every indication of having made up her mind to abandon Bob "to his own dreamy devices and illusions" (294). His marriage and family near ruin, Bob loses another, albeit dubious, mainstay when he discovers that Eddie, now desperately insolvent, has committed suicide by asphyxiating himself in his own garage (305). Eddie's pathetic demise demonstrates the futility of hustling the American Dream by relentless scheming and sheer bravado. It also liberates Bob from the suffocating burden of being a permanent adjunct to his brother's ego:

> In a flash, [Bob] realizes that Eddie is totally powerless now; a glowing red bed of coals has become a bag of waters. A spirit that shouted at Bob, that beat on him and prodded and directed him, scolded and shamed him for thirty-one years, has been miraculously transformed into a typed [suicide] note that claims only absence for itself.
>
> It's a terrible thing, Bob thinks. To go from being something to being nothing! A terrible thing for a man to endure ... And for the first time, Bob pities his older brother, and his pity instantly releases him, so that when he weeps aloud for Eddie, in sorrow, of course, like any brother, but more crucially, with pity as well, he weeps for himself, in joy. And as he weeps, torn by contending emotions that are called grief—pity and sudden potency, sorrow and joy, the horrified, abandoned child, bereft and frightened, and the exhilarated man, powerful and self-admiring. (308–9)

Pondering his recent dream, Bob had been unable to reconcile his sense of shame with his sense of pride, his fear of death with his longing to confront death's reality. Eddie's suicide removes a major obstacle to Bob's moral self-realization.

Determined to finally take control of his life, Bob approaches Avery Boone with a plan whereby he borrow money from Ave to buy the *Belinda Blue* outright (322–23). When Boone informs him that the bank owns title to the boat, Bob realizes that the $15,000 he put up (proceeds from the sale of his trailer) for his share of the *Belinda Blue* was actually used as the down payment for Ave's newer boat, the *Angel Blue*.

In yet another in a long series of chilling epiphanies, Bob now understands that he has "ruined everything, lost everything, he's given away everything" (324).

Though devastating on a material level, Bob's shattering realization affords him (and us, as readers) a remarkable insight into the seductive workings of contemporary American society:

> It's not bad luck, Bob knows, life's not that irrational an arrangement of forces; and though he's no genius, it's not plain stupidity, either, for too many stupid people get on in the world. *It's dreams. And especially the dream of a new life, the dream of starting over.* The more a man trades off his known life, the one in front of him that came to him by birth and the accidents and happenstance of youth, the more of that he trades for dreams of a new life, the less power he has. Bob Dubois believes this now. (325, emphasis added)

As Banks has noted elsewhere, the "dream of a new life, the dream of starting over" is the quintessential American Dream, the ideological keystone of American civilization from its inception to the present day.[15] More than merely duped by his friends and relatives, Bob Dubois has been taken in by the false promise of the dominant ethos.

Although he is finally enlightened as to the *real* conditions that govern his life, Bob's hard-won wisdom is inherently tragic because it comes too late to save him. As Banks's narrator puts it, Bob has now "fallen to a dark, cold place where the walls are sheer and slick, and all the exits have been sealed" (325). Essentially alone, without friends, resources, or prospects, Bob Dubois has become the latter-day equivalent of Harry Morgan in Hemingway's *To Have and Have Not;* he has little choice but to accept Avery Boone's offer to help him make some "quick money" by smuggling Haitians into Florida from the Bahamas (325–26). As Banks's laconic narrator notes, "This is how a good man loses his goodness" (325).

Final Acts

Among those Haitians are Vanise and Claude Dorsinville and the baby, Charles. Hence, Banks's two narrative strands finally converge. Given the book's exceedingly grim content thus far, the results of that convergence are not difficult to imagine. On the return voyage to Florida, the *Belinda Blue* is still a considerable distance from shore when it is spotted by a Coast Guard cutter: disastrous luck that precipitates the book's

most savage incident (362). Thinking fast, Tyrone, the *Belinda Blue*'s
Jamaican first mate, asks Bob's permission to throw the Haitians over-
board. His reasoning is that the Coast Guard will have to stop to pick
them up, thus allowing the *Belinda Blue* time to escape.[16] Bob naively
agrees and Tyrone, armed with a loaded rifle, proceeds to force the terrified Haitians to jump into rough seas. Bob looks on in horror as almost
all of them are immediately drowned.

Only Vanise survives. After washing ashore half-dead, she is taken to
her brother, Emile, who lives in Miami. Demented by the deaths of
Charles and Claude and all the others, Vanise believes that she alone has
survived to feed them to the bloodthirsty loa, Ghede (368).

In a sense, Bob Dubois fares worse. Returning to port, he and Tyrone
are arrested at the pier by Florida state troopers. Naturally assuming
that the police are there because they know about the Haitians, Bob
actually feels a kind of relief at being apprehended for his crimes: "It's as
if by holding guns on him, and arresting him and searching his boat,
they have brought him back into the community of man" (382). But
even the police prove unsuitable as agents of divine retribution, for no
sooner have they "welcomed Bob Dubois into the community than they
have rejected him again, sent him home in his car, with his awful secret
undetected" (383). (Ironically, the police are on the scene not because of
the Haitian deaths but because Ave Boone has just been caught smuggling drugs.)

In the end, Bob has to effect his own moral redemption, a fact made
brutally clear to him after the local papers report the tragedy at sea and
Elaine guesses the truth about her husband's involvement (400). Her
unmitigated horror makes Bob's already intense remorse unbearable. At
base, Bob still "wants to be a good man" so that "he can hope for
redemption" (416). He and Elaine decide to return north, but before
they go, Bob undertakes a final errand. He holds hundreds of dollars in
cash that the Haitians gave him to smuggle them into the United
States. Desperate not only to expiate his sins but also to rid himself of
what has now become blood money, Bob combs the bars of Miami's Little Haiti until he hears definite news about Vanise's survival and whereabouts (414).

In the novel's climactic scene, Bob Dubois is led to Vanise Dorsinville
by four young toughs. Recognizing her from the boat, Bob sees that, as
sole survivor of the drownings, Vanise is the only viable instrument of
his moral regeneration, "the woman whose fate now is to say his fate to
him, that he may live it out" (417–18). But when he pleads with her to

take the money and thereby "remove the sign of his shame," she refuses and turns away. A moment later, Bob is set upon and stabbed to death by the four teenagers when he refuses to give them the money that he hopes he can still convince Vanise to take (418).

Though certainly tragic, Bob's death does indeed constitute the moral redemption he so avidly sought. He dies defending the money not as a fetish of greed, power, and upward mobility but as the emblem of his renewed integrity, his desire to finally and decisively do the right thing. The irony, of course, is that money is a pathetic substitute for the lives of 15 human beings, ridiculous compensation that Vanise must decline as a testament to her own righteousness (although, given her unbalanced state, it is not clear that her refusal to take the money is conscious and deliberate). In the end, blood must be atoned with blood, the money appropriately ceded to thieves.

Chapter 7

American Dreams and Delusions: *Trailerpark* and *Success Stories*

We're living in a funny world, kid, a peculiar civilization. The police are playing crooks in it, and the crooks are doing police duty. The politicians are preachers, and the preachers are politicians. The tax collectors collect for themselves. The Bad People want us to have more dough, and the Good People are fighting to keep it from us. It's not good for us, know what I mean?

Jim Thompson, *The Killer Inside Me*

Trailerpark

In form, if not in content, Banks's third collection of short fiction, *Trailerpark* (1981), tends to recall Sherwood Anderson's *Winesburg, Ohio* (1919), American literature's most famous collection of interrelated stories. Anderson's aim was to blast open the pastoral myth that masked the increasingly moribund social reality of the rural Midwest in the early days of the twentieth century. His Winesburg stories vividly depict the widespread emotional anguish and neurosis that lay festering beneath a facade of placid industriousness.

Set 60 years later in New England during the Reagan era, *Trailerpark* effects a very different kind of demystification. The popular stereotype of the trailer park has nothing to do with some deluded nostalgia for a happy American countryside. On the contrary, trailer parks are generally regarded by the middle-class as rural eyesores, unsightly enclaves of a scruffy, disreputable, and sometimes dangerous underclass. Having lived in trailer parks in Florida 20 years earlier, Banks was able to draw on personal experience to create what he obviously felt was a more nuanced and humane vision of a house trailer community (his microcosm for the proletarian world). Indeed, Banks goes to some trouble in these 13 connected stories to both acknowledge and refute the prejudicial images that animate popular stereotypes of rural poverty.

True to the dictates of literary naturalism, Banks's characters are representative types. But each one also possesses the peculiar uniqueness that conjures a human being, as opposed to a cardboard cutout-constructed to prove a sociopolitical point. Part of Banks's agenda is to suggest to his middle-class readers that the poor and marginalized *also* have dramatic, even harrowing, personal histories. As he told Wesley Brown, "Part of the challenge of what I write is uncovering the resiliency of [working class] life, and part is in demonstrating that even the quietest lives can be as complex and rich, as joyous and anguished, as other, seemingly more dramatic lives" (Brown, 64).

"The Guinea Pig Lady"

The collection's first story, "The Guinea Pig Lady," is also its longest (some 20,000 words) and most sweeping in scope. The story serves dual purposes, as both a highly articulated portrait of the life of an underclass woman and as a general introduction to the denizens of Granite State Trailerpark. The so-called guinea pig lady is Flora Pease, a fortyish retiree on a small pension from the U.S. Air Force, where she worked, for more than twenty years, "as a maid or steward, in officer's clubs and quarters at various bases around the country" (64). Being a female of low status in the military, Airman Third Class Pease was subjected to brutal sexual exploitation. Banks's unnamed narrator hints darkly that she "was not badly treated by the Air Force itself, but numerous individual service-men, enlisted men as well as officers, treated her unspeakably" (64).

Flora Pease's route to the military was even more grim. Her mother died when she was still an infant. Her father was a "rough" (i.e., semi-skilled) carpenter, only seasonally employed, alcoholic, and alternately abusive to or neglectful of his four children. Flora's older brother had an arm blown off while playing with blasting caps found near a local lumber camp. Her only sister succumbed to something like catatonia after being raped by an uncle when she was eleven. Her other brother died of malnutrition at the age of 14, "at which point the remaining three children were taken away from their father and placed in the care of the state" (64). After four years of being warehoused in the juvenile wing of New Hampshire State Hospital, a mental institution, Flora was allowed to leave if she agreed to join the Air Force.

After her discharge, Flora Pease turned up at the Granite State Trailerpark and was allowed to rent trailer number 11 even though the park's manager, Marcelle Chagnon, immediately recognized her as "someone who seemed slightly cracked" (3). The full range of Flora's eccentricities quickly manifest themselves. Her body "was a little strange ... and people remarked on that. It was blocky and square-shaped, not exactly feminine and not exactly masculine, so that while she could almost pass for either a man or a woman, she was generally regarded as neither" (2). Furthermore, Flora has the odd habit of singing old Broadway show tunes to herself in a loud voice everywhere she goes. She never greets "the same way twice, or at least twice in a row, so you could never work out exactly how to act toward her" (4).

Yet all of these odd traits are soon eclipsed by a predeliction potentially disruptive to the entire trailer park: Flora begins to keep guinea pigs. At first she only has two, but they are male and female, and like rabbits, guinea pigs breed at an exponential rate. In a matter of a few months, Flora is housing dozens of the furry rodents in her trailer—a situation of growing concern to her neighbors. The park manager, Marcelle Chagnon, repeatedly tries to persuade Flora to get rid of the unhygienic guinea pigs, but to no avail; Flora Pease adamantly refuses to part with her "babies."

By virtue of her strangeness, Flora functions as a catalyst or mirroring figure for the other trailer park residents. Their varying reactions to the guinea pig dilemma reveal a range of ideological biases formed by personal experience—Banks's sly way of articulating his characters' mindsets and personalities en masse before dealing with them separately in subsequent stories. For example, Doreen Tiede (number 4), a struggling, single mother, has become a hardheaded pragmatist; she advocates evicting Flora and leaving it to the SPCA to deal with the guinea pigs. Terry Constant (number 10), a young and frequently unemployed black man, might be thought of as an adherent to Darwin. He proposes setting the guinea pigs free while Flora is away from the trailer and letting them fend for themselves out of doors: "The ones that [do not] learn to survive, well, too bad for them. Survival of the fittest" (60). Bruce Severance (number 3), a pseudo college student who is actually a small-time marijuana dealer, betrays an essentially capitalist mentality when he argues that "the profit motive ... needs to be invoked here," that Flora should be encouraged to grow her guinea pigs for sale to laboratories. Noni Hubner (number 7), a mentally ill young woman, reveals the fragility of her own sense of self when she voices the non-opinion that all the proposed plans should be tried in turn: "That would be the democratic way" (60). Leon LaRoche (number 2), an overly fastidious bank teller, admires the hard-line plan of retired Air Force Captain Dewey Knox (number 6) ("Either she goes, or the animals go. She decides which it's to be, not us" [61]) but favors Doreen Tiede's solution as the least potentially scandalous. Carol Constant, a black nurse living with her brother, Terry, in number 10, takes the stance of a liberal humanist, believing that, left to her own devices, Flora will come to her senses and curb the guinea pig population. Nancy Hubner (Noni's mother), a widow, formerly middle class, takes a characteristically thera-peutic approach to the problem, suggesting that Flora is probably keep-ing guinea pigs "as a substitute for family and friends" (61). In Nancy's view, Flora needs "Christian charity" in the form of neighborly socializ-ing. Marcelle Chagnon (number 1), Granite State's tough but compas-sionate manager, champions a "compromise" solution that would allow Flora to keep her guinea pigs as long as she refrains from breeding them (62). Merle Ring (number 8), a retired carpenter with a mischievously cynical nature, feels that Flora should be allowed to breed her guinea pigs indefinitely, as a kind of experiment: "It should be interesting to see what the woman does with her problem. And if it never becomes a problem that should be interesting too" (62).

In the end, after all the pondering and debate, nothing is done. Flora Pease is allowed to breed her guinea pigs over the next two and a half years, until they take over most of her trailer. Only then does catastrophe strike Flora's increasingly hermetic world. She gets ill and has to be taken to the hospital. Despite emphatic assurances by Carol Constant that Terry will care for her guinea pigs while she is laid up, Flora (rightly) fears that, in her absence, her "babies" will be disposed of by her untrustwor-thy neighbors. Stealing away from her hospital bed—despite a 105-degree fever—Flora returns to the trailer park in the middle of the night and burns her trailer to the ground, guinea pigs and all, in a final gesture of self-destructive defiance. Thereafter, she builds a squatter's shack in view of the trailer park and pretty much reverts to a feral state (78–80). Thus a woman who was never really integrated into the human commu-nity slips out of it forever. The trailer park was for her a kind of halfway house, a liminal place between an indifferent society and the desolate natural world to which she returns, like an outcast from Eden.

"Cleaving, and Other Needs"

That Banks uses the odd, archaic word *cleaving* as the key term for the title of this story about the failed marriage of Doreen and Buck Tiede bears comment. *To cleave* is an unusual verb in that it possesses diametri-cally opposite meanings. In one context, it may mean "to unite or be united closely in interest or affection." In another, it may mean "to sever or separate by cutting or splitting."[1] Both of these meanings hold true simultaneously when describing the tragicomic nature of the relationship between Doreen and her second cousin, Buck Tiede. The two fall in love and marry at an early age, when Doreen is only 17, and still a virgin, and Buck is 23 and not much more sexually experienced. Ironically, Doreen soon proves to be considerably more adept at, and passionate about, lovemaking than her husband.

Banks's narrator hints that Doreen's sexual superiority may have something to do with genetics. Doreen is descended from the branch of the Tiede family "that had risen in the world," whereas Buck hails from "the Tiedes who, generation after generation, had plowed the same old row" (81–82). Another important factor here is the sexual hypocrisy and prudishness that permeates American society but is, arguably, even more virulent in New England working-class culture and perhaps affects men more than women, because they bear the brunt of an anxiety-provoking macho ethic that equates sexual performance with normative notions of masculinity. Like the bizarrely neurotic Alvin Stock in "A Sentimental Education" (from *The New World*), Buck Tiede has come to learn that sex is shameful and dirty and, therefore, guilt inducing—but also titillating, with its furtive aura of taboo, mystery, and sin. When youthful inexperience and fear of pregnancy are added to all of these highly charged and conflicting associations, the results are predictable: after a sexual encounter, Buck "is left feeling dazed with guilt and overall feelings of inferiority" (83).

These feelings carry over into his marriage to Doreen. Their honeymoon "in a motel near Franconia Notch in the White Mountains" is a sexual disaster for both of them. The ironically named Buck, who happens to be a well digger by trade, is "awkward and too quick and then impotent for a while and then impatiently passionate and grabby, his head so full of blood from shame and lust that he [cannot] think, so finally, because she [can] think, Doreen just [gives] herself over to him and, without feeling, let[s] him have his ways with her" (84).

When Buck's sexual dysfunction proves to be chronic, conjugal relations between he and Doreen become more stress laden and infrequent. Commenting on the situation, Banks's omniscient narrator wryly notes that "[n]either of them was technically incompetent in the act. What was wrong was inside their heads. Her fantasies and his fears had no way of meshing together or of helping one another go away or even of becoming known to one another" (86). Almost inevitably, Doreen is compelled to relieve her libidinal frustrations with other men. Her first adulterous act is with Bruce Severance, in the adjacent trailer, from whom she buys marijuana as a sex aid for her and Buck. A month later, after recovering from pregnancy terror and feeling "dirty and almost evil," she "felt downright eager to do it again" (88). Her next liaison involves a lunchtime bout of oral sex with Leon LaRoche, the timid bank teller who lives in the trailer next to Bruce Severance's (89). Doreen then initiates a third encounter, with the aptly named Howie Leeke, "the recently divorced plumber who was awfully good-looking and had a funny, raspy way of talking and quick gray eyes . . ." (90).

Unfortunately for Doreen, Howie Leeke is a sexual braggart. When he makes lewd comments about her at the local bar, Buck gets wind of it and flies into a jealous rage. Doreen claims that Howie only kissed her but Buck knows, instinctively, that she is lying to protect his self-esteem. He gets out his .20 gauge shotgun and points it at Doreen's chest, threatening to kill her, Howie Leeke, and then himself.

In a strange, desperate ritual of self-abasement and sexual provocation, Doreen alternately praises Buck's goodness and begs him to kill her for letting "another man's lips touch mine" (93). He obliges her by pulling the trigger—but the gun is not loaded. Now utterly assured of Doreen's submissiveness, of her willingness to martyr herself for his approval, Buck is able, at least temporarily, to overcome his deep terror of women and the two make unihibited love for the first and only time in their marriage (which ends in divorce five years later). Such is the crushing power of sexual ignorance and emotional repression in the lives of working-class people that even though Doreen and Buck never forget "that snowy night and the shotgun," they are never able "to speak of it to each other," and did not, "even the night that it happened" (94).

"Black Man and White Woman in Dark Green Rowboat"

The black man and white woman referred to in this story's title are Terry Constant and Noni Hubner, yet Banks never identifies them by name. Other trailer park residents are also alluded to, but not by name—except for a fleeting reference to Merle Ring. Banks's refusal to name characters he clearly identifies in every other story in the cycle is not a narrative oversight or an example of the author being coy. The strategem is quite deliberate, its estrangement effect calculated to create both optimal reader objectivity and, somewhat paradoxically, optimal involvement. (Characters stripped of their societal labels take on a kind of primal immediacy. Concomitantly, the use of a highly detached point of view forces heightened reader engagement almost by default.)

The relatively plotless scenario of "Dark Green Rowboat" recalls, indeed conflates, elements of two modern classics of American fiction that deal with precisely the same subject matter (i.e., an unmarried couple agonizing over a pregnancy unwanted by only one of the pair): Theodore Dreiser's *An American Tragedy* and Ernest Hemingway's "Hills Like White Elephants." In Banks's story, Terry and Noni take a rowboat out on Skitter Lake in order to negotiate their dilemma in private: an image that rather eerily recalls Clyde Griffiths's homicidal boat excursion on Big Bittern Lake in upstate New York with his pregnant girlfriend, Roberta Alden. Likewise, Banks's couple engage in the same kind of oblique pleading and parrying around the question of abortion that Hemingway's miserable pair do in "Hills." But the difference between "Dark Green Rowboat" and its precursors is so vast as to be fundamental. In the Dreiser and Hemingway narratives, race is not a factor; both couples are white. And, in accordance with dominant mores and societal expectations, the woman is the one who wants to keep the baby.

In Banks's story, the *man* is the one who wants to keep the baby because the central issue at play here is not male supremacy but white racial hegemony. In the boat on the lake, Noni informs Terry that she has confessed her pregnancy to her mother the night before and that an abortion has been scheduled for that very day. Though societal taboos prevent him from voicing it openly, Terry knows that Noni's mother, Nancy, arranged the abortion for her daughter with breakneck haste because she was stricken with racial embarrassment and was desperate to erase the evidence that Noni had premarital sex with a black man. For his part, Terry wants the baby to live as incontrovertible evidence that he has successfully defied white racist proscriptions against miscegenation. But he also knows that Noni's inner resources and social supports are so shaky that it is unlikely she will forfeit her dependence on her mother to ally herself with a mostly unemployed black man who lives with his sister. Accordingly, the boat trip around the lake is circular to underscore its futility; a sense further enhanced by Terry's insistence on fishing even though it is too hot for the fish to be biting. Noni "won't bite" at Terry's wishes because their social environment is heavy with the oppressive heat of racism, poverty, and powerlessness. At one point, Terry tells Noni that he would like to leave her on an island in the middle of the lake: a statement that Ross Leckie interprets as Terry's wish to imprison Noni "in the fantasy of his [hypermasculine] sexual identity," a plot that "can redeem him neither sexually nor racially."[2] Overwhelmingly white and rightist, New Hampshire is no place for interracial couples, especially those with a biracial child.

"Dis Bwoy, Him Gwan"

Terry Constant's essential powerlessness and social detachment is dealt with from a different angle in "Dis Bwoy, Him Gwan," something of a companion piece to "Dark Green Rowboat." Terry's drinking and pot-smoking buddy, Bruce Severance, returns from one of his marijuana-buying trips to Revere, Massachusetts, in a panic. Exhibiting the gross naïveté of a latter-day hippie-romantic, Severance has made the monstrous faux pas of offering his suppliers some marijuana derived from hemp that grows wild in the area of the trailer park (an unintended leftover of the Second World War, when hemp was grown legally, for rope). Although he explains its source to them, the two men—a black Jamaican named Keppie and his white cohort—come to the mistaken conclusion that he has begun to deal with other suppliers.

Walking into the trailer park from the woods after hiding his van, Severance runs into Terry Constant, who tells him that two men were looking for him earlier. Now fully aware that he is in mortal danger, Severance hustles Terry into his darkened trailer and pleads for help moving the offending bales of homegrown into the woods. Reluctantly, Terry agrees, but it is already too late; Severance's erstwhile business partners suddenly arrive. Keppie, the Jamaican dealer, asks Terry to leave them alone with Bruce Severance. Terry readily complies, despite Severance's desperate plea to the contrary (114). Later, Terry returns to Severance's trailer and discovers that he has, indeed, been murdered. In a final act of evasion and denial, Terry later tells his sister, Carol, that he has not seen Severance "for a couple of days" (115).

More than a macabre story of underworld violence, "Dwis Bwoy" addresses the delicate question of loyalty between friends of different races. A racially guilty white liberal, Bruce Severance stupidly "admire[s] Terry for being black" (110). For his part, Terry Constant finds Severance a posturing narcissist forever pontificating about the glories of "organic gardening, solar energy, transcendental meditation" and the like (110). Terry tolerates Severance because his "boring" white companion is willing to share his drugs and ample spending money with him. Banks's laconic narrator also notes that "[w]hen you are a long way from where you think you belong, you will attach yourself to people you would otherwise ignore or even dislike" (110). Contrary to Severance's illusions, Terry Constant is nothing more than he pretends to be: a passive, shiftless social outcast. Indeed, Bruce Severance is mostly his own victim, with his insipid utopian fantasies about cosy race relations and a benign, comradely drug culture.   &

"What Noni Hubner Did Not Tell the Police about Jesus"

A year after her abortive romance with Terry Constant described in "Dark Green Rowboat," Noni Hubner has a "nervous breakdown." Under the influence of marijuana, she hallucinates a phone call from Jesus (the event she later neglects to tell the police about). Courteously speaking English with "a local New Hampshire accent," Jesus announces that he has "been thinking of giving a little visit" to Noni in order to relieve her depression (117). Two days later, on 22 February 1979, Noni walks out on the ice-covered lake by the trailer park and sees a bearded figure in "a heavy maroon poncho" and "bulky mucklucks" who waves to her from a distance (if real, probably Merle Ring). To Noni, half-psychotic from loneliness, depression, and drug abuse, the figure can only be Jesus, come to comfort her. Deeply frightened, she runs back to the trailer and tells her mother that "she had seen Jesus walking across the lake toward her, so she had run home" (120). In a masterpiece of comic understatement, her mother replies, "Oh, dear."

Some weeks later, "along about the end of March," Noni joins "The New Hampshire Ministry of Jesus Christ," a storefront church in nearby Catamount (120–21). After giving up marijuana, "alcoholic beverages, sex, cigarette smoking, cursing, and cosmetics," Noni has another vision of Jesus, this time "in the form of a body of light" (121). Now a completely "different person," Noni Hubner receives "her instructions, or what she regarded as instructions," from Jesus through the words of Brother Joel at a ministry prayer meeting. As she understands it, her divine warrant is to dig up her father's grave so as to prove to her mother, Nancy, that "Daddy" is, in fact, dead—a reality her mother has been in stubborn denial about for the five years since his demise (124). Fortunately, the police apprehend Noni before she completes her exhumation.

If the reader is inclined to think of Noni Hubner as a pathetic wreck of a human being, that judgment is leavened by the disclosure, late in the story, that she has been living under psychologically untenable conditions. In the spirit of the radical psychologist R. D. Laing, Banks suggests that insanity is the mind's way of coping with intolerable circumstances.[3] Though Noni's mission to the cemetary is bizarre, the underlying motivation for it is a reasonable desire to disabuse her mother of the delusion that her husband is "merely absent, as if he had driven downtown to get the paper" (123). In her public degradation, Noni achieves a kind of tragic nobility by taking on, and perhaps expiating, her mother's more subtle madness.

"Comfort"

With his early story, "The Lie" (from *Searching for Survivors*), Banks had explored the devastating effects that homophobia can have on victims and victimizers alike. "Comfort" takes up the same issue, but its approach to the topic is considerably less sensationalistic.

On a "frosty November night," Leon LaRoche, the young bank teller in trailer number 2, pays a visit to Captain Dewey Knox, "U.S. Army, ret.," in number 6. Over the course of the next several hours, the two men consume three six-packs of beer. His usually strong inhibitions loosened by the alcohol, Leon proceeds to tells Dewey Knox a story about an embarrassing incident involving himself and Buddy Smith, the ne'er-do-well son of Tom Smith (who used to live in trailer number 9 before his suicide, the circumstances of which are explained in a later story, "The Burden").

Telling his story within a story, Leon recounts a chance meeting with Buddy Smith at the Hawthorne House, the seedy local bar that Leon usually avoids but that he entered that night to get a drink because he was "angry, pissed off, from having been yelled at once too often by [his boss] at the bank" (128). The two men begin to chat and, after awhile, Leon invites Buddy back to his trailer to play chess, drink beer, and have something to eat. Destitute himself, Buddy readily agrees.

Things soon go awry, however, when Leon is suddenly struck by the impression that Buddy, sitting alone, with a beer in his hand, "looked so sad and alone, so pitiful" (131). In an effort to comfort him, Leon, as he passes behind Buddy's chair, lays a hand on his shoulder, "in a friendly way" (130). Misinterpreting Leon's kind gesture as sexual solicitation, Buddy flies into a "red-faced" rage, calling Leon "a fairy" and "all kinds of names," before upsetting the chess board and stomping out (130–31).

After hearing Leon's story, Captain Dewey Knox takes the opportunity to ask him the obvious question, ironic under the circumstances, "if it was true, was he a fairy?" (131). Though terrified to acknowledge it openly, even to someone as friendly and garrulous as Dewey Knox, Leon admits that he is. Somewhat surprisingly, the captain is unfazed by Leon's revelation; indeed, he seems amused. Assuring Leon "not to worry," that "his secret is safe," Knox claims to understand "that sort of thing" through ample exposure to it in the military (131). Braced for a torrent of scorn and ridicule, Leon LaRoche finds himself just as enervated by Dewey Knox's cheerful condescension as by Buddy Smith's fear and rage, perhaps more so, because Knox's mirth bespeaks the smug dismissal of a man confident in his innate superiority. Mortified once again, Leon hurriedly leaves Knox's trailer in an ironic reiteration of Buddy's flight from his own.

"God's Country"

A 28-year-old black divorcée from West Roxbury trying to reenter nursing after a three-year hiatus, Carol Constant has been unable to find work in the Boston area. When she travels north to "God's Country," to hire on as live-in nurse for dying Catamount real estate man, Harold Dame, she understands the social price she will have to pay, "that to live and work wholly among white people would continually embarrass her," but she quite desperately needs the job (138). As for her relations with her employers—Harold Dame's son, Ed, and his daughter-in-law, Sue—they remain "precisely distant, perfunctory, and routine" as the weeks pass, despite the fact that Carol is saving them a tremendous amount of money by facilitating the old man's death at home (146). (Indeed, the Dames show every evidence of regarding Harold's final illness as nothing more than a messy logistical problem to be dealt with as cheaply, efficiently, and discreetly as possible.)

Hired to do the white man's dirty work, Carol Constant is otherwise left to her own devices, except for the solicitations of Harold Dame's physician, Doctor Samuel F. Wickshaw.[4] "Sam" Wickshaw telephones every day, ostensibly to check on the old man's condition but more to engage Carol in idle chitchat. He is always courteous and friendly, even effusive, but Carol cannot help but be suspicious of his motives. As it turns out, Wickshaw *does* have ulterior motives. In part, he is friendly to Carol to salve his own conscience, inasmuch as he brokered her grim employment as a favor to the Dames, with whom he does lucrative real estate business. He also wants to court Carol's favor so that she will agree to work as his nurse after the old man dies; good nursing help is hard to find in rural New Hampshire. Finally, a later story ("The Child

Screams ...") clearly establishes Wickshaw as a lecher. In sum, Doctor Wickshaw's exploitative ways are even more crass and unsavory than the Dames' because they come disguised in a smarmy sugarcoating.

"Principles"

Like Bob Dubois and most other Banks characters, Claudel Bing is the product of a hardscrabble working-class upbringing. His father has imbued him with the standard, bitter proletarian outlook,

> that the world [is] a tough and miserly place, and that the best way to live in that place [is] to be careful and relentlessly efficient. Don't waste a thing. Don't take anything for granted. Don't put off for tommorow what you can do today, because tommorow might never come, and just in case in does, you better have something done today or else you're going to get beat tommorow. (154)

A stint in Vietnam inverts (but does not alter) Claudel's perspective. Witnessing American bombing wreaking destruction on Vietnamese farmers who are, in many ways, like the working-class Americans he knows, Claudel Bing comes to believe in "Luck" as a more dynamic principle than life's toughness; there is, for him, no other way to explain the arbitrariness of a fate that spares one people while it decimates another.

Convinced that, as an American, he is one of the lucky ones, Claudel returns home with an aggressive consumerist approach to life. He is "hot to get started making big money, buy a fast and fancy car, get himself a pretty girl and maybe marry her and buy one of those sixty-five-foot mobile homes to live in" (158). Quickly succeeding in all of those aspirations, Claudel comes to consider himself "one lucky son of a bitch!" (159).

Then disaster strikes. Claudel's wife, Ginnie, absentmindedly leaves the stove on when the couple depart for a weekend at the beach. They return home to find their house trailer reduced to a smoldering "sixty-eight-foot long barbecue pit" (159). To make matters worse, the trailer's loss is not fully covered by insurance; Claudel has to pay off the mortgage on a home that no longer exists. Worse still, Ginnie starts "running around" with the amorous plumber, Howie Leeke (and eventually moves in with him). Turning to drink, Claudel soon loses his job at the Public Service Company. He ends up on unemployment, living in a bare, rented room in Hawthorne House and spending every evening at the bar, downstairs, getting drunk. Having moved from an inherited philosophy of disempowerment to a superstitious belief in luck, Claudel Bing settles on the equally unfounded notion that he is now cursed with bad luck.

The fourth and final step in the evolution of Claudel's philosophy of life occurs only after a year of drinking and depression has reduced him to the basic foundations of self. On a Friday night at the Hawthorne House, Claudel overhears a young man named Deke tell two drinking companions the story of how he was arrested for speeding (164–68). After listening to Deke's tale with rapt attention, "watching the youth and attempting to understand him," Claudel realizes that, during the entire interim, "he hadn't thought about himself once" (168). The experience leaves him feeling "strangely refreshed" and with "a feeling of wholeness he hadn't even imagined possible before" (168).

Temporarily liberated from narrow self-absorption by the seductive power of narrative, Claudel has an extremely important epiphany, that "[i]t's all in the way you pay attention to things!" (168).[5] Consequently, he realizes that he had been deluded in thinking that he had held a genuine philosophy of life when he "had held nothing of the sort" (168). Though Claudel's life situation will continue to be grim, he will now at least face it with a degree of realism and equanimity that had previously eluded him. For that, he is "very thankful."

"The Burden"

Introduced in "Comfort" as the homophobic acquaintance of Leon LaRoche, Buddy Smith is more fully fleshed out in "The Burden." The product of a broken home, Buddy has been raised by his father, Tom Smith, with love and patience but has not turned out well. Having failed to graduate from high school, Buddy has since been dishonorably discharged from the Army for infractions "committed so compulsively and frequently that finally they had given up on him and sent him home to his father" (181). At 21 Buddy is handsome and charming, "the all-American boy" (173). Unfortunately, he is also a drinker and brawler, a sociopathic liar and petty thief who seems, to his father, not to "know the difference between right and wrong" (173).

"The Burden" alluded to by the story's title does not refer to Buddy himself. The real burden for Tom Smith is not Buddy's shiftlessness but rather the untenable emotional and moral position he is put in by his son's parasitic ways. For Tom, the burden is not in *giving* "love, trust, and protection" to a prodigal son, but in having to *withhold* those things to protect himself from exploitation (175). After Buddy steals some of his father's personal possessions and disappears, an invisible line of tolerance and trust is transgressed once too often. For the first time, Tom Smith feels compelled to lock his trailer (metaphorically, his heart) against his son's eventual return.

When Buddy returns three months later and tearfully pleads to be taken in again, Tom steels himself emotionally and sends his son packing (185). This wrenching act of self-preservation is made all the more poignant when we recall, from "The Guinea Pig Lady," the incidental disclosure that, "after his son had gone away, Tom had withdrawn into himself and one gray afternoon in February had shot himself in the mouth" (37).

"Politics"

In "What Noni Hubner Did Not Tell the Police about Jesus" we learn that Noni's father, Ronald Hubner, had died almost five years before the events related in that story, or sometime in the spring of 1974 (123). We also learn that Noni's mother, Nancy, has since been unable to come to terms with her husband's death: foreknowledge that casts a melancholy light on "Politics," the companion story to the Noni Hubner tale that examines the life of Nancy Hubner before Ronald's death.

On a rainy Thursday afternoon in October of 1973, Nancy Hubner is driving back to Catamount from an appointment with her psychiatrist in Boston. After six months of psychotherapy, Nancy has come to the realization that, after 25 years of marriage, "she not only [does] not admire her husband, she [does] not love him either" (187). As she drives north on the turnpike in an increasingly heavy rain, Nancy contemplates her recent affair with Dino, a young carpenter building her a solar greenhouse. She also reflects on her gradual evolution, from a conventional middle-class housewife and mother to a self-styled "political" woman with progressive ideas about sex, ecology, alternative energy, child care, and so forth, "principles and positions that she did not have as a younger woman and that she had acquired only after great thought and some reading and a considerable amount of conversation with people who shared those beliefs, principles, and positions" (189).

In the midst of her self-involved reveries, Nancy is nearly killed when a passing tractor-trailer startles her, causing her to momentarily lose control of her compact car on the slick highway (190–91). Shaken by her brush with death, Nancy imagines Ronald's "face breaking into pieces, shattered by grief and loss, tears swarming over his cheeks" (191).

A lesser writer might have ended the story there, with Nancy having a humbling epiphany about her deep ties and obligations to her husband and family. Instead, Banks brings the story to yet another dialectical level by having Nancy renew her thoughts about the constrictions of her life as a prisoner of "obligations to others—to the children, to Ronald, of course, even to the damned dog" (192). Her discontent is real and enduring, not the momentary wistfulness of a bored matron.

Nancy Hubner is fantasizing in vivid detail about the shape of her new life after leaving Ronald when she notices a female hitchhiker by the side of the road. She slows down to rescue the woman from the driving rainstorm but cannot quite bring herself to come to a full stop. Afterwards, Nancy does not understand "why she had tempted and then rejected the girl, why, by slowing almost to a stop, she had offered something she was not ready or willing to actually give" (195). Though she cannot comprehend her behavior, Nancy intuits its deeper significance. In a sense, the hitchhiker in the rain is her potential new self—young(er), adventurous, but also transient and vulnerable. By not stopping, Nancy discloses to herself that she is not ready to give up a meticulously structured life of material comfort, security, and social status for a risky experiment with fate. She decides not to leave her husband.

One of the strongest stories in the collection, "Politics" dramatizes the sometimes startling contradictions that can arise between lived experience and perception in contemporary consumer culture. Ironically, Nancy Hubner's sheltered and relatively affluent life has allowed for a degree of psychological and moral growth that tends to contradict the shallow materialism that made such growth possible in the first place. Though disaffected with the stultifying conformity of middle-class life, Nancy Hubner is ill equipped to embrace any other kind of existence. In effect, she has been permanently tamed by the same dynamic that has allowed her to achieve a modicum of inner liberation.

"The Right Way"

Set on Dewey Knox's 14th birthday in the winter of 1928 to 1929, "The Right Way" chronicles an important but mishandled moment in his coming of age. For what seems to be the first time, Dewey's remote and dour father, Fred, offers a ritual concession to his son's emerging maturity by allowing the boy to drive him into town on an errand. On the way back home, father and son stop at a rural speakeasy. Fred Knox drinks whiskey but does not allow his son to imbibe, despite the friendly urgings of the other men there (203 – 4). Holding out but ultimately denying Dewey a proper rite of passage, Fred Knox thoughtlessly compounds his error by indulging in an arm-wrestling contest with another patron that somehow seems designed to remind his son of his father's unassailable dominance. Fred Knox loses the contest but is too rigid to admit any fallibility or weakness to his son. The unconscious lesson that Dewey Knox takes away from his 14th birthday is that stoic, uncommunicative rigidity is the only "right way" to be masculine. That Knox has ended up a lonely army retiree living in a trailer park does not speak well for the world view with which he was indoctrinated as a boy.

"The Child Screams and Looks Back at You"

Having survived marriage to an abusive, alcoholic husband, Marcelle Chagnon later undergoes the worst nightmare of every parent: the death of a child.[6] In just a few short days after the onset of a high fever, Marcelle's eldest son, Joel, succumbs to a case of spinal meningitis that is not properly diagnosed until it is too late.

Much of the blame for Joel Chagnon's death falls on Doctor Wickshaw, whose initial examination of the sick boy seems casual at best (215). Indeed, Wickshaw shows more interest in propositioning Joel's divorced mother than in attending to his young patient. But the main point of the story is not to impugn the doctor's dubious morals (which Banks had already done with considerable effectiveness in "God's Country").

Set in "the early 1960s," "The Child Screams" is more centrally concerned with dramatizing the yawning disparity in social class between physicians and working-class people: institutionalized inequality that always makes for an exploitative doctor-patient relationship. Banks's narrator notes that, 30 years ago, the general practicioner made house calls and "usually knew all the members of the [patient's] family and frequently treated them for injuries and diseases" (214). He therefore "tended to regard an injured or ill person as one part of an injured or ill family. Thus it gradually became the physician's practice to minimize the danger or seriousness of a particular injury or illness" (214).

Doctor Wickshaw's cavalier treatment of Joel Chagnon's illness vividly illustrates the abject nature of blue-collar disempowerment in the face of the postwar professional's smug paternalism. Too familiar with his clientele, Wickshaw does not care as much as he should about Joel's fate. Likewise, Marcelle Chagnon is too cowed by Wickshaw's high social status to unambiguously ward off his sexual advances or demand more of him than platitudes regarding her son's health. Even when it is clear to her that Joel is dying, Marcelle hesitates to call Doctor Wickshaw in again because she remembers his kisses in the hallway "and what she had let him promise her with her eyes" (217). Though he is a lecher guilty of a kind of negligent homicide, Wickshaw comes out of the incident untouched, whereas Marcelle wrongfully assumes a burden of guilt and grief that penetrates "to the very bottom of her mind" (220).

"The Fisherman"

Companion story to "The Guinea Pig Lady," "The Fisherman" brings closure to *Trailerpark* by examining the reactions of the park residents to eccentric Merle Ring's winning the state lottery not once but twice. The first time, on 30 October 1978, Merle wins $4,500 by playing the daily numbers game (226). After paying the tax on his prize and spending "about $250 refurbishing his [ice-fishing] bobhouse," Merle gives the rest of the money away in increments of "$300 or $400 or $500" to anyone with a professed need (227). No wonder that his neighbors are anxious to importune him again after he wins $50,000 in the grand prize drawing on 15 January 1979 (253).

But to the deep chagrin of the other park residents, Merle Ring's sole passion in life is not money but ice fishing. Despite his newfound fortune, Merle spends the entire winter of 1978 to 1979 the way he spends every suitably cold winter: in utter isolation on Skitter Lake in his darkened bobhouse, drinking whiskey, tending his lines, peering into a half-dozen dark holes in the ice, and occasionally catching a fish.

Ordinarily ignored by the other trailer park residents, Merle Ring becomes the object of their obsessive fascination both before and after the grand prize drawing. Despite pretenses to the contrary, no one really cares about Merle as a person; he is thought of only in talismanic terms, as the living embodiment of the sort of wealth that buys liberation.

Once he wins the $50,000, Merle's privacy is more thoroughly expropriated by his desperate neighbors. They somehow consider the money a kind of imaginative community property, the locus of a group wish-fulfillment fantasy that involves everyone *but* Merle Ring, who seems to them to be largely oblivious to the implications of his own great good fortune. The truth is more subtle, however. Though Merle is quite sane and fully understands the value of $50,000, the money does not send him into utopian ecstasies because he has long since adopted an austere mentality that does not consider money to be tantamount to happiness. Having no immediate use for the cash, Merle opts to do nothing with it other than keep it in a cigar box in his bobhouse on the ice. Such apparent fiscal carelessness horrifies all interested parties and precipitates the story's tragicomic climax.

Bewildered by the fact that Merle Ring's winnings have resulted in no immediate change in his life or theirs, the trailer park residents delegate five-year-old Maureen Tiede as their emissary to Merle's bobhouse to gently inquire as to the status of the money (264). She is soon followed by the entire group, who descend on Merle's ice shack like a pack of hungry jackals and fight over custody of the cash. In a scene that recalls the culminating moment of B. Traven's *The Treasure of the Sierra Madre,* the cigar box full of $100 bills is accidentally spilled into the strong night wind that blows across the lake (272). Some of the money is later recovered, but most of it is lost, to Merle's despair and to the shame of the others.

While "The Guinea Pig Lady" explored the severe limits of neighborly compassion and altruism, "The Fisherman" is a parable that inversely mirrors the saga of Flora Pease by examining the seemingly limitless and often destructive energy of greed—especially for those in the lower social strata, who are most susceptible to the myth that sufficient wealth can redeem life. The money matters to Merle Ring, but he does not let it rule his imaginative life the way his neighbors do. Much like the coffin maker in *The Relation of My Imprisonment,* Merle (also a carpenter by trade) has somehow conquered the ideology of materialist consumption inside himself, a truer and more lasting form of liberation than the freedom provided by a lottery prize.

Success Stories

A year after the publication of *Continental Drift,* Banks gathered the short stories he wrote in the first half of the eighties into a fourth collection entitled *Success Stories* (1986), a book that seems implicitly designed to refute the opportunistic fervor of the Reagan era.

Always conscious of the subtle signifying power of the work's overall form, Banks organizes his dozen stories into two distinct types. Alternating six quasi-autobiographical tales (hereafter referred to as "The Earl Painter Stories") with six sociopolitical fables, Banks contrasts narratives that illuminate aspects of his personal history with stories that showcase his imagination at its most abstract: a characteristic oscillation of realism and allegory that some critics found problematic.

All of the fables are more than competently written, but the autobiographical stories have a psychological and emotional resonance that their more minimalist counterparts cannot match. The result is a collection of short fiction that is perhaps Banks's most jarringly bifurcated in tone and mood, despite the thematic unity provided by the success story motif. As Isabel Fonseca notes, "*Success Stories* is not a particularly coherent collection—it has the makings of two books (and one of them [i.e., the Painter stories] is a novel)."[7]

The Earl Painter Stories

"Queen for a Day"

Banks ("Earl Painter" in these stories) begins his fictive autobiography by dealing with the signal event of his young life: his father's abandonment of the family in 1952. In "Queen for a Day," the elder Banks is called Nelson Painter but is readily recognizable as the hard-drinking, irresponsible philanderer that caused so much pain to his family. In the story, as in life, the patriarch's desertion causes even greater grief. Each family member handles the trauma in a highly individual way, but all handle it badly. Earl's mother, Adele Painter (Florence Banks), is an emotionally fragile woman by nature. Left with three young children to raise without any outside support, she suffers from nearly crippling levels of depression and anxiety. Earl's brother, George (Steve Banks) and sister, Louise (Linda Banks), are ten and six years old respectively; too young to be of any emotional or material support to their mother.[8] The moral burden for the survival of the family falls on 12-year-old Earl, who is himself deeply traumatized by his father's flight.

Earl's way of coping with the family's ongoing catastrophe is pathetically naive but also deeply poignant in its bravery: he "decides to solve their problems himself" (6). After several failed attempts to fix up his mother with other men, Earl hatches an even more far-fetched scheme: to get her on *Queen for a Day*, a surreal fifties television show that actu-

ally awarded prizes to the contestant who had the day's most wrench-
ingly maudlin hard luck story.[9] Earl writes a painfully sincere letter
describing the family plight to host Jack Bailey but receives no reply
(10–11). Undaunted, he writes another, and then a third letter, but
never hears from anyone connected with *Queen for a Day.* Finally disillu-
sioned with fanciful schemes meant to bring "honor" to his "tiny,
besieged family" and make his mother "happy at last," Earl Painter is
able to apply his hard-won skepticism to the equally illusory promise of
his father's return.

"My Mother's Memoirs, My Father's Lie, and Other True Stories"

With pieces like "Principles" (*Trailerpark*) and "Envoi" (from *Continental
Drift*), Banks had discoursed on the redemptive power of narratives for
those who listen to or read them. With "My Mother's Memoirs" he
takes the opposite tack by exploring the story's therapeutic effects on
the storyteller.

Sifting through a pile of old newspaper clippings, Earl Painter discovers an obituary of 1940s film star Sonny Tufts (1911–1970). The clip-
ping prompts him to recall one of his mother's favorite stories, about
how his father beat out Tufts in courting her. Yet the obituary points out
that "Bowen Charleton Tufts III, scion of an old Boston banking family,
had prepped for Yale at Exeter" (37–38).[10] It occurs to Painter that
Tufts's "closest connection to the daughter of a machinist in Catamount,
and to [him], was probably through his father's bank's ownership of the
mill where the machinist ran the lathe" (38). In the same, deluded vein,
his mother claims to have known "the principals in Grace Metalious's
novel *Peyton Place* ... She also insists, in the face of [her son's] repeated
denials, that she once saw [him] interviewed on television by Dan
Rather" (33–34).

Knowing that his mother's stories about her past are simply not true,
Earl Painter interprets them as elaborate fantasies that provide clues to
his mother's psychology. He notices that there is "always someone
famous in her stories ... as if she hopes that you will love her more easily
if she is associated somehow with fame" (39).

As for his father, Nelson, Earl Painter notes that he was "a depressed,
cynical alcoholic, [who] did not tell stories," yet he vividly recalls a single anecdote the old man told him just "a few months before he died"
that concerned his being named Earl (35–36).[11] Nelson Painter claimed

that he named his firstborn son after his own Uncle Earl, an eccentric, drunken, Cape Breton bachelor with whom he spent the summers of his early boyhood. After his father's death, Earl tried to confirm the story with his aunt Ethel, the "unofficial family archivist" (37). When Ethel says "she never heard of the man," Earl is startled to realize that "the story was simply not true" (37). His father had fabricated an Uncle Earl "because for an instant that cold February morning he dared to hope that his oldest son would love him" (36). In sum, "My Mother's Memoirs" suggests that all familial anecdotes, no matter how fabulous or deluded, are in some sense "true," inasmuch as they express a genuine and otherwise inexpressible desire to be loved.

"Success Story"

The sequel to "Queen for a Day," "Success Story" fictionalizes another pivotal period in Banks's young life, beginning with his dropping out of Colgate University in the fall of 1958 and ending with his marriage to Darlene Bennett (i.e., "Eleanor Hastings") in Florida a year later. What intervened, of course, was Banks's attempt to join Fidel Castro's revolution, a desperate gambit motivated by what Banks later called "a cloud of shame" emanating from his "terrible failure" at Colgate.[12] With the wisdom of hindsight, Banks has since explained that he "converted that [failure], as one often converts shame when it feels intolerable, into a political romance" (Lee, 210).

"Success Story" is divided into three parts or phases. The first part chronicles Earl Painter's hitchhiking adventure from New England to St. Petersburg, Florida. His longest and most significant ride is from "a retired U.S. Army captain, named Heinz 'like the ketchup' " (54). A confident, worldly man in his forties, Heinz easily disabuses Painter of his heroic fantasies and urges his young charge to adopt an updated version of the Horatio Alger myth instead: "Kid, forget Cuba. Stay in St. Pete and you'll be a millionaire before you're twenty-five" (55).

Through Heinz's offices, Earl Painter lands a job as a furniture mover at the Coquina Key Hotel downtown. Oblivious to the fact that such unskilled and poorly paid work is really de facto wage slavery reserved for itinerant alcoholics, Painter decides, Candide-like, that he is going to "succeed" in his work so spectacularly that he will eventually rise through the ranks to become a hotel mogul (58). Fortunately, he is soon dissuaded of such foolishness by a fortyish alcoholic from Chicago named Bob O'Neil, who apprises Painter of his true status: "You're like a prisoner, never see the light of day, never make enough money to make a difference in your life, so you just gotta get your pay and leave. Get the hell out. Find a place or job that *does* make a difference" (61). O'Neil himself disappears the next morning, prompting Earl Painter to quit as well. Painter rents a room and quickly finds a job in the display department of Maas Brothers Department Store the next day (65–67). All goes well until he decides "to succeed in this new trade, to become the best assistant window trimmer that had ever worked at Maas Brothers" (70). In his overweening ambition to prove himself, Painter builds a display panel that proves too large for the escalator. The resulting accident, punctuated by "screams, shouts, cries for help, falling debris, wood grinding against concrete, metal bending under wood," plunges Painter into the depths of "endless shame" (74–75).

Once again he is rescued by a sympathetic stranger: this time, a 17-year-old coworker named Eleanor Hastings, who takes pity on him in his acute distress. Painter ends the story by claiming that "that is how I met my first wife, and why I married her" (76). For Banks and Darlene Bennett, it did not really happen that way, but no matter. Banks's point is that "success" is largely chimerical unless the term is applied to interpersonal relationships. Heinz, Bob O'Brien, and Eleanor Hastings have much more to do with Earl Painter's moral education and continued survival than any of his harebrained schemes to distinguish himself.

"Adultery"

The direct sequel to "Success Story," "Adultery" chronicles Earl Painter's angst-ridden sexual coming-of-age shortly before his marriage to Eleanor Hastings. On a more profound level, it describes Earl's entrance into adult morality, with its painful consciousness of guilt and sin. Furthermore, in sociohistorical terms, "Adultery" is a masterful depiction of the sexual repressiveness of the fifties, a furtive cultural milieu that only bred what it sought to eradicate: libidinal intensity.

Nineteen, drastically oversexed but still a virgin, Painter is horrified to discover that 17-year-old Eleanor has already lost her virginity. Thrown into an emotional crisis by Eleanor's confession, Painter flees in the night, "angry, betrayed, hurt and almost swindled by his own desire" (96). Looking back on that moment decades later, Painter has come to understand that his younger self was at the mercy of the "incoherence" of his desire, which was "too tangled in chains of insecurity, pride, fear, anger and mother love to move responsibly through the lives of decent people"

(97). Painter further reflects that the "loss of Eleanor Hastings's virginity meant that I could no longer idealize her, could not deal with her as an abstraction. It removed her, and therefore me, from ritualized sex, which was the only kind of sex that did not terrify me" (99).

His relationship with Eleanor at an impasse, Earl finds himself irresistibly drawn to Donna Pitman, the thirtyish wife of his "neighbor, boss, and landlord, Art Pitman" (97). Donna gladly initiates Earl into the mysteries of sex and the two begin an affair (99). When Donna eventually confesses the adulterous liaison to her husband—out of spite because Earl continues to love Eleanor—Earl Painter undergoes an agonizing confrontation with the cuckolded husband that should result in a moral reckoning but does not, at least not immediately.

> He [Art Pitman] stared up at me, a sea beast surfacing, tears streaming over his long face, mouth gaping, eyes wild and suffering from a pain I was not even able to be frightened of. Though I could open my eyes and see it, I could not imagine it. And I could not imagine his pain because I refused to know what I had done to him. (113)

Twelve hours later, driving toward Tampa to pick up Eleanor, Earl finally has his epiphanic moment. Looking into his rearview mirror, he sees his own eyes as he has never seen them before,

> an adult male's blue eyes, scared and secretive, angry and guilt-ridden, eyes utterly without innocence ... I saw in that moment that every terrible wound [that everyone I knew] had suffered I could inflict, and every terrible wound they could inflict I could suffer—abandonment, betrayal, deceit, all of them. Our sins describe us, and our prohibitions describe our sins. I had broken them all, I knew, every one. I was a human being, too, at last, and not a very good one, either, weaker, dumber, less imaginative than the good ones. (114)

Chastened by his confrontation with the evil inside himself, Earl Painter resolves to marry Eleanor Hastings, not to be happy (he knows that he does not love her), but to make her happy because she loves him: a deliberate act of penance that, paradoxically, both transcends and perpetuates Earl's neurotic tendency toward self-abasement.

"Mistake"

The weakest of the Earl Painter stories—a more nebulous and dilute version of "Adultery," of which it is the direct sequel—"Mistake" can be thought of as yet another installment in a long series of Banks tales that explore hopelessly troubled marriages.

Fired by Art Pitman and thrown out of his basement apartment, Earl Painter finds himself working days at a discount department store called Webb's City and selling women's shoes at a Thom McAn's store in West St. Petersburg in the evenings. For shelter, Painter shares a small apartment with a man named Martin Schram while he saves money for his impending but deeply dreaded marriage to Eleanor Hastings, which he considers "the biggest mistake of my life!" (132).

The two men are drinking beer at home one evening when the couple next door begin to make noise: "It was the sound of a man beating a woman. More precisely, it was the sound of a woman hollering that she was being beaten by a man" (134–35). The Smiths have fought before, but this incident is too loud and protracted to be ignored. After a tense interval, Painter decides to play the hero and intervene. Rebuffed by both combatants, he is also restrained and rebuked by his roommate, Martin Schram, who seems strangely affected by the incident, so much so that the reader surmises that Schram was having an affair with Mrs. Smith and that her crippled husband found out and is now exacting regular retribution on his wife in full earshot of her erstwhile lover—a possibility that did not enter Painter's naive mind until he sees Schram "frightened and very sad and deeply, painfully weary" of him (137).

"Firewood"

Set in winter, some time in the late seventies, "Firewood" presents a poignant glimpse of Earl Painter's father, Nelson, near the end of his troubled life. A lifelong alcoholic, Nelson Painter lives in a restored farm house in central New Hampshire with his second wife, Allie. Old at 61, "but [he] doesn't know it yet," Painter is a desperately lonely and guilt-ridden man who yearns for the love and forgiveness of the children he abandoned 25 years before (179).

Nelson's younger son, George, firmly believes that his wayward father ruined his life and will have nothing to do with the old man. Louise is not even mentioned in the story. Earl, however, has managed an uneasy rapprochement with his father and lives near enough to him to allow for some occasional contact. For Christmas, Nelson bought Earl a load of firewood over and above the ten cords he ordered for his own use. The only problem is that Earl has since neglected to come and pick up the wood, which sits in Nelson's front yard as an unmistakable emblem of his son's indifference.

As the first snow of that winter begins to fall one Sunday morning in January, Nelson Painter calls his son at 7:30 A.M. to come and get his wood before it is buried. Earl initially agrees but ends up putting off the chore until later in the day. He finally reneges altogether, vaguely promising to come some time during the week, when his father will not be home. Gravely disappointed (but unable to say so) and already drunk on vodka, Nelson Painter impulsively decides to take the firewood into his barn in the midst of the full-blown storm. A man who has decided that "he does not *respect* love . . . that being alone is the only clear route to happiness" because it is "the only way to avoid hurting other people," Nelson finds himself stumbling, alone, in the driving snow with a few sticks of wood in his arms to bring to the barn (181, 188). Trying to restore order to his world and his mind, Nelson Painter becomes an indelibly tragic image of self-inflicted loneliness and desolation in a bleak landscape—a fate that Painter hates but one that he is unable to avoid. Compared to Banks's harsh caricature of his father in *Family Life*, "Firewood" is a remarkably empathetic and poignant depiction.

Fables

Alongside Banks's vividly detailed Earl Painter stories, the book's fables seem somewhat abstract. But this is precisely the effect Banks had in mind. As he explained in his 1986 interview with Trish Reeves,

> Half the stories are coventionally realistic in their narrative mode[s] and formats and so they use a lot of devices of Realism. The other half of the stories are more like political fables or allegories and they have a different kind of intention and so they use different means. And one of those means is to sort of reach for emblematic or generic characters and use them the way a morality play might use them. Rather than to specify . . . Different kinds of specification so that you can deal more easily with the abstract qualities of the stories. *Part of the structure of the book is based on the tension between the two kinds of truth.* (emphasis added)[13]

While they may lack in emotional resonance, the fables enlarge the thematic scope of the collection by addressing larger social and political questions in ways that Banks's quasi-autobiographical tales cannot touch. Whether the two kinds of stories ultimately cohere is a matter best left to individual readers.

The parables themselves further divide into two types: a set of stories ("The Fish," "The Gully," "Hostage," and "Children's Story") that deal with the relationship between contemporary social conditions and political violence, and a pair of quieter tales that focus on interpersonal relationships.[14]

"The Fish"

In an unnamed Southeast Asian country, the appearence of a monstrously large fish in a pond disrupts the social and political equilibrium of an entire rural district. Colonel Tung, a Catholic and the district's political leader, orders his men to destroy the fish because it is attracting too many Buddhists to the area. Tung's soldiers attempt to shoot the fish, blow it up with mines, and feed it live hand grenades disguised as food. But violence is of no avail; the fish miraculously survives and continues to grow, as does its legendary reputation (it is "thought to be the reincarnation of Rad, the painter, an early disciple of Buddha" [44]). Thousands of pilgrims, Buddhist and Catholic alike, from all over Southeast Asia flock to the pond to glimpse the fish and to draw water from what is now widely regarded as a sacred pond. And with the crowds come the profiteers: "tentmakers, carpenters, farmers, storekeepers, clothiers, woodchoppers, scribes, entrepreneurs of all types, entertainers . . . musicians and jugglers, and of course the manufacturers of altars and religious images" (47–48). Unable to suppress popular idolatry for the strange fish through blunt force, Colonel Tung decides to get in on the profit-taking by collecting taxes on water extracted from the pond. Eventually, so much water is drained by devotees that the pond dries up and the fish dies.

The purport of "The Fish" is not too difficult to decipher. Colonel Tung (homophone for *tongue,* suggesting a purveyor of authoritarian propaganda) and his forces clearly embody the modern Marxist states that have tried to suppress human desire, specifically their peoples' yearning for consumer goods and the individualistic values that such goods foster (symbolized by the irrational cult of the great fish). Ultimately unsuccessful in their attempts to crush desire, some of these states have had to imitate their enemies in the West by embracing "free enterprise." Once the entire world converts to the unbridled consumerist dynamic of the modern capitalist state, a new and more intractable problem arises: the systematic destruction of the world's ecology (symbolized in the drying up of the pond). What "The Fish" implicitly calls for is a new way of relating to the material world that transcends capitalist and state socialist models, which both blindly affirm continual industrial expansion and mass consumption as the sine qua non of "progress."

"The Gully"

In his radio interview with Trish Reeves after the publication of *Success Stories,* Banks explained the specific genesis of "The Gully":

> What literally sparked it was a newspaper clipping that I stashed about ten years ago in Jamaica, when I was living down there. I clipped it from the *Kingston Daily Gleaner.* It was an account of three young guys who had gone into business in the ghetto, in Trenchtown (in Kingston), who were murdering thieves and taking their rewards. Taking the goods back to the victims of the robberies and getting a piece of it. And they were quite organized and they were protected by the community. When I reexamined the clipping, *I was struck by the impulse to upward mobility.* (Reeves, emphasis added)

In Banks's fable, his three protagonists are initially motivated by desperation or vengeance. After being robbed twice in one week, a bus driver known as "Freckle Face" (Naldo de Arauja) shoots and kills two would-be robbers. After his entire family is slaughtered, "Chink" (Felipe de Silva) tracks the three assailants to their van, traps them inside, douses the vehicle with gasoline, and burns them to death. After "Tarzan" (Saverio Gomez Macedo) witnesses the accidental shooting of his aged grandmother by two drug dealers, he hunts down the men and kills them with his bare hands.

"In the Gully, [where] true heroes [are] almost nonexistent," the three men are widely recognized as the genuine article (83). Freckle Face determines to capitalize on the trio's moment of glory "as swifty as possible, before people settled back into their old ways of dismissing heroism as a trick" (84). The three folk heroes set up a partnership that specializes in spotting and killing thieves and recovering stolen property. "In short order, Freckle Face, Chink and Tarzan [are] making more money than they ever imagined possible" (85). Their operation is so successful that the men are able to move out of the Gully, buy lavish cars, houses, condos, and 40-foot cabin cruisers. Most of all, they are able to deny that they ever lived there. Indeed, Freckle Face manages to convince himself that "the people who go on living there must want to live there, or they'd leave that place. Look at Tarzan, look at Chink, look at me!" (87). Thus, the inexorably predatory logic of capitalism transforms

populist heroes into a new breed of overlord. Summing up the story for
Trish Reeves, Banks notes that "this is a description of how anyone gets
ahead from out of the ghetto. This is what everyone advises you to do.
They never advise you to become a better person" (Reeves).

"Hostage"

Schmidt, the German ambassador of some unnamed Third World country, is being held hostage at a secluded farm house by four "terrorists."
As government commandos assault the house in an effort to free
Schmidt, he hallucinates five different scenarios ("Plans A–E") that
would lead to his freedom and safety, much in the way that the confed-
erate soldier, Peyton Farquhar, imagines his miraculous escape from
hanging in Ambrose Bierce's famous story, "An Occurrence at Owl
Creek Bridge."

Herr Schmidt's "plans" are increasingly absurd and outlandish. At
first he imagines simply walking away from his captors while their car is
stuck in traffic in order to elicit the help of a policeman. He next imagines becoming two people: his sleeping self and his own rescuer. In plan
C he becomes *three* people, two of whom overpower his guard, Odem,
and take him to safety. In plan D Schmidt imagines himself becoming
invisible, and, in plan E ("a desperate last resort"), he visualizes "slaying
everyone in the house and burying the bodies under the gravel walk-
way" (126). In the end, though, Schmidt commits suicide after all his
captors have been killed or have taken their own lives in the raid: a
bizarre, incongruous act that bespeaks the relentless and horrific psychological pressures that attend hostage situations, pressures that can
compel hostages to identify with their captors.

"Children's Story"

According to the dust jacket of the cloth edition of *Success Stories,* "Children's Story" is "an allegory of the relationship between citizens of the
first and third worlds" (Fonseca, 920). Subject to surprise attacks by
their increasingly restive, violent, and cunning children, the parents in
Banks's story defend themselves with "fulsome protestations of love and
concern for [their children's] welfare, assurances of endless devotion,
actual monetary gifts, a plethora of fondling, cooing, stroking of cheeks
and patting of little heads" (140). Once they regain control by deceit
and manipulation, the parents spirit their children to roofs and over-

passes and toss them off, a grostesque symbol of the containment and counterinsurgency tactics practiced by the rich nations against their impoverished client states.

Banks's assessment of the relationship between the First and Third Worlds is probably accurate. The problem with "Children's Story" is that it is too pat and simplistic in its didacticism to convert anyone except the already converted. "Children's Story" is, however, the exception. Considered in their totality, the almost two dozen stories that comprise *Trailerpark* and *Success Stories* form one of the most thoroughgoing indictments of American Dream idealogy offered by contemporary American literature.

Chapter 8

Worlds of Pain: *Affliction, The Sweet Hereafter,* and *Rule of the Bone*

No one that night turned into literature, nothing that we did or didn't
entered the mythology of boys growing into men or girls fighting to be
people. Everyone went home because that was how the world was before
God turned to prime-time TV and kids still rose early to catch the bus
for school and everyone was innocent.

Philip Levine, "Coming of Age in Michigan"

Taken together, Banks's three most recent novels, *Affliction* (1989), *The
Sweet Hereafter* (1991), and *Rule of the Bone* (1995), form his most comprehensive and cogent treatment of working-class life in the Northeast.
All three books are written in a blunt neorealist idiom that one critic has
aptly described as "vigorous and gritty."[1] To the chagrin of some critics,
Banks still insists on experimenting with his narrators and narrative
points of view, but he largely refrains from complicated metafictional
tropes that might detract from the immediacy of the narrative.

Very much alike stylistically, the three novels are thematically complementary as well. *Affliction* focuses on adult male rage and violence instilled
by childhood abuse at the hands of an alcoholic father. *The Sweet Hereafter*
also examines abuse but is more centrally concerned with the guilt and
grief of a small town that has lost its children to a bus accident. *Rule of the
Bone* reprises *Affliction* from a different angle by focusing on a dangerously
alienated young man in flight from a broken, abusive home. Taken
together, these fictions form a chilling depiction of the kinds of psychological and emotional traumas that children and youth are apt to suffer growing up in families situated near the bottom of the socioeconomic heap. In
a larger sense, though, Banks's main concern in these works is to plot contemporary America's wholesale abandonment of the family as a basic
social structure, a phenomenon that cuts across all demographic and class
lines. As Banks put it in a recent talk to college students: "We're losing
the children in our culture now unlike any time since the Children's Crusade. We're at a period where the social structure is undergoing such radi-

cal transformation that none of the social units that provided respect and protection for children have survived."[2]

· Affliction

Constructing a Narrator

A compelling but underdeveloped feature of *Continental Drift* is the sadomasochistic relationship between Bob Dubois and his older brother, Eddie. In stark contrast to the confused but basically scrupulous Bob, Banks uses Eddie to typify the kind of arrogant, working-class thug who relies on macho audacity to get over on "the system," and the people around him. Both men ultimately succumb to forces greater than themselves, but Eddie, for all his exaggerated nastiness and vulgarity, at least avoids his younger brother's abject passivity. Bob's failing is that moral courage comes to him too little and too late. Eddie's is a more radical and spectacular failure of imagination; he is unable to conceive of a life that does not involve being either predator or prey. Though both figures are tragic in their own ways, Eddie is arguably the more vivid and emblematic character in the sense that he *actively chooses* to enter into the class warfare going on all around him. Unfortunately, Banks is too intent on having Eddie serve as a dramatic foil to Bob to grant him the full complexity and "roundness" of character he deserves.

As if to make amends for positing such a glaringly lopsided relationship between brothers who are too insistently portrayed as polar opposites, Banks places a more nuanced and thoroughly examined fraternal relationship at the center of *Affliction*. His protagonist is Wade Whitehouse, a 41-year-old well digger, snowplow operator, and small-town New Hamsphire policeman, who slides headlong into depression, paranoia, and violence when the life he once knew inexorably slips away from him. A "loner with a mean streak," Wade combines the viciousness of Eddie with the nagging sense of impotence that haunts Bob.[3] Wade's misanthropic tendencies strongly recall Hamilton Stark as well.

Indeed, Banks takes the narrator-protagonist relationship at the center of *Hamilton Stark* and adapts it to somewhat different purposes in *Affliction*. While Wade Whitehouse conflates Stark and the Dubois brothers into a single catastrophe, Wade's younger brother, Rolfe, the first-person narrator of *Affliction,* closely resembles the narrator Banks employs in *Hamilton Stark*. Gifted with superior self-awareness and moral acuity, Rolfe has managed to escape Wade's fate by leaving town, getting a college education ("the first in the family" [3]), and becoming a high school history teacher in the Boston area. An organized, self-disciplined man "of meticulous routine," Rolfe narrates from the safe distance of a suburban middle-class perspective, thus allowing Banks to fully engage his literate readership by articulating Wade's shattered life with a precision of language and feeling that Wade himself would not be capable of mustering. Yet Rolfe is also deeply implicated in his brother's life, so implicated that, in the aftermath of Wade's disappearence (another trope borrowed from *Hamilton Stark*), Rolfe becomes obsessed with explaining Wade's inner life. Hence, *Affliction,* like *Hamilton Stark,* is a meticulous narrative reconstruction of a subject that is absent from the outset. Yet it also represents an advance over the earlier novel, a further closing of the gap between investigative narrator and doomed protagonist-as-doppelganger that testifies to Banks's continued progress in merging the wounded, violent man of his youth with the circumspect man of letters he has become.

"Someplace Halfway Between Other Places"

As he did with Hamilton Stark and Bob Dubois, Banks assiduously pursues his vocation as postmodern naturalist by delineating the family, community, and regional (even topographical and climatic) structures that have worked together to shape his protagonist's character and fate.

For generations, the Whitehouse clan has resided in Lawford, New Hampshire, a fictive but highly credible representation of the typical New England mill town: grey, moribund, languishing like dozens of others "in the region's dead economy" (10). Rolfe Whitehouse evocatively decribes Lawford as "one of those towns that people leave, not one that people come back to" (5).

Situated on a river "fished for centuries by the Abenaki Indians," Lawford briefly prospered in the nineteenth century, staggered into the twentieth century, and was finally driven under by the Great Depression, when "the mills got taken over by the banks, were shut down and written off, the money and machinery invested farther south in the manufacture of shoes. Since then, Lawford has existed mainly as a place between other places, a town people sometimes admit to having come from but where almost no one ever goes" (9). Indeed, the several recent generations of Lawford's "most talented and attractive" children (people like Rolfe) have abandoned their dying hamlet "for the smarter life in the towns and cities" (6, 9–10). Those grown children, like Wade, who do stay behind or return to town after "being wounded in one of the wars or messing up a marriage elsewhere . . . are regarded by their parents as failures; and they behave accordingly" (10). In sum, Lawford is a ghostly anachronism, a town with "no connection to modern life" (5).

Wade Whitehouse's particular living situation is even more desolate than average for Lawford or the gloomy backwater in which it is situated. As is typical of so many of Bank's underclass protagonists, Wade lives in lonely, alcoholic squalor in a decrepit lakeside trailer park built "on a brush-covered rocky spit of land" in a windswept glacial valley: an unforgiving locale "enclosed by a fierce geometry of need, placement, materials, and cold" (50).

Wade's Past and Present

In accordance with naturalist precepts, Banks bases Wade's personal desolation in family poverty as well as Lawford's socioeconomic and cultural sterility. At the same time, Banks is well aware that there is never a simple and direct correlation between the subject and his or her surroundings. The wider world is always mediated by a complex web of subjective influences. In Wade's particular instance, his innate character makeup and the unique family dynamic that acted upon it are the salient factors.

Writing *Hamilton Stark*, Banks worked like a literary mason, systematically building up contextual matter from the broadest perspective to the most intimate details about his protagonist. True to the more conventional narrative requisites of neorealism, which call for a fluid, diachronic presentation, Banks fills in the social and familial context of Wade Whitehouse's life in scattered middle chapters that are tangential to the plot but essential to its ultimate meaning.

For example, in chapter 7, Rolfe recalls Wade's asocial personality as a child:

> We all thought of him as a dreamer. Most people saw him as tense, quick, unpredictable and hot-tempered, and indeed he was all those things too. But since childhood, he seemed ... sometimes almost to let go of consciousness and float on waves of thought and feeling of his own making. (94)

Dreamy, detached, and introspective by nature, a "country boy and the third child in a taciturn family that left children early to their own devices, as if there were nothing coming in adult life worth preparing them for, Wade from infancy had found himself, often and for long periods of time, essentially alone" (94).

Having established Wade as a lost boy, a surplus human being who "was generally ignored, treated like a piece of inherited furniture that had no particular use or value," Banks further delineates the toxic emotional climate in which the Whitehouse family operated (94). Rolfe confesses that "Glenn, our father, was a turbulent man who drank heavily, and though Glenn loved Sally [his wife], he beat her from time to time and had beaten the boys" (95).

To illustrate the tortured, rage-instilling emotions that Wade felt growing up, Rolfe recounts the first time that he (Wade) was beaten by his father. The incident is particularly telling because it involves Wade being used by his mother in a covert battle of wills with her husband. When Glenn Whitehouse comes downstairs drunk one Friday evening and angrily demands that the television be turned off so that he can get some sleep, Sally tells Wade to merely turn down the volume. Enraged that Wade chooses to side with his mother, Glenn strikes the boy in the face with his fist, picks him up again, slaps him, and calls him "a little prick" (101–2). When Sally tries to comfort her stunned and bleeding son, he rightly rejects her by "shov[ing] her hands away, wildly, as if they were serpents" (102).

Almost 100 pages later (in chapter 13), Banks again interrupts his main narrative with a flashback to an incident that happened 29 years earlier, when Wade was 12. This interlude centers on an impromptu arm wrestling contest between Wade's older brother, Charlie, and their father that recalls the arm wrestling incident in "The Right Way" (*Trailerpark*). When it appears that Charlie is going to beat his father at arm wrestling for the first time, Glenn Whitehouse claims victory by default when his son inadvertently places his free hand on the table (188). Thus Charlie and Wade are reminded that their father's churlish need to be dominant is a hopeless barrier to love and understanding.

Chapter 14 is taken up with a third flashback that builds on the previous two incidents by detailing a particularly devastating moment in Wade's young life. Four years after the arm wrestling incident, Wade, now 16 and physically larger than his father, puts his young manhood on the line when he arms himself with a cast iron skillet and attempts to confront his father over the man's violent ways: "If you touch her [Sally] or me, or any of us, again, I'll fucking kill you" (198). Unfazed, Glenn Whitehouse reacts swiftly and mercilessly:

> Without hesitation, Pop walked quickly around the table, came up to his son and punched him straight in the face, sending the boy careening back against the counter and the skillet to the floor. Grabbing him by his

shirtfront, Pop hauled the boy back in front of him and punched him a second time and a third. A fourth blow caught him square on the forehead and propelled him along the counter to the corner of the room, where he stood with his hands covering his face. "Come on!" his father said, and he advanced on him again. "Come on, fight back like a man! Come on, little boy, let's see what you're made of!" (198–99)

Wade's older brothers, Elbourne and Charlie, had each eventually managed to stand up to their father (though all for naught, as both are later killed in Vietnam). Considerably younger, Rolfe was spared his father's abuse and the need to eventually confront him. Of the four Whitehouse sons, Wade is the only one who is unable to successfully negotiate *his* Oedipal conflict, a failure that has devastating psychological consequences in the long run. Unable at that critical moment in his maturation to surpass his father, Wade unwittingly begins to *become* his father: a sadistic, self-pitying narcissist who approaches everything in life with fear and loathing.

Chapter 14 also explains why Wade's girlfiend (and future wife), Lillian Pittman, is initially attracted to him. Lillian's maternal instincts are activated by a profound sense of pity when Wade confesses to her that his bruises were inflicted upon him by his father. Reading the "map of pain and humiliation" manifest in his "misshapen and discolored face," Lillian comes to know that "Wade's pain went on and on, way beyond her imaginings" (194). The couple marry young and are happy for a time but eventually divorce, only to marry each other again and divorce again, after having a daughter together. Such a protracted and tortured pattern of involvement suggests genuine love that reluctantly succumbed to deeper malaise, undoubtedly rooted in Wade's horrific emotional scars.

In the narrative present, Lillian has since remarried to Bob Horner, a prosperous insurance man. Horner, Lillian, and Jill live in a handsome colonial in fashionable Concord (the state capital), dress impeccably, and own a late-model silver Audi. Lillian's dramatic improvement of her station in life, from the rural working class to the sophisticated suburban bourgeoisie, is an implicit rebuke to Wade's static existence, constant notice to him that he has been left behind by a former spouse more clever, attractive, and resilient than himself.

More vexing to Wade, though, is his increasingly tenuous relationship with his 10-year-old daughter, Jill. Arriving in Concord from Lawford on Halloween night too late to take her trick-or-treating back in Lawford, Wade tries to salvage the evening by bringing Jill to the public Halloween party in Lawford's town hall. Feeling displaced and alienated among people she hardly knows anymore, Jill keeps her Halloween mask on, a chilling symbol of her growing emotional distance from her father and his world. She soon telephones her mother to come and get her, an act of rejection that sends Wade into paroxysms of helpless frustration and anger. When Lillian and her husband arrive in Lawford to pick up Jill, Wade desperately tries to prevent his daughter from leaving so abruptly and prematurely, but there is nothing he can do. Lillian, Jill's mother and primary parent, has clearly won the battle for her heart and mind. Instead of an emotionally redemptive weekend, father to daughter, Wade ends up humiliated and alone, "his stomach tighten[ing] with resentment" (46).

Severely traumatized in his youth, bitterly disappointed by marriage, and feeling emasculated by noncustodial fatherhood, Wade also suffers daily indignities in his working life. As Lawford's part-time cop, he is nothing more than "a private security guard hired by the town, a human alarm system whose main functions [are] to call for the emergency vehicle at the fire station or the ambulance service in Littleton" (82). In his other capacities, as well driller and snowplow driver, Wade works for Gordon LaRiviere, Lawford's only successful entrepreneur, a tyrannical boss who despises Wade as a man incapable of real success and treats him accordingly.[4]

As for Wade's recent love life, he carries on a desultory relationship with Margie Fogg, a former girlfriend from his high school days. Old friends now, they are "too familiar with each other ever to fall in love, but in the absence of particular strangers, there were many cold and lonely nights when they depended on each other's kindness" (32).

In sum, every aspect of Wade Whitehouse's existence brings him disappointment, sadness, and unremitting pain—pain aptly symbolized by a raging toothache that plagues him in the last weeks of his known life. Without romanticizing Wade or absolving him of moral responsibility, Banks's exhaustive and deeply evocative depiction of the man's sorrows—many self-inflicted, some the function of social forces—not only serves to humanize him but also makes him an understandable, even sympathetic character. All of these considerations mitigate the portrait of Wade that emerges from his actions in the narrative proper, which are often deluded and destructive.

A Season in Hell

"Psychological portraiture of a high order," *Affliction* is, at the same time, a sweeping indictment of the male propensity for violence that is passed from one generation to the next.[5] Appropriately, most of its action is set during New Hampshire's deer hunting season, a grisly autumn festival of macho brutality and death that Banks describes with unstinting exactitude:

> There is a roar of gunfire, a second, a third, then wave after wave of killing noise, over and over, sweeping across the valleys and up the hills. Slugs, pellets, balls made of aluminum, lead, steel, rip into the body of the deer, crash through the bone, penetrate and smash organs, rend muscle and sinew. Blood splashes into the air, across tree bark, stone, onto smooth white blankets of snow, where scarlet fades swiftly to pink. Black tongue lolls over blooded teeth, as if the mouth were a carnivore's; huge brown eyes roll back, glassed over, opaque and dry; blood trickles from carbon-black nostrils, shit spits steaming into the snow; urine, entrails, blood, mucus spill from the animal's body as heavy-booted hunters rush across the frozen snow-covered ground to claim the kill. (68–69)[6]

Indeed, the event that drives the novel's main plot is a mysterious hunting accident. On the first day of the season, Evan Twombley, a wealthy and powerful union official but a neophyte hunter, loses his footing and accidentally shoots himself dead (87). Or does he? Indulging in what Madison Smartt Bell aptly refers to as "a little metafictional trickery," Banks supplies an alternate version of the "accident" that has Twombley deliberately shot to death by his hunting guide, Jack Hewitt (79).[7] These equally plausible but mutually exclusive versions of Twombley's fate are apt to confuse the reader. Banks takes that risk in order to lend some credence to Wade's growing conviction that Twombley met with foul play.

As it so happens, the circumstances surrounding Twombley's demise are genuinely suspicious, not merely a figment of Wade's increasingly paranoid imagination. As president of the New England Plumbers and Pipefitters Union, Twombley was due to testify in Washington concerning alleged connections between his union and organized crime. It is Rolfe, not Wade, who theorizes that Twombley's death was arranged by his son-in-law, Mel Gordon, the union's vice president and treasurer, possibly to cover his own wrongdoings and to pave the way for his accession to the union presidency. Together, Rolfe and Wade speculate that Jack Hewitt took on the job as amateur assassin because he was offered a sufficiently large sum of money by Mel Gordon (242–43).

His imagination fired by conspiracy theories, Wade embarks on a personal crusade to uncover the supposed truth behind Twombley's killing.

Wade cannot or will not allow himself to realize is that his actions are being driven by deeper compulsions: an urge to strike back at Mel Gordon, a LaRiviere crony who has humiliated him in the past; a desire to prove himself stronger than the young turk, Jack Hewitt; a need to vindicate and redeem himself through moral one-upmanship. But most of all, Wade's growing obsession with the Twombley case is fueled by displaced rage—rage at his father, his former wife, himself, and his life in general. While the Twombley saga unfolds, Wade engages in an equally quixotic campaign to win legal custody of his daughter. Wisely discouraged by his lawyer, J. Battle Hand, from pressing what is an essentially hopeless case, Wade renews his quest for Jill after he makes the chance discovery that Lillian smokes pot and is having an affair (166 – 68).

Ultimately, inevitably, Wade's desperate attempts to recast his life and bolster his deflated sense of self lead to tragedy. The beginning of the end is signaled by a hideously depressing event beyond Wade's control. On a Sunday in early November, when he and Margie Fogg visit Wade's parents, Wade discovers his mother frozen to death in bed because his drunken, addled father could not muster the wherewithal to call someone to repair the furnace (212).

When the surviving members of the Whitehouse family convene for Sally's wake and funeral (chapter 16), Banks uses the moment to deepen his already substantive characterizations of Glenn, Wade, and Rolfe. Lena, the only Whitehouse daughter, is also introduced. Bedraggled proletarians, Lena, her husband, Clyde, and their five children subscribe to a particularly noisome brand of fundamentalism that Banks satirizes with savage humor:

> I [Rolfe] spotted the VW microbus that belonged to Lena and her husband, their fifteen-year-old recidivist hippie van plastered with born-again Christian bumper stickers ... [asking the] cryptic question: "Are you ready for the Rapture?" and "Warning: Driver Of This Vehicle May Disappear at Any Moment!" along with the more usual crosses and fishes in profile and mottoes like "Jesus Saves" and "Christ Died for Our Sins" were stuck all over the sides of the van, as if the vehicle were a huge cerulean cereal box promoting apocalypse and everlasting life and promising redeemable gift certificates inside. (222–23)[8]

Rather to his credit, Glenn Whitehouse flies into a rage when his son-in-law attempts to lead everyone present in fervent, unctuous prayer (226–31). In one of the most powerful confrontations in the novel, Glenn castigates his adult children as "Jesus freaks and candy-asses" in a transparent attempt to engage Wade, his real nemesis, in a fist fight (230). To *his* credit, Wade merely restrains the flailing old man in a bear hug until he collapses onto the floor. Belatedly, then, in a scene that inversely mirrors his humiliation 25 years earlier, Wade finally has his Oedipal triumph—too late to do him any good. Rolfe's reaction is to applaud the rucus as if it were theater of the absurd, an instance of emotional perversity that prompts Margie Fogg to judge him "weird, even weirder in his own tight-assed way, than Lena . . . The woman had feelings. But Rolfe did not . . . He was the strange one, not Wade or Lena" (232–33).

Going Down Fast

His anger liberated and unmoored by his mother's death and his belated victory over his father, Wade loses the last vestiges of his reason. Like some latter-day Captain Ahab, with an ego inflated by a maniacal conviction of righteousness and driven by unfathomable rage and terror, Wade gives in to his obsessive delusions about the Twombley killing. The result of such surrender is a dangerous ego elation different in kind but similar in effect to the blissfully smug assurance of Lena and Clyde: "The world was full of secrets, secrets and conspiracies and lies, plots and evil designs and elaborate deceptions, and knowing them—and now he knew them all—filled Wade's heart with inexpressible joy" (249).

In a wild sequence that recalls Bob Dubois's reckless chase after Cornrow in *Continental Drift,* Wade suddenly takes it into his head to follow Jack Hewitt's pickup after it passes his father's house one evening. Chasing Hewitt up and over Parker Mountain at high speeds in one of Gordon LaRiviere's pickup trucks, Wade corners his prey on an ice-covered beaver pond. Unnerved by the pursuit and frightened that the ice will break, Jack Hewitt warns Wade away at rifle point and makes his escape. Predictably, the thin ice then breaks, and LaRiviere's truck sinks into the shallow waters—an obvious metaphor for Wade's ongoing break with reality, with the vehicle embodying his obsession, the ice his fragile sanity, and the sinking of the truck symbolizing the psyche's immersion in the unconscious (265).

Hitchhiking back into town, Wade has to endure the wrath of Margie and his father (who had to accompany her to work at Wickham's Restaurant because of Wade's failure to show up at home at the appointed time). Later that evening, Wade glances at himself in the mirror as he is washing up and is startled to see a "stranger's face," another sign of his accelerating alienation from himself (273).

Next morning Wade learns from Alma Pittman, the town clerk, that Gordon LaRiviere and Mel Gordon are quietly and deviously buying up all of Parker Mountain, probably to build a ski resort. His paranoia seemingly confirmed, Wade bursts in on LaRiviere in a rage—and is promptly fired (287). Later that morning he discovers that he has also been fired from his job as town cop. Out of work, penniless, his toothache now raging, Wade returns home in a state of manic agitation so frightening to Margie Fogg that she decides to move out (294). After getting drunk on his father's whiskey, Wade takes a pair of pliers and yanks out his own rotting tooth (296–97). His next move is to visit officer Asa Brown of the state police, but feeling "trapped, hot, guilty, angry," he is unable to relate his conspiracy theories (305). In a bizarre but excruciatingly poignant encounter, he then visits Hettie Rodgers, Jack Hewitt's girlfriend, whom he seduces, all the time insisting she let him call her "Lillian." More than merely wreaking imaginary vengeance on Hewitt, Wade tries to conjure, at least for a moment, the best part of his former life.

Thereafter, when Wade is decisively discouraged by his lawyer from pursuing the custody case, his mania dissipates: "He had tried, Lord, how he had tried to break through the pain and confusion of his life to something like clarity and control, and it had come to this—this dumb helplessness, this woeful thickened shameful inadequacy" (320). Moving beyond blind urgency into its mirror state—leaden despair—Wade leaves his lawyer's office to pick up his reluctant daughter, Jill, for a day's visit.

For the novel's penultimate chapter (chapter 23), Banks shifts out of Rolfe's exclusive point of view into a series of first-person testimonies, supposedly taped, transcribed, and recounted by Rolfe, that detail Wade's final hours. The effect is twofold: to speed up the already gripping momentum of the narrative and to formally enact Wade's psychic fragmentation.

Nick Wickham recalls Wade's visit to his restaurant, with Jill in tow. When Wickham teases Wade about mispronouncing a menu item, Wade flies into a rage and grabs Wickham by the shirt collar, badly frightening him and causing Jill to burst into tears. To distract Wade, who is giving off the aura of "a hand grenade with the goddamned pin pulled," Wickham relates a message from Jack Hewitt, the new town cop, "to clear your stuff out of his office down to the town hall" (329).

Jill's testimony adds little to Rolfe's investigative efforts; she is too traumatized by events to want to recall much beyond the restaurant incident.

Chick Ward, the mechanic at Chubb Merritt's garage where Wade's car is being repaired, relates a nasty encounter with Wade following the ugliness at Wickham's. Unable to pay his repair bill, Wade flies into a frustrated rage when Ward refuses to turn over his car to him. Ward is forced to threaten Wade with a Stillson wrench to get him to leave the premises (332).

Buddy Golden, the proprietor of Golden's Store in Lawford, adds another piece to the puzzle by informing Rolfe that Wade and Jill came into his store that day. Queried by Wade as to the whereabouts of Jack Hewitt, Golden made the mistake of telling him that Hewitt went up to Parker Mountain to hunt deer (333–34).

Margie Fogg's testimony is the most crucial of all. She tells Rolfe that she was in the midst of packing to move out when Wade came home with Jill. She tries to lie to Wade, of whom she is now afraid, but he sees through her. The emotional dilemma reduces Margie to tears. When Wade tries to comfort her with an embrace, Margie pushes him away, an act that causes Jill to think that Wade is somehow assaulting Margie. In the ensuing melee, Wade strikes Jill—"half by chance and half through the internal force of his programmed and terrible destiny"—and bloodies her nose, thus losing her forever.[9]

The rest of the story, though extremely violent, is anticlimactic. Shorn of all loving connection to other people, Wade fufills his tragic fate by murdering his hated father (342–43). After burning the old man's corpse, Wade seeks out Jack Hewitt and murders him as well. In the wake of these killings, Banks could have had Wade commit suicide or be captured or killed by law enforcement. Instead he chose to have his protagonist fade into oblivion, like Hamilton Stark. Such a fate is infinitely more tragic because it describes a kind of posthumous existence, a twilight life of extreme loneliness, isolation, and anonymity that knows no closure. Marginalized from the outset, Wade Whitehouse is pushed out of life altogether—the archetypal fate of the American blue-collar Everyman at the end of the twentieth century.

The Problem of the Narrator

As was noted at the outset, Banks's construction of Rolfe as narrator allowed him to articulate his protagonist's sorrows with a degree of moral and psychological insight far beyond Wade's ken. Furthermore, Rolfe, self-repressed and solitary, provides a foil to Wade's violent personality. To absent himself from "the tradition of male violence," Rolfe has had to "grimly accept the restraints of nothingness—of disconnection, isolation and exile" (340). In establishing a complex and often collusive dynamic between Rolfe and Wade, Banks suggests that there is no easy way out of the cycle of violence, that renunciation also carries a heavy price.

Important as these elements are to Banks's purposes, more than a few critics have found Rolfe's narrative voice awkward and unconvincing. Michiko Kakutani's comments are typical: "We constantly wonder how Rolfe could know what was happening at any given moment in Wade's mind. We're mystified by his nearly omniscient narration, and vaguely irritated by his nervous philosophizing about the meaning of Wade's life."[10] Even Fred Pfeil, a highly sympathetic Banks critic, complains that he "simply can never believe Rolfe can know all he's saying or execute this masterful narration; nor do I believe in or care about him as an individual character whenever he is roped into the plot."[11]

Such observations contain more than a little truth, but they also ignore the consequences of excising Rolfe from the narrative. Without his mediation, Wade's story would surely lose psychological and moral depth, because Wade's story is also Rolfe's. As Elizabeth Tallent points out, "Pursuing his investigation, Rolfe—scholarly, self-protective Rolfe—exposes himself to the impulsiveness and fury dominating Wade's inner life. [Thus a] fastidious and isolated consciousness is dissolved into a disturbed, passionate one; the result is an enormously complex point of view for the novel" (Tallent, 7).

The Sweet Hereafter

A Polyphonic Novel with the Community as Hero

Continental Drift and *Affliction* were long, complex, and richly textured naturalist tragedies that mostly centered on working-class male protagonists. With his next novel, *The Sweet Hereafter* (1991), Banks moved away from the brooding Dreiserian epic to a decentered narrative of more modest proportions. Instead of a single narrator and one or two protagonists, Banks employs four successive first-person narrator/protagonists. In an expository approach made famous by Kurosawa's *Rashomon,* all four narrators reflect on the same incident from their inevitably subjective, partialized, and somewhat self-serving points of view. But there the parallel ends, for Banks advances the plot with each version rather than merely reiterating it from another angle, and Banks is less interested in creating epistemological tension between his narratives than he is in depicting the life of an entire community. As he told interviewer Richard Nicholls, "I wanted to write a novel in which the community was the hero, rather than any single individual. I wanted to explore how a community is both disrupted and unified by a tragedy."[12]

The tragedy to which Banks refers is a particularly horrific one: a school bus accident that takes the lives of 14 young children, all from Sam Dent, a mythical town in upstate New York's Adirondack Park. The idea for the book came from news reports of a fiery school bus crash in rural Texas that killed 14 children in 1989. Banks told Elizabeth Mehren, in a 1991 interview, that he "kept dwelling on the aftermath of the accident. How did the families carry on in the face of such a tragedy? What of the survivors, those who must forever balance guilt at having lived against a blessed relief in being spared? What of the community and its struggle to restore some semblance of order?"[13]

Dolores Driscoll

Dolores Driscoll, the school bus driver responsible for the accident, narrates the first and last of the novel's five sections. Dolores's opening monologue, delivered with plainspoken directness and sincerity, establishes her as eminently sane, responsible, and caring. An experienced bus driver with an impeccable driving record, she characterizes herself as "the kind of person who always follows the manual. No shortcuts" (4). To her further credit, Dolores bears her crosses in life gracefully. Having suffered a stroke in 1984, her husband, Abbott, has since been confined to a wheelchair, a daunting reality that Dolores confronts with energy and good humor.

In sum, Dolores Driscoll is an almost eerily sympathetic character. A stalwart, good-hearted country matron, she seems the type who would never knowingly harm others, especially the children in her charge. Such a characterization adds enormous irony and pathos to her involvement in the accident and to her role as community scapegoat in its aftermath.

Recounting her routine the day of the accident, Dolores carefully decribes every one of her young passengers and the families they hail from: Banks's skillfully economical way of (1) humanizing the victims, (2) introducing most of the story's characters, and (3) creating an evocative portrait of Sam Dent, a typical Banksian rural hamlet—isolated, economically depressed, "one of those towns that's on the way to somewhere else" (21).

More importantly, Dolores's leisurely paced and laconic account has the effect of creating enormous reader suspense. It begins with an oblique reference to the accident ("A dog—it was a dog I saw for certain" [1]) but does not return to that moment until the end of the section: ". . . the children of my town—their wide-eyed faces and fragile bodies swirling and tumbling in a tangled mass as the bus went over and the sky tipped and veered away and the ground lurched brutally forward" (34–35). But there is something missing from all this: emotion. Dolores's oddly sanguine account of events seems to bespeak a woman who has made peace with herself, but it may also indicate that she is either obtuse or in stubborn denial as to the full implications of the hideous accident she caused.

Billy Ansel

The second narrator, Billy Ansel, represents all the grieving survivors in Sam Dent; he has lost both of his twin children. He even witnessed the accident, assisted with the rescue operations, and saw his childrens' lifeless bodies. A recent widower and Vietnam vet, Ansel has "already learned a few things about the precariousness of life" yet finds himself as devastated as anyone by the psychic shock of so monstrous a tragedy (39). But unlike Dolores, who prefers not to talk about it, or other survivors who find refuge in religion, blame fixing, or some other form of evasion or denial, Billy Ansel is too scrupulous about the truth of life to allow himself an easy out.

Like the coffin maker in *The Relation of My Imprisonment,* Ansel's intellectual and moral vision rests on a firm belief in the all-conquering reality of death. His existentialist ethos undoubtedly had its roots in his combat experiences, but Ansel identifies its full flowering as occurring years later, when he and his wife, Lydia, took their children to Jamaica on vacation in the early eighties. Deliriously high on marijuana, Ansel accidentally left his daughter, Jessica, in a store in Montego Bay and had driven many miles away before he realized it. Jessica was retrieved unharmed, but "[t]hat headlong terrified drive back" to the store "began the secret hardening of [Ansel's] heart" (53).

The subsequent death of his wife is another turning point in his life, but, with the death of his children, Billy Ansel's moral universe is

utterly transformed, as he believes it is for all of Sam Dent whether the
others acknowledge it or not:

> People who have lost their children—and I'm talking about the peo-
> ple of Sam Dent and including myself—twist themselves into all kinds of
> weird shapes in order to deny what has happened. Not just because of
> the pain of losing a person they loved . . . but because what has happened
> is so wickedly unnatural, so profoundly against the necessary order of
> things, that we cannot accept it. It's almost beyond belief or comprehen-
> sion that the children should die before the adults. It flies in the face of
> biology, it contradicts history, it denies cause and effect, it violates basic
> physics, even. It's the final contrary. A town that loses its children loses
> its meaning. (78)

His nihilism now fully confirmed, Ansel withdraws into himself and
begins to drink heavily. And the secret affair he was having with Risa
Walker, the wife of a friend, instantly collapses after the accident. A
fragile liaison that had been "permanently suspended halfway between
fantasy and reality," it could not withstand the destructive force of so
much grief (Risa has also lost a child: her only son, Sean).

Though clearly no role model for healthy coping, Billy Ansel is the
novel's moral ballast. His refusal to indulge in *any* form of comforting
illusion or escape (other than alcohol) is unduly extreme, perhaps insane,
but it stands as a scathing indictment to the standard cop-outs employed by his friends and neighbors. To him, "the religious explanation
[is] just another sly denial of the facts" (79). Nor does he have any use
for the lawyers who converge on Sam Dent after the accident, "like
sharks from Albany and New York City," with their facile promises of
moral closure through litigation (74). Considering himself "beyond
help," Billy Ansel is convinced that, indeed, "most people are"—a moral
philosophy that places him at society's ultima Thule (76).

Mitchell Stephens, Esquire

The third narrator, Mitchell Stephens, embraces a world view that is
diametrically opposed to Billy Ansel's. A highly successful New York
City attorney who specializes in accident cases, Stephens has made his
living by assigning blame. To Stephens, "[t]here are no accidents"; every
human catastrophe is the result of negligence (91). Yet he has no delusions about what he accomplishes; he knows "that in the end a million-
dollar settlement makes no real difference" to the survivors (98). Indeed,

he confesses that "these awful cases" humiliate him, that he "always come[s] out feeling diminished, like a cinder" (98).

Not a social avenger in the conventional sense, Mitchell Stephens admits that he is on a "personal vendetta" because he, too, has lost a child; his daughter, Zoe, has run away from home and is hopelessly immersed in drugs and prostitution. (He later discovers she is AIDS infected as well.) Stephens copes with his pain by being permanently "pissed off," which he defines as "a very special kind of anger" that mixes conviction with rage (99). Though exhausting, it is a stance that enables him to avoid the self-pity of the victim. Stephens's rage also positions him to be Banks's mouthpiece regarding the sad state of child welfare in contemporary America:

> We've all lost our children. It's like the children of America are dead to us. Just look at them, for God's sake—violent on the streets, comatose in the malls, narcotized in front of the TV. In my lifetime something terrible happened that took our children away from us. I don't know if it was the Vietnam war, or the sexual colonization of kids by industry, or drugs, or TV, or divorce, or what the hell it was; I don't know which are the causes and which are the effects; but the children are gone, that I know. So that trying to protect them is little more than an elaborate exercise in denial. (99)

Nichole Burnell

The fourth narrator, Nichole Burnell, is a bright, attractive eighth grader who survives the accident but is left a paraplegic. Ironically, Nichole's terrible fate constitutes a kind of liberation. Up until the accident she had been sexually molested by her father, a dirty secret that has kept her "isolated in an inexpressible silence," to use Chuck Wachtel's apt phrase.[14] After the accident, her father dare not touch her, but her injury also transforms Nichole morally: "Before the accident, I was ashamed all the time and afraid. Because of Daddy. Sometimes I even wanted to kill myself. But now I was mostly angry and never wanted to die" (173). Empowered for the first time in her life, Nichole appropriates her father's secret: "His secret was mine now; I owned it. It used to be like I shared it with him, but no more" (180).

When Nichole finds out that her father has signed on with Mitchell Stephens in a lawsuit against the state and town, she has moral trepidations but reluctantly agrees "to say what they wanted me to say" (181). But after Billy Ansel visits the Burnells and pleads with Nichole's father to drop the suit, Nichole has a change of heart. She decides to lie during sworn testimony, falsely claiming that she could see the speedometer and that Dolores Driscoll was driving the bus at 72 miles per hour when the accident occurred—making Dolores exclusively liable (213). Nichole lies to get back at her father but the effect is to derail all pending lawsuits, thus paving the way for the town to begin healing without any further distractions.

Denouement

Set at the annual Sam Dent County Fair in August, the novel's last section depicts the community's coming together for the first time since the accident half a year before. In virtual seclusion during that period, Dolores, Nichole, and Billy Ansel attend the fair's demolition derby, thereby reentering the life of the town—but under markedly different circumstances. Ansel, spiritually ruined by the accident, shows up drunk, with a woman of dubious repute in tow. Dolores wheels in her husband, Abbott, but both are pointedly shunned by their neighbors; Billy Ansel helps Dolores get Abbott's wheelchair up in the grandstand when no one else will assist. When Nichole is wheeled in, she is treated as a heroine, with smiles and applause, and a number of men lift her wheelchair "like it was a throne" and carry it up the stairs of the grandstand (239).

One of the entrants in the demolition derby is "Boomer," an old station wagon that belonged to Dolores Driscoll but is now owned by Jimbo Gagne, an army buddy of Ansel's. To exact a kind of symbolic revenge on Dolores, the infamous Boomer is singled for punishment by the other drivers in the derby. After being hit and battered time after time, Boomer not only survives but emerges victorious. Its resiliency wins over the fickle crowd.

Thankfully, Banks avoids the pitfall of a simplistic, upbeat ending by having Billy Ansel tell Dolores and Abbott about Nichole's lie. Apprised that the town has judged her guilty of negligence, Dolores is glad that Boomer won the derby but also feels "utterly and permanently separated from the town of Sam Dent and all its people" (253). Indeed, she comes to feel that Sam Dent has been transformed into "a town of solitaries living in the sweet hereafter" (254). There *is* the possibility of forgiveness—Abbott's wheelchair is carried down by his neighbors after the derby—but there is no chance that Sam Dent will ever overcome its fragmentation in the wake of the accident. As Dolores puts it, "we were absolutely alone, each of us, and even our shared aloneness did not modify the simple fact of it. And even if we weren't dead, in an important way which no longer puzzled or frightened me, and which I therefore no longer resisted, we were as good as dead" (254). Contrary to the hoary cliché averring that tragedy brings people closer together, Banks suggests a more painful truth, that tragedy rips people apart.

Rule of the Bone

Chappie Dorset, Antihero

Banks's eighth novel, *Rule of the Bone* (1995), demonstrates that the stylistic directness and verve of *The Sweet Hereafter* was no fluke. *Bone* also marks another step in Banks's evolution as a political writer who understands that "politics" is not really about government, political parties, voting, and the like; that politics in the deepest sense actually plays out in terms of lifestyles, in modes of thought and emotional attitudes, in the myriad ways that marginal groups are ignored, exploited, or made war upon by the hegemonic powers that be. As Banks told an interviewer, "We dismiss people too easily. We put them aside through stereotyping. It's easier to deal with unpleasantness if the people we dislike are reduced to a convenient label."[15]

Banks's case in point is Chapman "Chappie" Dorset, also known as "Bone," a 14-year-old "mall rat" from a broken home in upstate New York who sports earrings, a nose ring, a mohawk haircut, and a massive marijuana habit. Yet, appearances to the contrary, Chappie is not a social degenerate, just the contemporary version of a lost, lonely, and alienated teenager. Ten years earlier his father abandoned the family and was eventually replaced by Ken, an alcoholic pederast who makes lewd demands on his stepson.

Creating a credible version of such a protagonist would be an ambitious imaginative endeavor for a successful writer in his mid 50s, but Banks attempts the even riskier gambit of telling Chappie's story from the first-person point of view. Asked by Pinckney Benedict if he should even be writing about such a character, Banks replied, "Well, if I didn't I wouldn't be using the gift I have. Mark Twain was a middle-aged bourgeois gentleman living in Hartford, Connecticut when he wrote *Huck Finn*; and he wasn't telling the story of himself as a boy."[16]

Banks's choice of protagonist and narrative approach is more astute than it might seem at first glance; half boy, half man, with one foot in society and one foot outside it, Chappie Dorset is well positioned to see the naked workings of "the system" in ways that more respectable folk would never dare to imagine. Furthermore, Banks refuses to condescend to his subject; he makes Chappie intelligent and aware, with a sardonic view of the state of things. The result of these narrative decisions is a generally gripping story that only falters in its last stages.

Homeless

Driven to the end of his endurance by Ken's abuse and his mother's indifference, Chappie leaves home in the midst of an angry confrontation over some coins that he stole from his mother. He and another homeless friend, Russ, soon find themselves living with members of a biker gang called "Adirondack Iron" in a slum apartment over a video store in Ausable Forks. But even that dubious situation sours when the bikers discover that Russ has been stealing their stolen loot. Fearing for their lives, the boys flee in the night, but not before inadvertently starting a fire that kills Bruce, one of the bikers, who dies trying (he thinks) to save Chappie.

All connections with family and surrogate family broken, Russ and Chappie steal a pickup truck, take a joy ride, abandon the vehicle, and end up at the wrecked school bus that figured so prominently in *The Sweet Hereafter,* now put to pasture and occupied by the "Bong Brothers," drug-addled college dropouts. In trouble with bikers and the police, Russ and Chappie decide to slough off their old identities and assume new ones. They develop aliases ("Buck" and "Bone" respectively) and acquire corresponding tattoos before moving on to their next temporary haven, an unoccupied summer house nestled in the woods of Adirondack State Park in Keene, New York. Holed up in the house for a number of weeks, the boys eat what food is available, break up the furniture for firewood, and generally make a shambles of the premises. Eventually abandoned by Russ, Bone has no choice but to set out on the road before the owners arrive on the scene. In a Dickensian coincidence, Bone is picked up hitchhiking by Buster Brown, an itinerant child molester and kiddy porn purveyor with whom Bone has already had a run-in at the local mall some weeks before. Though he fears this unpredictable, predatory adult, Bone dares to steal several hundred dollars from Buster Brown. He also manages to liberate Sister Rose, also known as "Froggy," a nine-year-old girl who was "given" to Buster Brown by her own drug-addicted mother, to be used as his sex slave.

Bone takes Froggy back to the abandoned school bus in Au Sable. The Bong Brothers are gone now, having been replaced by I-Man, a Rastafarian migrant worker from Jamaica with outsized dreadlocks. Kind, patient, and openhearted, I-Man becomes Bone's friend, mentor, and father surrogate, schooling the boy in Rastafarian ways. Under I-Man's gentle tutelage, Bone begins to grow spiritually and emotionally, for the first time in his life. The beginning of Bone's moral transformation occurs when he decides to take moral responsibility for Rose and sends her back to her mother in Milwaukee. (Sadly, she later dies.) When I-Man decides to return to Jamaica, Bone opts to go with him, travel finances provided by Buster Brown's cash.

"Into the Promised Land"

The final chapters of the novel take place in Jamaica and feature the rather farfetched coincidence of Bone finding his real father, Doc, who turns out to be a mean-spirited narcissist. Equally obnoxious is Doc's "old lady," Evening Star, a wealthy dilettante obsessed with sex, drugs, astrology, and all things fashionably hip. Life at their elegant compound, Starport, is an orgy of food, liquor, drugs, and faux Rastas who provide stud service to affluent white women from the States avid for exotic sexual experiences.

Although Bone grows dreadlocks and comes to consider himself a full-fledged Rastafarian, he is not immune to the corrupt influences of life at Starport. Discovering I-Man having sex with Evening Star, Bone opts to tell his father about it out of some craven sense of familial obligation. In a jealous rage, Doc has I-Man and a cohort murdered. Bone stumbles on the bloody scene just as the killers are leaving and is only spared because he is Doc's *white* son.

Though undeniably tragic, I-Man's death is Bone's redemptive moment; it grants him the resolve he needs to finally repudiate his amoral parents, their scabrous lovers, and everything they stand for. In the end, Bone is free of most of his cherished illusions regarding the sanctity of blood ties over chosen loyalties. As Bone puts it, "Stealing is only a crime but betrayal of a friend is a sin ... when you commit a sin it's like you create a condition that you have to live in" (366). Through I-Man's death, Bone also comes to the equally important realization that he is merely a make-believe Rasta, ultimately and always white, with all the attendant privileges of his race. But far from a cause for disappointment, the realization is actually liberating: "Even though I was a white kid I could still become a true heavy Rasta myself as long as I didn't ever forget I was a white kid, just like black people could never forget they were black people" (360). In the end, Bone exacts revenge on his father by eschewing the man's violent ways. Instead of killing his father, Bone seduces Evening Star, an act of Oedipal rebellion that ritualizes a moral shift back to I-Man's otherness. Though he embraces the biological fact of his whiteness, Bone succeeds in turning his back on the oppressive self-absorption of the First World. He comes to know who his friends really are—and were.

Huck Finn for the Nineties

If all this sounds vaguely familiar, it should. On one level, *Rule of the Bone* is a masterful retelling of Mark Twain's *The Adventures of Huckleberry Finn* (1885). Both novels fall under the aegis of *bildungsroman* (formation or upbringing novel). Both novels feature a homeless white youth from a broken family on the run from the bourgeois world. Both books also feature evil biological fathers counterpoised by black father-surrogates who act as spiritual and moral mentors. More through deed than word, Twain's Jim and Banks's I-Man teach their charges the importance of acceptance, love, and loyalty over prejudice, convention, and fear. Where the books really differ is in terms of their respective endings. In the final chapters of Twain's novel, Jim is toyed with by Huck Finn and Tom Sawyer but finally freed from slavery. In Banks's novel, I-Man is brutally murdered, surely a comment on the increasingly violent and unforgiving nature of life in the late twentieth century.

In the final analysis, Banks's rendition of the inner life, perceptions, and diction of a homeless 14-year-old is beautifully realized and almost wholly convincing. Tough, stoical, and nobody's fool, Chappie is, like Huck, an extremely likable character, though sometimes, understandably, a less than reliable narrator.

Unfortunately, Banks's brilliant handling of character and narrative point of view is not matched by his management of plot. The novel loses credibility when Banks transports Bone to Jamaica (chapters 15–22). In real life, impoverished homeless boys seldom make it out of the country, and those that do are unlikely to find their long-lost fathers in a foreign land. Furthermore, the unambiguous villainy of Ken, most of the bikers, Buster Brown, Froggy's mother, and Doc—contrasted with the forlorn goodness of Chappie, Froggy, and I-Man—makes for a black and white moral universe that seems too pat to be true. Similarly, the murder of I-

Man adds a sensationalist element that suggests the triumph of melo-drama over verisimilitude. Yet, despite these flaws, *Rule of the Bone* effec-tively presents a scathing critique of adult selfishness and irresponsibility while it pays homage to the perennial resilience of youth—a tentative signal that Banks's sombre vision of life at the margins is being sup-planted by a more optimistic assessment of human nature, especially the capacity to endure, and by enduring prevail.

Notes and References

Chapter One

1. Russell Banks, "Russell Banks," *Contemporary Authors Autobiography Series,* vol. 15 (New York: Gale, 1993), 33–45; hereafter cited in text as "Banks."

2. Wesley Brown, "Who to Blame, Who to Forgive," *New York Times Magazine,* 10 September 1989, 52–53, 66, 68–70; hereafter cited in text as "Brown."

3. Russell Banks, "Success Story," in *Success Stories* (New York: Ballantine, 1986), 52; hereafter cited in text as *SS.*

4. Don Lee, "About Russell Banks," *Ploughshares* (Winter 1993–1994): 210.

5. Russell Banks, interview by author, Keene, N.Y., 19 May 1993; hereafter cited in text as "19 May 1993."

6. Giroux did publish a long novel near the end of his life, entitled *The Rishi* (New York: M. Evans, 1985).

7. Curtis Wilkie, "Grit Lit," *Boston Globe,* 25 August 1991.

8. Russell Banks, "Nelson Algren: The Message Still Hurts," *New York Times Book Review,* 29 April 1990, 34; hereafter cited in text as "Banks, 1990."

9. Marcelle Thiébaux, "PW Interviews Russell Banks," *Publishers Weekly*, 15 March 1985, 121; hereafter cited in text as "Thiébaux."

10. By prior agreement, Banks and Matthews terminated the journal with its 14th number, in 1974; see *The Little Magazine in America: A Modern Documentary History,* ed. Elliott Anderson and Mary Kinzie (Yonkers, N.Y.: Pushcart Press, 1978), 710–11.

11. Russell Banks, William Mathews, and Newton Smith, *15 Poems* (Chapel Hill, N.C.: Lillabulero Press, 1967), 1–5.

12. Russell Banks, interview by author, Burlington, Vt., 12 August 1993; hereafter cited in text as "12 August 1993."

13. Russell Banks, *Waiting to Freeze* (Northwood Narrows, N.H.: Lillabulero Press, 1969), n.p.

14. Russell Banks, *Snow: Meditations of a Cautious Man in Winter* (Hanover, N.H.: Granite Publications, 1975); *Family Life* (New York: Avon, 1975); *Searching for Survivors* (New York: Fiction Collective, 1975).

15. "Impenetrable": *New York Times Book Review,* 20 April 1975, 30; "heavy-handed and pretentious": *Publishers Weekly,* 6 January 1975, 59; "appallingly clumsy": Bruce Allen, *Library Journal,* 15 September. 1975, 1650.

16. "Homage to Che Guevara," *Quest* 3, 2 (Winter–Spring 1969): 28–29.

17.   *Publishers Weekly*, 31 March 1975, 52.
18.   Thomas LeClair, review of *Searching for Survivors, New York Times Book Review*, 18 May 1975, 7.
19.   Russell Banks, *Hamilton Stark* (Boston: Houghton Mifflin, 1978); *The New World: Tales* (Urbana, Ill.: University of Illinois Press, 1978); hereafter cited in text as *The New World*.
20.   Ann Birstein, "Metaphors, Metaphors," *New York Times Book Review*, 2 July 1978, 12.
21.   The exception is "The Adjutant Bird," written considerably earlier (in or before 1967), discussed above.
22.   At least two critics use the word *pretentious* in their reviews: William Koon, review of *The New World, Library Journal*, 1 February 1979, 419, and Edward Butscher, review of *The New World, Booklist*, 15 January 1979, 793.
23.   Robert Kiely, "Tales and Stories," *New York Times Book Review*, 25 February 1979, 27.
24.   Anonymous review of *The New World, Publishers Weekly*, 6 November 1978, 74.
25.   Russell Banks, *The Book of Jamaica* (Boston: Houghton Mifflin, 1980).
26.   Darryl Pinckney, "Seductive Setting," *New York Times Book Review*, 1 June 1980, 15, 35.
27.   Jerome Klinkowitz, "From Banks, a Novel That's the Real Thing," *Book World {Chicago Sun Times}*, 9 March 1980, 12.
28.   Anonymous review of *The Book of Jamaica, Booklist*, 15 May 1980, 1343.
29.   Russell Banks, *Trailerpark* (Boston: Houghton Mifflin, 1981).
30.   Jonathan Yardley, "Life Behind the Fiberglass Curtain," *Book World—The Washington Post*, 4 October 1981, 3; hereafter cited in text as "Yardley."
31.   Anonymous, "Russell Banks," in *World Authors 1980–1985*, ed. Vineta Colby (New York: H. W. Wilson, 1991), 66.
32.   Mary Soete, review of *Trailerpark, Library Journal*, 15 October 1981, 2047.
33.   Anna Shapiro, review of *Trailerpark, Saturday Review*, October 1981, 76.
34.   Anonymous review of *Trailerpark, Kirkus Reviews*, 15 August 1981, 1016.
35.   Russell Banks, *The Relation of My Imprisonment* (Washington, D.C.: Sun & Moon Press, 1983); hereafter cited in text as *Relation*.
36.   Jodi Daynard, review of *The Relation of My Imprisonment, Boston Review* 9, 4 (July–August 1984): 28; hereafter cited in text.
37.   Deirdre Bair, "Parable From a Coffin," *New York Times Book Review*, 1 April 1984, 8.

38. Banks culled the phrase "Remember death" from an eighteenth-century gravestone in New Hampshire. He first used it in one of his own short stories, "A Sentimental Education," which appears in *The New World*.

39. Russell Banks, *Continental Drift* (New York: Harper & Row, 1985).

40. Janet Fletcher et al., "The Best Books of 1985," *Library Journal*, January 1986, 45.

41. James Atlas, "A Great American Novel," *Atlantic Monthly*, February 1985, 97.

42. James Marcus, "Symmetrical Migrations," *Nation*, 27 April 1985, 506.

43. Wendy Lesser, review of *Continental Drift*, *Hudson Review* 38 (Fall 1985): 467; hereafter cited in text.

44. *New York Times*, April 29, 1985.

45. In an important interview with Trish Reeves, Banks explains his philosophy of narration: "To [narrate] without irony was a goal for me, and it wasn't just an abstract or theoretical goal, it grew out of a kind of frustration that I felt with the realistic convention of the author as merely a window on the world—a kind of Flaubertian presentation of the experience with the author out somewhere behind the clouds paring his nails so that there is an illusion of reality in front of you. And it *is* an illusion; you're aware of that as soon as one starts to write ... This is all artifice, folks, I wanted to say on the one hand; but I still want to tell you something, I still want to tell a story. I don't want to simply comment on the artifice and reveal the artifice, which seems boring after a point, and obvious and redundant, so why bother? So I set out to reinvent, for myself anyhow, a narrator that I could trust and that the reader could trust." Russell Banks, interview by Trish Reeves, in *New Letters* 53 (Spring 1987): 56.

46. Jean Strouse, "Indifferent Luck and Hungry Gods," *New York Times Book Review*, 24 March 1985, 12.

47. Robert Towers, "Uprooted," *New York Review of Books*, 11 April 1985, 37.

48. Isabel Fonseca, "Moving Upwards," *Times Literary Supplement*, 22 August 1986, 920.

49. Anonymous review of *Success Stories* in *Booklist*, 14 June 1986, 1434.

50. Anonymous review of *Family Life* (revised ed.), *Publishers Weekly*, 1 April 1988, 78.

51. Anonymous review of *Family Life* (revised ed.), *Booklist*, 15 May 1988, 1570.

52. Russell Banks, *Affliction* (New York: HarperCollins, 1989); quote from Eric Larsen, "Generations of Abuse," *Los Angeles Times Book Review*, 20 August 1989, 10; hereafter cited in text.

53. Laurel Graeber, "The Perspective of the Perpetrator," *New York Times Book Review*, 17 September 1989, 7.

54. The phrase is from Robert Towers's review of *Affliction*, "You Can't Go Home Again," *New York Review of Books*, 7 December 1989, 47.

55. Julian Loose, "Hunters and Hunted," *Times Literary Supplement*, 26 October 1990, 1146.

56. Judith Graham, ed., *Current Biography Yearbook, 1992* (New York: H. W. Wilson, 1992), 47.

57. Elizabeth Tallent, "Ice That Breaks Before it Melts," *New York Times Book Review*, 17 September 1989, 7.

58. Alice Bloom, review of *Affliction, Hudson Review* 43 (Spring 1990): 156.

59. Jon Saari, review of *Affliction, Antioch Review* 48 (Winter 1990): 118.

60. Russell Banks, *The Sweet Hereafter* (New York: HarperCollins), 1991.

61. Richard Nicholls, "The Voices of the Survivors," *New York Times Book Review*, 15 September 1991, 29.

62. Charles E. May, "The Sweet Hereafter," *Magill's Literary Annual 1992* (Pasadena, Calif.: Salem Press, 1992), 790.

63. "Gripping": Michiko Kakutani, "Small-Town Life After a Huge Calamity," *New York Times*, 6 September 1991; "beautifully written": Michael Boodro, review of *The Sweet Hereafter, Vogue*, September 1991, 388; "a very good book": anonymous review of *The Sweet Hereafter, New Yorker*, 28 October 1991, 119; "a very accomplished book, well planned and well executed": Ben McNally, review of *The Sweet Hereafter, Quill & Quire*, September 1991, 54.

64. Anonymous review of *The Sweet Hereafter, Kirkus Reviews*, 15 June 1991, 742.

Chapter Two

1. Russell Banks, ed., *30/6* (Poetry Pamphlet Number Two), supplement to *Quest* 2 (Winter-Spring 1969); hereafter cited in text as *30/6*.

2. Paul Carroll, comp., *The Young American Poets* (Chicago: Follett Publishing Co., 1968).

3. Curtis Zahn, *American Contemporary*; with an introduction by Herbert Gold (Harmondsworth: Penguin, 1968).

4. Alfred Kazin, introduction to John Dos Passos' *The Big Money* (New York: New American Library, 1969), xvi.

5. *The Random House College Dictionary* (New York: Random House, 1975).

6. In this later version, one line is slightly altered to move the setting from Chapel Hill to Northwood: "twelve Carolina pines" in the first version become "twelve black-tipped pines."

7. "The Song of Cellach," trans. W. S. Merwin, in *Selected Translations, 1948–1968* (New York: Atheneum, 1968).

8. Published in 1975, *Snow* may have been completed as early as 1970. In line 340 Banks refers to himself as "a thirty year old."

9. Don Lee, "About Russell Banks," *Ploughshares* (Winter 1993–1994): 211–12.

Chapter Three

1. Twelve of the 14 stories that comprise *Searching for Survivors* were previously published. Only the two title stories ("Searching for Survivors," I and II) were written specifically for this collection.

2. Carll Tucker, "Failed Utopia," *Village Voice*, 30 June 1975, 44.

3. Struck down in his prime, Banks's elegant "Prince" certainly evokes the slain Kennedys. Perhaps another reference is to Gregorios Lambrakis, the Greek pacifist leader whose 1963 assassination by the Greek military was the subject of Costa-Gavras's political thriller, *Z* (1969). In the film, the Lambrakis figure, played by Yves Montand, is supposedly killed by a small van careening through the streets.

4. The name, Robert LeBrun, is something of a literary in-joke. Robert Lebrun is the name of Edna Pontellier's lover in Kate Chopin's novel, *The Awakening* (1899).

5. Originally published in *New American Review*, "With Che in New Hampshire" was reprinted in *Best American Short Stories of 1971* (Boston: Houghton Mifflin, 1971).

6. "With Che at Kitty Hawk" was selected as one of the O. Henry Prize stories for 1974.

7. For a brief period, in the winter of 1962, Banks himself worked as a timekeeper at the Boston naval shipyard.

8. "Impasse" has autobiographical underpinnings. Banks himself was a Boston bookstore clerk in the early sixties. Charleen is loosely based on Banks's first wife, Darlene Bennett, and Rosa is a fictionalized version of Banks's second wife, Mary Gunst, then a music student also living in Boston.

Chapter Four

1. Though completed on the island of Jamaica in 1977, *The Relation of My Imprisonment* was not published until 1983.

2. Blurb from Ballantine Books edition of *Hamilton Stark*.

3. Anonymous review of *Family Life*, *Publishers Weekly*, 6 January, 1975, 59.

4. Banks, letter to the author, dated 5 November 1993; hereafter cited in text as "Banks, 5 November 1993."

5. Don Lee, "About Russell Banks," *Ploughshares* (Winter 1993–1994): 212.

6. Banks, E-mail posting to author, dated 4 February 1995; hereafter cited in text as "Banks, 4 February 1995."

    7. Terence Winch, "The Man Who Wasn't There," *Book World—Washington Post*, 2 July 1978, F4.
    8. Jodi Daynard, review of "The Relation of My Imprisonment," *Boston Review* 9, 4 (July-August 1984): 28.
    9. Deirdre Bair, "Parable From the Coffin," *New York Times Book Review*, 1 April 1984, 8.

Chapter Five

    1. The wandering folksinger, Oakes, is a punning allusion to the sixties folksinger Phil Ochs (1940–1976), a leftist activist who committed suicide a few years after the collapse of the sixties counterculture.
    2. Cate is oddly vague about the incident but the implication is that he was suspected of having caused the man's injury in the first place.
    3. J[ohn] B[rande] Trend, *Bolivar and the Independence of Spanish America* (n.p.: Bolivarian Society of Venezuela, 1951), 97.
    4. Peter Quennell, *Hogarth's Progress* (New York: Viking, 1955), 71; hereafter cited in text as "Quennell."
    5. Hogarth hailed from petit-bourgeois stock while the Thornhills were of the landed gentry.
    6. Poe is known to have lectured on "The Poetic Principle" in Richmond on 17 August and, again, on 24 September 1849. He ended both lectures with a recitation of "The Raven." Kenneth Silverman, *Edgar A. Poe: Mournful and Never-Ending Remembrance* (New York: HarperCollins, 1991): 324–32; hereafter cited in text as "Silverman."
    7. As for Poe's father, David Poe Jr., he abandoned his family a few months after Edgar's birth and was never heard from again.

Chapter Six

    1. Curtis Wilkie, "Grit Lit," *Boston Globe,* 25 August 1991.
    2. Russell Banks, interview by author, Burlington, Vt., 20 August 1995; hereafter cited in text as "20 August 1995."
    3. *Kirkus Reviews,* 15 January 1980, 76.
    4. As the narrator later explains, the document in Mann's possession is likely a parchment copy of the 1739 treaty, probably no more than 100 years old (170–71).
    5. Switching from first to second person also serves to increase the immediacy of the account for the reader.
    6. Marcelle Thiébaux notes that Banks also designed and "built the Cornell box that forms the book jacket's collage of the novel's elements: maps, a ganja (marijuana) leaf, a skeleton, a Renaissance Virgin and Child." Marcelle Thiébaux, "PW Interviews Russell Banks," *Publishers Weekly* 5 March 1985, 120.

7. Banks admits that the name Dubois is an ironic reference to W. E. B. Dubois (1868–1963), the distinguished black sociologist and writer who authored *The Souls of Black Folk* (1903).

8. Ralph B. Sipper, "Drifters: America's Unwashed" (Review of *Continental Drift*) *Los Angeles Times*, 17 February 1985, 95; hereafter cited in text as "Sipper."

9. In an article on the art of James T. Farrell, "James T. Farrell and the 1930s," critic Donald Pizer defines *indirect discourse* as the literary device "of depicting in a third-person narrative voice the thoughts and feelings of a character, yet doing so as [Roy] Pascal notes, 'with the vivacity of direct speech, evoking the personal tone, the gesture, and often the idiom of the … thinker reported.' The dual voice of the device derives from the circumstance that the narrator is present as reporter, structurer, and summarizer of the character's frame of mind but he presents this material in the language and grammatical form habitually used by the character." Ralph F. Bogardus and Fred Hobson, eds., *Literature at the Barricades: The American Writer in the 1930s.* (University, Ala.: University of Alabama Press, 1982), 75.

10. Also contributing to Bob's desperation is the lack of a sophisticated understanding of the *structural* causes of his victimization, such an understanding usually being the product of an expensive education.

11. Kyle Kristos, *Voodoo* (Philadelphia: J. B. Lippincott, 1976), 80; hereafter cited in text as "Kristos."

12. Leslie G. Desmanglas, *The Faces of the Gods: Vodou and Roman Catholicism in Haiti* (Chapel Hill: University of North Carolina Press, 1992), 118.

13. The situation recalls Banks's own sense of entrapment as a newly married and expectant father in Florida in the early sixties.

14. For Bob Dubois, Ted Williams is the very embodiment of heroic masculine competence and success that he wants so desperately to emulate.

15. Russell Banks, interview by Trish Reeves, in *New Letters* 53 (Spring 1987): 59.

16. Tyrone knows full well that the Haitians will drown before the Coast Guard arrives on the scene.

Chapter Seven

1. *Webster's New International Dictionary of the English Language,* 2d ed., s.v. "cleave."

2. Ross Leckie, "Plot-Resistant Narrative and Russell Banks's 'Black Man and White Woman in Dark Green Rowboat,' " *Studies in Short Fiction* 31, 3 (Summer 1994): 408.

3. R. D. Laing, *Self and Others* (New York: Penguin, 1978), 33–43.

4. "Wickshaw" conjures "rickshaw," an English bastardization of the Japanese word, "jinrikisha," literally, "man-power-carriage." Something of a

symbol of white, Western imperialism, the (wo)man-powered Asian taxi aptly symbolizes Carol Constant's subordinate relationship to Dr. Wickshaw and the Dames.

5.   The idea that a narrative can make its reader/listener at least temporarily more empathetic to the concerns of others is voiced in the concluding statement of *Continental Drift:* "Good cheer and mournfulness over lives other than our own, even wholly invented lives—no, especially wholly invented lives—deprive the world as it is of some of the greed it needs to continue to be itself" (421). Likewise, the notion that everything depends upon the quality of one's attention is expressed through the halting words of Abbott Driscoll in *The Sweet Hereafter:* "Biggest ... difference ... between ... people ... is ... quality ... of ... attention" (26). Obviously, both of these concepts are central to Banks's thought.

6.   Banks would explore this tragic theme much more fully in his 1991 novel, *The Sweet Hereafter.*

7.   Isabel Fonseca, "Moving Upwards," *Times Literary* Supplement, 22 August 1986, 920.

8.   Christopher Banks (1951–1968), the youngest of the Banks children, is omitted from the story for some reason.

9.   Actually, *Queen for a Day* was not yet on television in 1953. After a 10-year stint on NBC radio, the program aired on the CBS television network on 1 January 1955. Banks also mentions *{The Many Loves of}* *Dobie Gillis,* but that program did not air until 1959. Lester L. Brown, *Les Brown's Encyclopedia of Television,* 3d ed. (New York: Gale Research, 1992), 337, 444–45.

10.   Banks is either mistaken about Tufts's real name or has deliberately modified it for dramatic effect. "Sonny" Tufts was actually born Bowen Charleston Tufts 2d.

11.   Banks gives a factual account of this incident in "Russell Banks," *Contemporary Authors Autobiography Series,* vol. 15 (New York: Gale, 1994), 36.

12.   Banks quoted in Don Lee, "About Russell Banks," *Ploughshares* (Winter 1993–1994): 210; hereafter cited in text as "Lee."

13.   Russell Banks, interview by Trish Reeves, in *New Letters* 53 (Spring 1987): 00.

14.   See chapter 1 for a discussion of "Sarah Cole: A Type of Love Story."

Chapter Eight

1.   Review of *Affliction* in *New Republic*, 11 September 1989, 38.

2.   Buff Lindau, "Fiction Writer Russell Banks Comes to Saint Michael's," *Founders Hall* 17, 5 (April 1996), n.p.

3.   Quotation from cover copy, Harper Perennial edition.

4.   Gordon LaRiviere's contemptuous, bullying relationship to Wade bears a strong resemblance to Eddie Dubois's relationship to his brother, Bob.

Indeed, LaRiviere shares Eddie's view of life as war: "Either you are able to use people or they use you. Nothing in between" (119).

5. Elizabeth Tallent, "Ice That Breaks Before It Melts," *New York Times Book Review,* 17 September 1989, 7; hereafter cited in text as "Tallent."

6. Banks has New Hampshire's rifle deer hunting season as starting at the beginning of November. Actually, it runs from 13 November to 8 December. (Shotgun deer hunting season runs from 2 November to 12 November.)

7. Madison Smartt Bell, "Banks Continues to Pour Out Exceptional Fiction," *Journal* [Atlanta, Georgia], 17 September 1989.

8. Banks's portrayal of Lena's family of religious zealots is an unmistakable allusion to Clyde Griffiths's family in Theodore Dreiser's *An American Tragedy* (1925).

9. Eric Larsen, "Generations of Abuse," *Los Angeles Times Book Review,* 20 August 1989, 10.

10. Michiko Kakutani, "A Violent Crime and What Led Up to It," *New York Times,* 8 September 1989, 16.

11. Fred Pfeil, "Beating the Odds: The Brechtian Aesthetic of Russell Banks," in *Another Tale to Tell: Politics and Narrative in Postmodern Culture* (New York: Verso, 1990), 80.

12. Richard Nicholls, "The Voices of Survivors," *New York Times Book Review,* 15 September 1991, 29.

13. Elizabeth Mehren, "After a Tragedy, a Portrait of Hope," *Los Angeles Times,* 30 September 1991.

14. Chuck Wachtel, "Character Witness," *Nation,* 16 December 1991, 787.

15. Michael Blowen, "The Voices of Russell Banks," *Boston Sunday Globe,* 14 May 1995.

16. Pinckney Benedict, "Russell Banks," *Bomb* 52 (Summer 1995): 27.

Selected Bibliography

PRIMARY SOURCES

Poetry

15 Poems. With William Matthews and Newton Smith. Chapel Hill, N.C.: Lillabulero Press, 1967.
Snow: Meditations of a Cautious Man in Winter. Hanover, N.H.: Granite Publications, 1974.
30/6. With Peter Wild, Charles Simic, Robert Morgan, William Matthews, and Doug Collins. Supplement to *The Quest* 3, 2 (Winter–Spring, 1969).
Waiting to Freeze: Poems. Northwood Narrows, N.H.: Lillabulero Press, 1969.

Short Story Collections

The New World: Tales. Urbana, Ill.: University of Illinois Press, 1978; 2d ed., 1996.
Searching for Survivors. New York: Fiction Collective/George Braziller, 1975.
Success Stories. New York: Harper & Row, 1986.
Trailerpark. Boston: Houghton Mifflin, 1981.

Novels

Affliction. New York: Harper & Row, 1989.
The Book of Jamaica. Boston: Houghton Mifflin, 1980.
Continental Drift. New York: Harper & Row, 1985.
Family Life. New York: Equinox Books/Avon, 1975. 2d ed. Revised. Los Angeles: Sun & Moon Press, 1988.
Hamilton Stark. Boston: Houghton Mifflin, 1978.
The Relation of My Imprisonment. Washington, D.C.: Sun & Moon Press, 1983.
Rule of the Bone. New York: HarperCollins, 1995.
The Sweet Hereafter. New York: HarperCollins, 1991.

Coedited Books

Banks, Russell, Michael Ondaatje, and David Young, eds. *Brushes with Greatness: An Anthology of Chance Encounters with Greatness.* Toronto: Coach House Press, 1989.

Uncollected Short Stories

"Crossing the Line." *New York Times Magazine,* 20 December 1992, 21.

"Just Don't Touch Anything." *GQ*, May 1993, 126–31.

"That." In *Statements: New Fiction from the Fiction Collective*, compiled by John Baumbach, 28–33. New York: George Braziller, 1975.

"The Travel Writer." *Antioch Review* 47, 3 (Summer 1989): 354–62.

"The Visitor." In *Disorderly Conduct: The VLS Fiction Reader*, edited by M. Mark, 15–24. New York: Serpents Tail, 1991.

"Xmas." *Antaeus* 64/65 (Spring–Autumn 1990): 176–80.

Reviews

"The Abuse Had to Stop." Review of *A Hole in the World: An American Boyhood*, by Richard Rhodes. *New York Times Book Review*, 28 October 1990, 14.

"Border Country." Review of *The Beet Queen*, by Louise Erdrich. *Nation*, 1 November 1986, 460.

"Distant as a Cherokee Childhood." Review of *Homeland And Other Stories*, by Barbara Kingsolver. *New York Times Book Review*, 11 June 1989, 16.

"Duffy Deeter and the Guru of Wholesome Acceptance." Review of *All We Need of Hell*, by Harry Crews. *New York Times Book Review*, 1 February 1987, 9–11.

"A Dyspeptic View of Nineties Fiction." Review of *Talents and Technicians: Literary Chic and the New Assembly-Line Fiction*, by John Aldridge. *Atlantic Monthly*, May 1992, 120–27.

"One Man in 25." Review of *Life Sentences: Rage and Survival Behind Bars*, by Wilbert Rideau and Ron Wikberg. *New York Times Book Review*, 30 August 1992, 5.

"Paychecks before Art." Review of *Hard to Be Good*, by Bill Barich. *New York Times Book Review*, 14 December 1987, 7.

"We're All Shockproof These Days." Review of *The Coming Triumph of the Free World*, by Rick DeMarinis. *New York Times Book Review*, 30 October 1988, 7–9.

Miscellaneous Essays and Articles

"Caribbean Compass." *Conde Nast Traveler*, October 1989, 124–45.

"Going to the Source: A Lesson in Good Manners." *Paideuma* 9 (1980): 17–18.

Introduction to *Gringos and Other Stories*, by Michael Rumaker. New Edition. Rocky Mount, N.C.: Wesleyan College Press, 1991.

Introduction to *The Lonely Voice: A Study of the Short Story*, by Frank O'Connor. New York: HarperCollins, 1985.

"The Last Birds of Paradise." *Conde Nast Traveler*, September 1991, 104–15.

"Nelson Algren: The Message Still Hurts." Foreward to *A Walk on the Wild Side*, by Nelson Algren. New York: Thunder's Mouth Press, 1990. [A slightly altered version appears in *New York Times Book Review*, 29 April 1990, 34.]

"A Place Between Places." *Natural History* (May 1992): 26–27.

"The Place of Primeval Mystery." *Conde Nast Traveler*, April 1989, 158–65.
"R (&I)." *Antaeus* 73–74 (Spring 1994): 8–10.
"Red, White, Blue, Yellow." *New York Times*, 26 February 1991.
"Russell Banks." *Contemporary Authors Autobiography Series*, vol. 15, 33–45. New York: Gale, 1994.
"Strictly in the Interests of Plausibility." *Ploughshares* 19, 4 (Winter 1993): 7–9.

Interviews

Checkoway, Julie, and English 497. "An Interview with Russell Banks." *AWP Chronicle* 28, 6 (May/Summer 1996): 1–8.
"Author tests work on high school students." *Weekend Edition*—Sunday— National Public Radio, 4 June 1995, program no. 1126. [Transcripts available from Journal Graphics, Inc., 1535 Grant St., Denver, CO 80203.]
Interview by Kay Bonnetti. Recorded in November 1985 at Banks's home in Brooklyn, N.Y. [Tape available from Columbia, Mo.: American Audio Prose Library, 1986.]
Interview by Terry Gross. *Fresh Air*—National Public Radio, 10 October 1995. [Tape available from Spencer Retail Services, (609) 520–7955.]
"Itchy Feet and Pencils: A Symposium." [Transcript of a panel discussion on travel writing between Banks, Jan Morris, William Styron, and Robert Stone.] *New York Times Book Review*, 18 August 1991, 1, 23–25.
"Obsession—Author Russell Banks Tells Writers: Find Yours." Interview by Linda Brinson. *Salem Journal* [N.C], 1 November 1987.
"*PW* Interviews Russell Banks." Interview with Marcelle Thiebaux. *Publishers Weekly*, 15 March 1985, 120–21.
"Russell Banks." Interview with Pinckney Benedict. *Bomb* 52 (Summer 1995): 24–29.
"The Search for Clarity: An Interview with Russell Banks." Interview by Trish Reeves. *New Letters* 53, 3 (Spring 1987): 44–59.
"Talking about American Fiction." Edited transcript of a panel discussion between Marilynne Robinson, Russell Banks, Robert Stone, and David Rieff, moderated by Robert Boyers, August 1990, New York State Summer Writer's Institute, Skidmore College. *Salmagundi* 93 (1992): 61–77.
"Willem Dafoe." *Interview*, January 1993, 82–87.
"Writers Must Reach Out to Minorities, Author Says." Interview by C. R. Hoover. *Daily Camera* [Boulder, CO], 16 September 1992.

SECONDARY SOURCES

Aldridge, John W. "Blue-Collar Enigmas." *New York Times Book Review*, 22 June 1986, 22. [Review of *Success Stories*.] In this harsh evaluation of Banks's career as a neorealist writer, Aldridge finds fault with Banks's

tendency to step outside of his narratives, Brechtian fashion, to discourse
on their social and political significance (cf. Fred Pfeil).

Atlas, James. "A Great American Novel." *Atlantic Monthly,* February 1985, 94,
96–97. [Review of *Continental Drift.*] Atlas compares Banks's proletarians
to Raymond Carver's drunks and Robert Stone's "nihilistic drifters" but
goes on to observe that Banks's writing is distinguished "from these
other chroniclers of the desperate and depressed" by "a quality of moral
outrage" the others lack.

Bair, Deirdre. "Parable from the Coffin." *New York Times Book Review,* 1 April
1984, 8. [Review of *The Relation of My Imprisonment.*] Bair notes that
Relation is "a strong and radical departure" from Banks's earlier work, a
"solid and convincing work" only marred by certain details that are
inconsistent with a "pre-realist" narrative.

Birkerts, Sven. "Bleak House." *New Republic,* 11 September 1989, 38–41.
[Review of *Affliction.*] In this well-informed and fair-minded review,
which is also a capsule survey of Banks's literary career, Birkerts places
Banks in the company of writers like William Kennedy, Andre Dubus,
and Larry Woiwode, neorealists "who have worked to sustain what may
in time be seen as our dominant tradition."

Birstein, Ann. "Metaphors, Metaphors." *New York Times Book Review,* 2 July
1978, 12. [Review of *Hamilton Stark.*] Birstein characterizes *Stark* as "a
one-man show, or, rather a kaleidoscope" of a novel that features a varied
array of narrative techniques but wonders if "Hamilton Stark is worth all
this, either philosophically or as a character."

Brown, Wesley. "Who to Blame, Who to Forgive." *New York Times Magazine,*
10 September 1989, 53, 66, 68–70. In an extremely revealing biographical portrait of Banks (based on extensive interviews), Brown pays particular attention to family violence as a formative influence on Banks's psyche and as a major theme in his fiction.

Domini, John. Review of *Success Stories. Boston Review* 11, 4 (August 1986):
27–28. Comparing Banks, favorably, to the "heartlessly flashy" post-
modernists and "tamped down" minimalist writers, Domini cites Banks's
"great gift" for "naming sources, reasons, first causes."

Eder, Richard. "A Small Town Copes with Tragedy." *Los Angeles Times Book
Review,* 1 September 1991, 3, 8. [Review of *The Sweet Hereafter.*] Eder
judges *The Sweet Hereafter* "a remarkable book, a sardonic and compas-
sionate account of a community and its people" that may well be Banks's
"best book."

———. Review of *Success Stories. Los Angeles Times Book Review,* 22 June 1986,
3, 10. In reviewing these stories, Eder places particular emphasis on
social protest in Banks's fiction.

Graham, Julie, ed. "Russell Banks." *Current Biography Yearbook, 1992.* New
York: H. W. Wilson, 1993. A concise survey of Banks's life and literary
career.

Hitchens, Christopher. "The New Migrations." *Times Literary Supplement,* 25
    October 1985, 1203. [Review of the British edition of *Continental Drift.*]
    Although Hitchens judges the novel's resolution, "in which [Bob]
    Dubois tries to realize a sort of community with the Haitians," as "rather
    improbable and sentimental" and finds the envoi "silly and posing," he
    nonetheless praises "the vigour and the wit" of *Continental Drift.*
Klinkowitz, Jerome. "From Banks, a Novel That's the Real Thing." *Book
    Week—Chicago Sun Times,* 9 March 1980, 12. [Review of *The Book of
    Jamaica.*] In a highly adulatory review, Klinkowitz hails *The Book of
    Jamaica* as "the breakthrough novel for commercially innovative fiction in
    America."
Leckie, Ross. "Plot-Resistant Narrative and Russell Banks's 'Black Man and
    White Woman in Dark Green Rowboat.' " *Studies in Short Fiction* 31, 3
    (Summer 1994), 407–14. In this turgidly written critical essay that
    focuses on a story from *Trailerpark,* Leckie borrows interpretive concepts
    from postmodern theorists Fredric Jameson and Julia Kristeva in order to
    argue that Banks's two main characters misunderstand "each other's
    structures of desire, for each has adopted a semiotic [code] of sexual
    advertisement that suggests that he or she is available to be appropriated
    into the other's constructs." Too ratiocinative to be truly illuminating.
LeClair, Thomas. Review of *Searching for Survivors. New York Times Book Review,*
    18 May 1975, 6–7. In this, the first wholly positive review of Banks's
    work, LeClair finds that Banks's stories "have an assurance few
    younger—or established—writers can match."
Lee, Don. "About Russell Banks." *Ploughshares* 19, 4 (Winter 1993): 209–13. A
    brief but perceptive review of Banks's life and career as a writer.
May, Charles. "The Sweet Hereafter." *Magill's Literary Annual 1992.* Pasadena,
    Calif.: Salem Press, 1992. A review-essay that finds *The Sweet Hereafter*
    well written and constructed but ultimately faults the novel for striving
    too hard for social relevance.
Niemi, Robert. "Rule of the Bone." *Magill's Literary Annual 1996.* Pasadena,
    Calif.: Salem Press, 1996. A review-essay that characterizes *Bone* as a
    modern retelling of Twain's *The Adventures of Huckleberry Finn*—both
    "coming-of-age" novels that are also moral parables about adult irre-
    sponsibility.
Pfeil, Fred. "Beating the Odds: The Brechtian Aesthetic of Russell Banks." In
    Another Tale to Tell: Politics & Narrative in Postmodern Culture. New York:
    Verso, 1990. In this indispensible review-essay, Pfeil discusses Banks's
    narrative techniques in *political* terms, affirming Banks's conscious iden-
    tity "as a writer from the white working class, writing explicitly about
    the rage and damage [the capitulations, self-corruptions, and small resis-
    tances of subordinated lives."
Rosenblatt, Roger. "An Inescapable Need to Blame." *New York Times Book
    Review,* 15 September 1991, 1, 29. [Review of *The Sweet Hereafter.*] An

astute and appreciative discussion of the novel as a moral parable that
instructs acceptance of life's inexplicable tragedies.

Strouse, Jean. "Indifferent Luck and Hungry Gods." *New York Times Book
Review,* 24 March 1985, 11–12. [Review of *Continental Drift.*] Though
she praises Banks's "vivid" writing, Strouse is perplexed by Banks's
authorial intrusions; she ultimately cannot decide what Banks is trying
to accomplish.

Towers, Robert. "Uprooted." *New York Review of Books,* 11 April 1985, 36–37.
[Rev. of *Continental Drift.*] Comparing Banks to Dreiser and Dos Passos
as "a novelist-historian" of "uprootedness and anomie," Towers judges
Bank's duel-voiced narrative risky but ultimately effective.

————. "You Can Go Home Again." *New York Review of Books,* 7 December
1989, 46–47. [Review of *Affliction.*] Towers pronounces *Affliction*
"unremittingly grim" but finds the grimness redeemed, "if only partly
relieved, by the sympathetic insight which the author brings to Wade."

Wachtel, Chuck. "Character Witness." *Nation,* 16 December 1991): 786–88.
[Review of *The Sweet Hereafter.*] A highly perceptive evaluation of Banks's
brand of realism, which Wachtel characterizes as "both old fashioned and
new. New because his characters feel as if he first discovered them outside of fiction, not from pre-existing literary or cultural models. Old fashioned because his work is dedicated to what Cynthia Ozick has called . . .
'explicit and definitive portraiture and the muscular trajectory of whole
lives.' "

Wilkie, Curtis. "Grit Lit." *Boston Globe,* 25 August 1991. An insightful survey
of Banks's life and career, based on an interview at the time of the publication of *The Sweet Hereafter.* Particular emphasis is placed on Banks's
racial politics.

Index

The Author

Robert Niemi received his Ph.D. from the University of Massachusetts at Amherst in 1990. He is currently an assistant professor of English at Saint Michael's College in Colchester, Vermont, where he teaches courses in American literature, film, and critical theory. His scholarly interests include studies in American popular culture, literary realism and naturalism, and contemporary literature, especially by writers from working-class backgrounds. Dr. Niemi has published articles on John Dos Passos, Robert Frost, Weldon Kees, Langston Hughes, Phil Ochs, and other figures in literature and the arts.

The Editor

Frank Day is a professor of English and head of the English Department at Clemson University. He is the author of *Sir William Empson: An Annotated Bibliography* (1984) and *Arthur Koestler: A Guide to Research* (1985). He was a Fulbright lecturer in American literature in Romania (1980–1981) and in Bangladesh (1986–1987).